Religious Trauma

EMERGING PERSPECTIVES IN PASTORAL THEOLOGY AND CARE

Series Editor: Phillis I. Sheppard, Vanderbilt University

The field of pastoral care and counseling, and by extension pastoral theology, is presently at a crossroads, in urgent need of redefining itself for the age of postmodernity or even post-postmodernity. While there is, to be sure, a rich historical foundation upon which the field can build, it remains for contemporary scholars, educators, and practitioners to chart new directions for the present day and age. Emerging Perspectives in Pastoral Theology and Care seeks to meet this pressing need by inviting researchers in the field to address timely issues, such as the findings of contemplative neuroscience, the impact of technology on human development and wellness, mindfulness meditation practice for reducing anxiety, trauma viewed through the lens of positive psychology and resilience theory, clergy health and wellness, postmodern and multicultural pastoral care and counseling, and issues of race and class. The series will therefore serve as an important and foundational resource for years to come, guiding scholars and educators in the field in developing more contemporary models of theory and practice.

Titles in the Series

Religious Trauma: Queer Stories in Estrangement and Return by Brooke N. Petersen
Tilling Sacred Grounds: Interiority, Black Women, and Religious Experience by Phillis I. Sheppard
Christianity, LGBTQ Suicide, and the Souls of Queer Folk by Cody J. Sanders
Warriors Between Worlds: Moral Injury and Identities in Crisis by Zachary Moon
Pastoral and Spiritual Care in a Digital Age: The Future Is Now by Kirk A. Bingaman
Women Leaving Prison: Justice-Seeking Spiritual Support for Female Returning Citizens by Jill L. Snodgrass
The Chaplain's Presence and Medical Power: Rethinking Loss in the Hospital System by Richard Coble
Neuroplasticity, Performativity, and Clergy Wellness: Neighbor Love as Self-Care by William D. Roozeboom

Religious Trauma

Queer Stories in Estrangement and Return

Brooke N. Petersen

LEXINGTON BOOKS
Lanham • Boulder • New York • London

Published by Lexington Books
An imprint of The Rowman & Littlefield Publishing Group, Inc.
4501 Forbes Boulevard, Suite 200, Lanham, Maryland 20706
www.rowman.com

86-90 Paul Street, London EC2A 4NE, United Kingdom

Copyright © 2022 by The Rowman & Littlefield Publishing Group, Inc.

All rights reserved. No part of this book may be reproduced in any form or by any electronic or mechanical means, including information storage and retrieval systems, without written permission from the publisher, except by a reviewer who may quote passages in a review.

British Library Cataloguing in Publication Information Available

Library of Congress Cataloging-in-Publication Data

Names: Petersen, Brooke N., 1979- author.
Title: Religious trauma : queer stories in estrangement and return / Brooke N. Petersen.
Description: Lanham : Lexington Books, 2022. | Series: Emerging perspectives in pastoral theology and care | Includes bibliographical references and index.
Identifiers: LCCN 2022029084 (print) | LCCN 2022029085 (ebook) | ISBN 9781793641144 (cloth) | ISBN 9781793641168 (paper) | ISBN 9781793641151 (electronic)
Subjects: LCSH: Church work with sexual minorities—Case studies. | Psychological abuse—Religious aspects—Christianity—Case studies.
Classification: LCC BV4437.5 .P48 2022 (print) | LCC BV4437.5 (ebook) | DDC 261.8/35766--dc23/eng/20220803
LC record available at https://lccn.loc.gov/2022029084
LC ebook record available at https://lccn.loc.gov/2022029085

For Josh, Sam, and Hannah

Contents

Preface	ix
Acknowledgments	xiii
Introduction	1
Chapter One: Trauma History and Critique	9
Chapter Two: Homosexuality in Psychology and Pastoral Theology	23
Chapter Three: What Was Lost: Describing the Attachment to Religious Community as Selfobject	41
Chapter Four: Estrangement: Leaving Church	75
Chapter Five: Psychological Analysis: Return	95
Conclusion	151
Bibliography	163
Index	169
About the Author	171

Preface

At the earliest stage of this project I was sitting in a coffee shop in my neighborhood with a pastor from a well-known queer accepting and progressive church. I had all sorts of notes in front of me, thinking that this meeting would be the time that I could "prove" that religious trauma was a real experience for many queer people in the church. I was ready with data, believing that if I could convince this pastor that religious trauma was present in their church community they might help me to find people willing to share their stories.

My notes were unnecessary. Once I spoke the words "religious trauma" the conversation ground to a halt. "Tell me how many people you need," he told me, "because I have more people who would raise their hand and say this is me than you could interview in a lifetime."

When I have gone into congregations and classrooms, what I hear over and over again in response to the concept of religious trauma is, "yes, this is me. That phrase tells my story." In my own clinical practice I regularly receive inquiries from queer folks who feel in their bodies and spirits that something like religious trauma has happened to them, and they aren't sure how to process the experience. I come to this research as a pastor, a pastoral theologian and a psychotherapist. It is these three lenses that inspired me to research and write about religious trauma, because I was seeing it in the pews, I was encountering it in my office as a pastoral caregiver, and I was working through it with clients in my psychotherapy practice. It is also these three lenses that inform my approach to this book: it is not just a description of the psychological framework and history of queerness and trauma in psychotherapy, but also a story of the complicated history of the church and the power of pastoral caregivers in the work of healing and recovery.

I wanted to engage in research that allowed me to enter into the complexity of lives and stories. This project seeks to understand and describe the "lived world of everyday experience" for queer people in accepting congregations.[1] I wanted to know what it felt like to leave non-accepting congregations, if that leaving-taking felt like a part of their trauma, and why they eventually returned to accepting faith communities. What was drawing them back? Was there something healing about the return? I wanted to know how people made meaning when what mattered most to them was taken away, what kind of sense they made in their lives of past trauma and new experience, and how they existed as social beings within particular social worlds in which they found themselves.[2]

This kind of qualitative research begins with a broad research question related to a particular phenomenon, and requires simultaneous data collection and analysis. In this particular study, I sought to understand the "lifeworld" of LGBTQIA+ people who had grown up in non-accepting religious communities, left those communities and later in life returned to accepting religious communities. Though I suspected that trauma theory might offer a helpful lens through which to understand their stories, the application of a theory in this constructivist grounded theory model does not come first, but rather during and after data collection. Theory is "grounded" in the data, or the narratives of the participants themselves. This research is centered not just in complex institutions, but in the psychological experiences of people in those institutions, and qualitative research is the kind of work that can unearth the complexity of the human experience.

Throughout this book you will encounter the stories of eight participants who describe their own experiences of growing up in conservative, non-accepting religious communities, leaving those communities and returning to progressive churches. Their stories, though they talk about the healing that has occurred for them, are not gathered into this book because the best or only way to work through religious trauma is to return to a progressive religious community. Many people find a way to work through their trauma outside of the church, and like with all stories of trauma, the way toward healing is to trust and support the agency of the person who was harmed. However, as more and more denominations are making public statements of their support for queer folks, it is imperative that we recognize that throwing open the church doors is not sufficient when the queer people forced to wait outside for so long carry with them a story of trauma. You can't love people out of their trauma, but you can bear witness to the stories, do the work of repentance, and reimagine a new future together.

All eight of my research participants grew up in non-accepting religious communities, which are defined, for the purpose of this study, as religious communities which do not have explicit statements of welcome for LGBTQIA+ people. All of the participants are now members of accepting religious communities, which are defined as communities with explicit statements of welcome for LGBTQIA+ people either specific to their congregation or as a larger denominational body. The category of accepting or non-accepting does not always employ neat boundaries. Though there are certainly accepting communities that do not have explicit statements of welcome, this marker helped to isolate participants that could clearly differentiate between the congregation they were estranged from and the congregation to which they later returned. Many participants made an initial return to a congregation that did not have an explicit statement of welcome before finally joining one that was clearly welcoming to them. Of the eight participants, three attend an Evangelical Lutheran Church in America congregation, four attend an accepting Methodist congregation, and one attends an Episcopal congregation. Several participants identify as members of the denominational body of the church they attend, others prefer to call themselves "Christ-followers," or something similar rather than Methodist, Lutheran, or Episcopalian. The participants ranged in age from 26 to 50. Participants came from a variety of non-accepting congregations, including Baptist, Non-denominational, Christian Reformed, Evangelical, and Missouri Synod Lutheran. Four participants identify as female, three as male, and one as gender queer. Three participants were married at the time of their interviews, two were in a relationship, and three were single. Only one participant had previously been married to a person of the opposite sex. Six participants were white, one was Black, and one was Latino. Four participants identified as lesbian, three participants as gay, and one participant as specifically queer. One participant noted comfort in using both the word lesbian or gay, another used either lesbian or queer to describe her sexuality. Four participants used the pronouns she or her to describe themselves, one used the pronouns they or them, and three used the pronouns he or him.

Some might suggest that a project like this is too small, or can't teach us anything about what might be happening out in churches. Is it possible that stories of eight people can say anything about what our church can do in the face of the immensity of religious trauma? How can this research matter if it is so firmly rooted in the lives of particular people in particular social contexts? What might the narrative of participants in this study tell us about the experiences of LGBTQIA+ people in non-accepting congregations and their later return to accepting faith communities? What can be determined in qualitative research like this project are values that underlie particular human experiences. These stories can teach us how people who have experienced religious trauma have found their way into healing and recovery.

NOTES

1. Finlay, L. *Phenomenology for therapists: researching the lived world.* Hoboken, N.J.: J. Wiley, 2011, p.11.
2. Lareau, Annette. "Using the terms hypothesis and variable for qualitative work: a critical reflection." *Journal of Marriage and Family* 74 (2012): 673.

Acknowledgments

It feels difficult to offer enough gratitude to the people who helped make this book possible. I have been surrounded by a community of mentors and friends who have been integral to bringing this book into being.

First, to my husband, Josh, and my children, Sam and Hannah—you are the best part of my life. I could not have written without you. I hope that if there is anything that I can pass on in our family it is that questions matter, and that reading and writing is one way we really can change the world around us.

My advisor, Dr. David Hogue, was central to shaping me into the scholar I am today. His challenges, edits, and encouragement when this was in dissertation form were invaluable.

My dearest friends, Ian Burch and Collette Broady-Grund, have changed my life and encouraged me every step of the way. Your friendship is one of the greatest gifts I have ever known.

My colleagues, students and friends at the Lutheran School of Theology at Chicago push me to think more clearly about ministry and what it means to be faithful in the world. You all make me believe that the church can be better.

Immense gratitude also goes to the unnamed pastors of congregations represented in this study who have stood in the midst of trauma and have done the hard work to reach out to people in pain. I am grateful for your willingness to give me access to your parishioners. I hope I have done justice to the work you are already doing.

Finally, to April, Lucas, Oliver, Alex, Beth, Jorge, Jasmine and Sarah, it was truly a gift to share your stories. I am honored by your trust in me. I can only hope that this work will benefit those who have yet to claim the healing you have found. This work would be nothing without you.

Introduction

It is a warm spring afternoon when I first meet April.[1] She sits across from me at the dining room table in my apartment, drinking a glass of water, having just come from her work as an advocate for undocumented immigrants who are victims of domestic violence. She tells me stories about growing up as the daughter of a pastor in a very conservative Southern Baptist family. Her Southern Baptist parents were so enraged when she came out to them that she now holds a legal order or protection against them. She feared that if they had been able to afford to send her to conversion camp, they would have taken her against her will. She secured her order of protection when she could no longer stand the continued harassment and stalking of her and her now wife. When I ask her if she feels as if her experience in her family and the Southern Baptist Church might qualify as something like religious trauma, she looks at me as if I am silly for even asking the question. "Oh, absolutely," she says. She describes having

> anxiety attacks all through high school, where I thought I was having a heart attack, or something, but now I know it was anxiety because I really thought I was going to die and go to hell, and I was really really afraid of dying.

She paints vivid pictures of what she believed was going to happen to her when she died, of being tortured while in eternal pain and anguish. April says,

> It is just really hard to be okay, and live and move and breathe in the world when you are like, I can't *not* be gay, and if I am gay and I am not adequately repentant about it I could get hit by a bus and go to hell in a moment. It is really hard to be like, "I should do my Chinese homework," you know? It just doesn't seem important. I think that is where it started and then worsened into clinical depression which was shitty.

Some might read stories like April's and wonder if a word like "trauma" fits, or if perhaps it makes more sense to suggest that April simply went through a truly significant and deep period of suffering. Some might suggest that unless her symptoms fit the requirements in the Diagnostic and Statistical Manual of Mental Disorders (DSM), the guide used by most health care providers to diagnose mental disorders, we cannot really call her experience trauma, even if she wants to use that word herself. Yet, April's story, along with the stories of others you will read in these pages, shed light on a new way of thinking about trauma and what it takes to heal.

WHAT ABOUT POLITICAL AND RELIGIOUS ACCEPTANCE?

Working as a pastor and a clinician, I have encountered many LGBTQIA+ people who were practicing their faith in accepting communities, while carrying within them stories of deep pain and suffering inflicted by non-accepting faith communities in their past. Like April's fears of being spirited off to conversion camp, it was common to hear about prayer groups who showed up out nowhere to "pray the gay away," the loss of beloved friends and family, or being harassed with threats of eternal damnation. This left me wondering why, when they have faced such intense rejection from these congregations, have they continued to seek after a faith community? Why didn't they just give up on God and on faith in general?

I began this project in 2015, at a time when the political gains within the LGBTQIA+ community suddenly felt much more tenuous than they ever had before. All interviews with participants in this study took place when Donald Trump was a candidate for the presidencyt. President Trump's candidacy was mentioned by several participants during our interviews: the anti-Muslim, racist, xenophobic, heterosexist, misogynistic rhetoric popularized by the campaign loomed large in the cultural conversation outside of the interview room. Participants in this project were intensely aware that as a base of voters was mobilized on the premise that America could be "made great again," the Trump administration was subtly suggesting that the new rights guaranteed to LGBTQIA+ people were part of what made the America of right now decidedly *not* great. The selection of Vice President Pence, a politician who as governor of Indiana attempted to dismantle the civil rights of LGBTQIA+ people, only increased the fear that this new administration might seek to overturn the right to same-sex marriage, and protections against discrimination on the basis of sexual orientation or gender identity.

Now, as the Trump administration draws to a close, we live in a time when mainline Protestant denominational bodies are, with surprising frequency, making statements of welcome and, on occasion, repentance for the ways they have treated LGBTQIA+ people. In 2013, the Defense of Marriage Act was repealed by the Supreme Court, making same-sex marriage legally recognized in all 50 states. Many states have adopted laws protecting LGBTQIA+ people from discrimination on the basis of their sexual orientation. The speed at which secular and religious institutions are changing long held stances is, at times, shocking. At the same time, the recent election of politicians who are either silent or openly oppose the rights of LGBTQIA+ people, the potential for the loss of these rights is not outside of the realm of possibility. Even with what can feel like radical shifts in both our political communities and faith communities, it seems that the gulf between communities who seek to support and care for LGBTQIA+ people and those who believe that the sexual "choices" of LGBTQIA+ people are anathema to the Christian faith grows only wider. Now more than ever, welcoming churches have the opportunity to proclaim an inclusive gospel that speaks to the anxiety and fears of LGBTQIA+ people.

SPIRITUAL ABUSE AND RELIGIOUS TRAUMA SYNDROME

When this project began, the question of why a person might return to an accepting faith community after rejection from a non-accepting faith community was central to my research. Though one can access a wealth of information about how religion helps or hinders coping with trauma, there is little (beyond some self-help books) that seeks to examine what happens when the religious community itself is the source of trauma.[2]

Spiritual abuse has been a growing area of interest and research since the 1990s.[3] *The Subtle Power of Spiritual Abuse,* one of the earliest texts focused on this phenomenon, suggests that it is best defined as "the mistreatment of a person who is in need of help, support or greater spiritual empowerment, with the result of weakening, undermining, or decreasing that person's spiritual empowerment."[4] Johnson and Van Vonderen recognize both the ability of leaders to spiritually abuse, and of congregations to create an atmosphere of spiritual abuse. However, Johnson and Van Vonderen's work faces criticism for its focus on the victims of spiritual abuse as vulnerable and needy, subtly suggesting that victims of spiritual abuse may suffer from a characterological deficit.[5] Ken Blue, in his book, *Healing Spiritual Abuse,* shifts from the victim of the abuse to the perpetrator, defining spiritual abuse as "when a leader with spiritual authority uses that authority to coerce, control, or exploit a follower, thus causing spiritual wounds."[6] Blue is clear that though the wounds of spiritual abuse are often intense, its perpetrators usually do not intend to harm. Blue suggests that we view abuse on a continuum, from the violation of trust experienced in seemingly minor manipulations, to the "deliberate exploitation of the weak by a grandiose and authoritarian spiritual dictator."[7] Blue's focus on the abuser offers a correction to Johnson and Van Vonderen, but also faces critique for focusing too specifically on religious leaders as the primary actors in this abuse. Lisa Oakley and Kathryn Kinmond argue that spiritual abuse "is coercion and control of one individual by another in a spiritual context. The target experiences spiritual abuse as a deeply emotional personal attack." Drawing on interviews with survivors of spiritual abuse, Oakley and Kinmond suggest that this kind of abuse often includes "manipulation and exploitation, enforced accountability, censorship of decision making, requirements for secrecy and silence, pressure to conform, misuse of scripture or the pulpit to control behavior, requirement of obedience to the abuser, the suggestion that the abuse has a 'divine' position, and isolation from others, especially those external to the abusive context."[8]

Without a doubt, in the stories of participants in this project, one can clearly note instances of spiritual abuse. However, throughout the spiritual abuse literature, the focus often rests on the experience of abuse as it exists between an abuser and the abused. Many examples of spiritual abuse highlight an authoritarian pastor who uses scripture to demand adherence and respect. This project, however, seeks to look beyond just an abusive relationship to understand how concepts like abuse and trauma exist in the expanded context of an entire religious community. Additionally, though spiritual abuse is a growing area of interest, few authors extend their argument to recognize spiritual abuse as a source of trauma. This project pushes the boundaries of current scholarship in spiritual abuse to ask what happens when the abuse is not at the hands of an authoritarian leader, but feels, to the victims, much bigger than just one relationship. Participants often located their trauma in the sum total of the theology of their community, not in an abusive relationship with a leader.

Marlene Winell was the first to use the term "religious trauma syndrome," but focused almost exclusively on the process of leaving a religious community or cult to heal.[9] Winell imagines that "recovery" from toxic and traumatic religious communities occurs when one can finally rid oneself of the teaching of that community and to "think for yourself," in a world now free of fundamentalist religion.[10] None of the research currently available explores the return of people traumatized by a religious community to a new accepting religious community. Understandably, it seems counterintuitive to imagine that those who have been abused or traumatized in the church would also find healing in the church. I was intrigued, however, by the potential for people to find healing after religious trauma, not by a complete break from the church, but in their return to a supportive religious environment. As I engaged with faith leaders in accepting communities, all had numerous stories about parishioners who had been deeply wounded by a church, but now talked about recovering or healing from their trauma in a new and supportive environment. I felt that these stories needed to be told to offer a new view of people who worked through trauma and were able to forge a lasting and deep relationship with a religious community.

In contrast to Winell's assumptions, the stories of participants in this study suggest that healing or recovery from religious trauma can happen within a religious community. The trauma they describe resonates with the work of Laura Brown and Maria P.P. Root who argue that trauma is not adequately understood as only a function of direct traumatic events, but is rather "a destruction of basic organizing principles by which we come to know self, others and the environment; traumas wound deeply in a way that challenges the meaning of life."[11] If trauma is wider than the more traditional view of an event which causes feelings of "intense fear, helplessness, loss of control, and threat of annihilation," then perhaps trauma generally, and religious trauma specifically, is a helpful lens through which to understand the experience of LGBTQIA+ people in non-accepting faith environments.[12] Root and Brown both argue that a feminist analysis of trauma reveals that the definition of what might be considered a traumatic experience is inherently political. Historically trauma studies focus almost exclusively on those events in which white men, a dominant class with social power, can participate as victims rather than perpetrators.[13] Real trauma, in this view, is what happens publicly: it is war, natural disasters, car crashes. Victims of private traumas like domestic abuse, rape, incest, etc., have to "prove" their trauma, demonstrating that they didn't bring their trauma on themselves.

Within counseling circles, we are beginning to see a change in how trauma is discussed, even if there has been little change in the DSM-IV criteria for most trauma related disorders. Therapists and pastoral counselors have begun to talk about what we might think of as "Big T trauma"—violence, sexual trauma, fatal accidents or natural disasters, and "little t trauma"—long-term experiences of chronic stress, dysregulation, or adversity. This wider view of trauma resonates for LGBTQIA+ people whose lives were centered around a religious community which preached hate, told them they were disgusting, and that God wanted to punish them for eternity in the fires of hell. For many LGBTQIA+ people, once they have been abandoned by the church or left it on their own, the pain they experienced goes far beyond simple suffering. The world they knew has been completely broken down, the ethical system by which they arranged their lives now no longer includes them. This study examines their stories in hopes that by knowing what happened to them, and how they recovered, the church and pastoral caregivers may practice the kind of care and witnessing that assists in the recovery process.

Numerous scholarly works focus on the question of whether LGBTQIA+ people are welcomed in scripture or tradition.[14] Many participants in this study received books to warn them about God's view of homosexuality from one church, only to later find an entirely new set of books about how homosexuality and Christianity are not opposite but compatible. This book does not wade too far into those waters, instead focusing not on whether homosexuality ought to be permitted in the church, but what happens to LGBTQIA+ people when it isn't. LGBTQIA+ people are at higher risk for suicide attempts, substance use, depression and other mental health problems.[15] Yet, it is not just the sexual orientation of LGBTQIA+ people, but the levels of support for their sexuality that impact the health risks they experience. A 2012 study suggested that in supportive environments LGBTQIA+ people often experience high self-esteem and lower levels of depression and anger, while in communities of lower support, coming out as LGBTQIA+ does not correlate with lower levels of anger and depression.[16] A recent quantitative study links health risk behaviors among LGB youth such as substance use and an increased number of sexual partners to the presence of a negative religious climate.[17] This project recognizes that at the heart of the stories of these participants is not just a scholarly debate, but real life and death struggles for LGBTQIA+ people.

In Chapter One I will offer a brief history of homosexuality within both psychological and pastoral circles, with the hope that by setting the scene for the current rift between non-accepting and accepting churches we can better understand the experience of participants in this study. I will examine how we moved from a pathological view of homosexuality to homosexuality as an identity category, and why the church appears so sharply divided. Though terms like homosexuality and heterosexuality are outdated language and anemic terms that no longer adequately describe the variety of sexual orientations and gender identities within the queer community and human experience, because these historical terms still form the basis of divisions within Christian circles I will use them to describe the positions of some accepting and non-accepting churches.. In Chapter Two I will further expand on the widened view of trauma suggested by Brown and Root, while making a case for the reality of religious trauma. I will offer a short history of the concept of trauma, while arguing that throughout the history of trauma studies, the scholarly community has slowly expanded the definition and can continue to do so now. In Chapter Three I will analyze the narratives of estrangement and trauma shared by these participants, using the work of Heinz Kohut to explore the concept of religious idealization and the impact of idealization on the traumatic stories of these participants. In Chapter Four I will deepen the examination of their stories by exploring what we can learn about the patterns within non-accepting churches that can lead to religious trauma. In Chapter Five I will explore the narratives of return, using the work of Judith Herman in trauma recovery to understand how accepting communities might accompany LGBTQIA+ people who have been religiously traumatized. Finally, in conclusion, I will offer a future oriented view of how religious communities might care for those people who have been traumatized with an eye toward how participants in this project think about what a just resolution might be for the harm that was caused.

NOTES

1. Names and identifying details of all participants in this study have been changed to protect their privacy.

2. For further reading see: Aten, J D. and D F. Walker. "Religion, spirituality, and trauma: an introduction." *Journal of Psychology & Theology 40.(*2012): 255–256; Walker, D F. and J D. Aten. "Future directions for the study and application of religion, spirituality, and trauma research." *Journal of Psychology & Theology* 40.(2012): 349–353; Bridgers, Lynn. " The Resurrected Life: Roman Catholic Resources in Posttraumatic Pastoral Care." *International Journal of Practical Theology* 15.1 (2011): 38–56. https://doi.org/10.1515/ijpt.2011.025 Web; Swain, Storm. *Trauma and Transformation at Ground Zero: A Pastoral Theology*. Minneapolis: Fortress Press, 2011. Print; Walker, Donald F., Christine A. Courtois, and Jamie D. Aten. Spiritually Oriented Psychotherapy for Trauma. First edition. Washington, DC: American Psychological Association, 2015. Print.

3. For further reading see: Johnson, D and J VanVonderen. *The Subtle Power of Spiritual Abuse*. Minneapolis, Minn.: Bethany House Publishers, 1991.; Enroth, R M.. *Churches that abuse*. Grand Rapids, Mich.: Zondervan, 1992; Purcell, Boyd C. "Spiritual Abuse." *American Journal of Hospice and Palliative Medicine®*, vol. 15, no. 4, July 1998, pp. 227–231, doi:10.1177/104990919801500409; David J. Ward (2011) "The lived experience of spiritual abuse." *Mental Health, Religion & Culture*, 14:9 (2011): 899–915, DOI: 10.1080/13674676.2010.536206; Oakley, Lisa, and Kathryn Kinmond. *Breaking the Silence on Spiritual Abuse*. Basingstoke: Palgrave Macmillan, 2013. Print.

4. Johnson, D and J VanVonderen. *The Subtle Power of Spiritual Abuse*. Minneapolis, Minn.: Bethany House Publishers, 1991, 20.

5. Oakley, Lisa, and Kathryn Kinmond. *Breaking the Silence on Spiritual Abuse*. Basingstoke: Palgrave Macmillan, 2013, 20.

6. Blue, Ken. *Healing Spiritual Abuse: How to Break Free from Bad Church Experiences*. Downers Grove, Ill: InterVarsity Press, 1993, 12–14

7. Blue, Ken. *Healing Spiritual Abuse: How to Break Free from Bad Church Experiences*. Downers Grove, Ill: InterVarsity Press, 1993, 12–14.

8. Oakley, Lisa, and Kathryn Kinmond. *Breaking the Silence on Spiritual Abuse*. Basingstoke: Palgrave Macmillan, 2013, 20–22.

9. Winell, M. *Leaving the fold*. Oakland, CA: New Harbinger Publications, 1993, 2.

10. Winell, *Leaving the Fold*, 253.

11. Root, M.P.P. *Reconstructing the Impact of Trauma on Personality*. In L. S. Brown & M. Ballou (Eds.), Personality and Psychopathology: Feminist Reappraisals (pp. 229–265). New York, New York: The Guilford Press, 1992, 229.

12. Herman, J L. *Trauma and Recovery* (Rev. ed.). New York: BasicBooks, 1997, 33.

13. Brown, L. *Not Outside the Range: One Feminist Perspective on Psychic Trauma.* In C. Caruth (Ed.), Trauma: Explorations in Memory (pp. 100–112). Baltimore: The Johns Hopkins University Press, 1995, 102.

14. For further reading see: Moore, G. *A Question of Truth: Christianity and Homosexuality*. London; New York: Continuum, 2003; De La Torre, Miguel A. *Out of the Shadows into the Light: Christianity and Homosexuality*. St. Louis, Mo: Chalice Press, 2009; Grenz, Stanley J. *Welcoming but Not Affirming: An Evangelical Response to Homosexuality*. 1st ed. Louisville, Ky: Westminster John Knox Press, 1998; Vines, Matthew. *God and the Gay Christian: The Biblical Case in Support of Same-Sex Relationships*. First edition. New York: Convergent Books, 2014; Myers, David G., and Letha. Scanzoni. *What God Has Joined Together?: A Christian Case for Gay Marriage*. First edition. San Francisco: HarperSanFrancisco, 2007.

15. Ryan, C, D Huebner, R M. Diaz and J Sanchez. "Family rejection as a predictor of negative health outcomes in white and latino lesbian, gay and bisexual youth adults." *Pediatrics* 123 (2009): 346–352.

16. Legate, N, R M. Ryan and N Weinstein. "Is coming out always a 'good thing'? Exploring the relations of autonomy support, outness, and wellness for lesbian, gay, and bisexual individuals." *Social Psychological and Personality Science* 3 (2012): 145–152.

17. Hatzenbuehler, M L., J E. Pachankis and J Wolff. "Religious climate and health risk behaviors in sexual minority youths: a population-based study." *American Journal of Public Health* 102 (2012): 657–663.

Chapter One

Trauma History and Critique

DEFINING TRAUMA

To understand the clinical category of trauma, one must follow the development of trauma theory through history. From the battlefield to the bedroom, what does and does not qualify as traumatic has changed shape over time, and even now, leaves us with some important questions. What qualifies as traumatic? Where lies the power to claim trauma—is it in the traumatized themselves, or in the credentials of the pastor, the counselor, the doctor or the psychiatrist? If we expand the definition of what qualifies as traumatic, do we suddenly dilute it into meaninglessness? If April says she was traumatized, who gets to decide if she is telling the truth? We will see, as we explore the history of trauma, that trauma always has been a nebulous category, with boundaries that are prone to the shifts and changes within our sociopolitical world.

In ancient Greek, τραύμα was a "wound" or "injury inflicted upon the body by an act of violence."[1] Trauma defined in this way is nothing new; the wounding of the body through violence and war are generally accepted traumas; well-equipped hospitals can be called "trauma centers" when they offer care for those who have been gravely wounded. In the field of trauma studies, however, the view of trauma extends beyond just the physical wounds to the internal, psychological wounds that manifest themselves as a result of events one might call traumatic. At the most basic level within the field of trauma studies, trauma is "the response to an unexpected or overwhelming violent event or events that are not fully grasped as they occur."[2] The wounds found in the mind are a result of violent events which overwhelm the capacity of the psyche to cope. What constitutes a traumatic wound on the psyche is a much more difficult event to define than the traumatic wounds of the body.

Despite the difficulty in defining a traumatic event, when we encounter trauma we are brought "face to face with vulnerability in the natural world and with the capacity for evil in human nature." Judith Herman argues that when hearing stories of trauma we must "constantly contend with the tendency to discredit the victim or to render her invisible."[3] Much as victims of trauma often dissociate during or repress the memory of the trauma, stories of trauma tempt those who hear them to push them out of our consciousness. It is this struggle, to hear stories of trauma, to see people who were broken under the weight of what happened to them, and to remain engaged with their stories that is always at the heart of understanding trauma.

FREUD, HYSTERIA AND TRAUMA

We can potentially locate the early study of trauma under another name, in the work of Jean-Martin Charcot, Pierre Janet and Sigmund Freud at the Salpetriere Hospital with women suffering from hysteria.[4] Freud suggests in these early studies of hysteria that the cause of the often bizarre and disturbing symptoms is a trauma located in the experience of women. His early studies, collaborating with Joseph Breuer, suggest that these women suffering from hysteria were stuck in "reminiscences" of traumatic events. These events, often sexual in nature, form the basis for Freud's 1896 presentation of the *Aetiology of Hysteria*, a paper which suggests that hysteria is caused by the early trauma of premature sexual experience. For Freud, women suffering from hysteria are not weak victims of an overwhelming desire to become mothers, they are victims of sexual abuse, incest, and trauma. To put it simply, Freud makes in the *Aetiology of Hysteria* a startling claim, that women suffering from hysteria, to the one, are all victims of sexual trauma. Hysteria results from the internal attempt to control these early uncontrollable events. Addressing the symptoms of hysteria required putting into words the buried memories and feelings surrounding this trauma.[5] The way back from the hysteria resulting from the trauma of these premature sexual experiences was to find the path back to this early memory.[6]

It was only shortly after presenting the *Aetiology of Hysteria* that Freud began to reject his own hypothesis. Its icy reception among the academy left him feeling ostracized and abandoned, fewer patients were knocking on his door, and his colleagues saw his work as a "scientific fairy tale."[7] If hysteria was as common as it appeared, and if hysteria was truly the result of sexual trauma, often perverse acts by a father, this kind of perversion must be nearly universal, given that there must be fewer cases of hysteria than causes of it; not all victims of perverse acts would necessarily manifest the symptoms of hysteria.[8] How could all these women, especially women of high social standing, be victims of sexually perverse men? Freud began to wonder if his own enthusiasm for the seduction theory led him to believe that the stories his patients reported were valid reflections of reality instead of their own sexual fantasies. He slowly set aside his argument that "at the bottom of every case of hysteria there are one or more occurrences of premature sexual experience," and instead begins to disbelieve the stories that his patients recounted, wondering if rather than victims of sexual exploitation, they were claiming as truth what was their own fantasy.[9] For Freud the basis of this "scientific fairy tale" becomes one spun by the patients themselves.

SHELL SHOCK AND THE INFLUENCE OF WAR ON CONCEPTS OF TRAUMA

As interest in hysteria wanes, so does the study of traumatic experiences of women. With the onset of the First World War, however, the response to trauma becomes front and center again, though this time, it manifests itself in the "shell shock" of veterans returning from war. Men return from the battlefield broken down and acting like "hysterical women." Shell shock as a diagnosis suggests that the disease results from the physical experience of being close to exploding shells, despite the emergence of hysterical symptoms in men who were never exposed to the physical trauma of explosions.[10] Treating shell shock becomes a point of contention—is the "fault" for this hysteria located in a weak soldier? Or are these soldiers victims of a circumstance beyond their control? In a world that wants heroes to return from war triumphant, not vulnerable and broken, there is an overwhelming desire to place the "fault" of trauma on the soldier rather than acknowledge our own responsibility for sending the military to war.[11]

This reaction to military experience continues throughout the history of modern warfare. In his early work with soldiers in the Vietnam War, Arthur Blank recalls, "the psychiatric line was, 'yes, combat events are disturbing to people, but it's temporary, it goes away, and we mustn't treat it.'"[12] Blank describes a widespread denial of symptoms of trauma among soldiers, and a hope that as long as psychiatrists did not "dwell" on the experiences of soldiers, there would be no "significant amount of lingering trauma symptoms."[13] Refraining from both diagnosis and treatment was the only way to help soldiers move forward. There was no diagnosis in the Diagnostic and Statistical Manual of Mental Disorders (DSM), the standard classification of mental disorders used by mental health professionals in the United States, to support the kind of symptoms that soldiers described, and so over and over again Blank saw soldiers misdiagnosed with schizophrenia, alcoholism, panic disorders and the like.[14] It wasn't until 1980, in the aftermath of anti-war sentiments, that the American Psychiatric Association would include post-traumatic stress disorder as a diagnosis in the DSM.[15]

For Freud, the experience of soldiers was also a source of puzzlement. The talking cure, centered on the work of the analyst to "discover the unconscious material that was concealed from the patient, put it together, and at the right moment, communicate it to him," to make the unconscious conscious. In *Beyond the Pleasure Principle* Freud describes how in the cases of trauma-neurosis, this communication of the concealed unconscious material fell flat, the patient has "no sense of conviction of the correctness of the construction that has been presented to him. He is obliged to *repeat* the repressed material as a contemporary experience instead of, as the physician would prefer to see, *remembering* it as something belonging to the past."[16] This compulsion to repeat in cases of trauma expands Freud's views of the pleasure principle; the traumatized continue to attempt to repeat something that has "no possibility of pleasure, and which can never, even long ago, have brought satisfaction."[17] Even in their dreams, patients suffering from trauma-neurosis continue to return to the moment of terror, something which an outsider might imagine is simply due to the overwhelming nature of the event. Yet in their waking hours these patients are not interested in thinking about the trauma; in fact, Freud argues they are most interested in avoiding thoughts about the trauma at all costs. For Freud, these patients present a challenge to his theories—they both attempt over and over again to return to experiences that mimic the trauma they faced, and they cannot seem to integrate the event into their consciousness no matter how many times they repeat. The trauma, in these cases, is outside of the "normal" developmental responses a child might have to the loss of love they experience from a parent. Freud recognizes that in cases of war neurosis resulting from the fright of trauma, our mental capacities are so overwhelmed that our minds and bodies must compensate in unique ways.

There is significance in the influence, though slow to enter the popular consciousness, of war and war trauma as a basis for the inclusion of post-traumatic stress in the DSM. The earliest diagnostic description suggested that trauma was "outside of the range of normal human experience." What could be more outside of the "normal range" of human experience than the very particular trauma of war? Yet what does "normal human experience" even entail? Trauma, when we conceive of it in this way, privileges the trauma of war, "war and genocide which are the work of men and male-dominated culture, are agreed-upon traumas; so are natural disasters, vehicle crashes, boats sinking in the freezing ocean."[18]

Currently, post-traumatic stress, the most commonly diagnosed condition resulting from trauma, classifies trauma as "exposure to actual or threatened death, serious injury, or sexual violence," with symptoms including recurrent dreams or flashbacks to the event, psychological or physiological reactions to external events that symbolize the trauma, avoidance of memories, people or places that arouse distressing feelings about the traumatic event, alterations in cognition or mood related to the event (detachment, personal beliefs about self, inability to remember the event, etc.), and heightened arousal (hypervigilance, reckless behavior, sleep disturbances).[19] The specific trauma of war affects the way we conceive of trauma. Even our most recent DSM-5 symptomology still privileges the one-time, extreme, direct kind of trauma. This excludes the more complex ways we might understand the concept of trauma and can lead to the discarding or discrediting of trauma that may look different or result in parallel but unique symptoms.

Events like war, sexual assault and threat of death are traumatic, but this project seeks to question whether those are the *only* kinds of trauma, or, if expanding our view of trauma may help us to see the ways in which people like April struggle to understand what happened to them, why they reacted the way they did, how to move forward in relationships that are healing and meet the challenges they face integrating the experience of trauma into their larger life narrative. Widening our view of trauma to include people like April, as well as other marginalized groups who often experience trauma outside the "range of normal" is not simply to give them access to mental health care, though this is an important result. Naming their experiences as trauma, especially when the victim desires to claim that language for themselves, forces us to examine the structures which have allowed that trauma to occur. If people like April, or women who have been raped, or people of color who have been consistently harassed by law enforcement are actually victims of real trauma, then as a result our recognition of the severity of these experiences and their effects suggest that we must evaluate and change the structures which surround these events.

FEMINIST AND WOMANIST VIEWS OF TRAUMA: DIRECT, INDIRECT, AND INSIDIOUS TRAUMA

Feminist and Womanist scholars have taken up this challenge to expand the foundations of our understanding of trauma. Rather than discarding trauma as a category because it is not inclusive enough to contain the experiences of women and other marginalized groups, these scholars instead attempt to widen the boundaries of our view of trauma. Laura Brown, a feminist psychotherapist, argues that in defining trauma as outside of the "normal human experience," trauma easily becomes separated from the claims of those who have been traumatized, it becomes not outside of the range of all human experience, but outside of the range of male human experience, "trauma is thus that which disrupts these particular human lives, but not others."[20] For Brown, what makes trauma "real" is at the heart of her work. She argues that we have been so captivated by trauma in which the "dominant group" in power within our society can be seen as a victim and not a "perpetrator or etiologist" of the trauma that we are unable to recognize the pervasiveness of trauma within groups on the margins. She argues that feminist psychoanalysis must "look beyond the public and male experiences of trauma to the private, secret experiences that women encounter in the interpersonal realm and at the hands of those we love and depend upon."[21] These nondominant stories of trauma often lead to the kind of "victim blaming" that belittles or ignores the reality of trauma; there is no writing about the "characterological pathology of people who seek out floodplains or tornado alleys to live in," whereas women in particular are often excluded or experience the location of "blame" for the trauma placed upon them.[22]

Brown argues that a response of psychic pain or severe distress to oppression, whether that oppression is based on gender, class, race, or other variables, is often regarded as something to be tolerated. Those who respond to oppression by claiming it is traumatic must suffer from a characterological disorder which leads us to suspect emotional problems in the oppressed rather than to see their distress as a healthy response to oppression itself. Brown argues,

> To admit that these everyday assaults on integrity and personal safety in the daily lives of women and other nondominant groups, admits to what is deeply wrong in many sacred social institutions and challenges the benign mask behind which everyday oppression operates. A collusion of the mental health professions with this oppressive dominance can be found in the rigid insistence that these events, regardless of their felt and lived impacts, cannot be 'real' trauma.[23]

Even though the American Psychiatric Association, the organization which publishes the DSM, removed the requirement that trauma be "outside of the range of human experience" in the fourth edition of the DSM, Brown still argues that our way of understanding trauma continues to resist the potential for trauma to occur as a response to the presence of frequent traumatic stressors in the lives of women and other nondominant groups. She joins with another feminist psychoanalyst, Maria P.P. Root, in arguing for a category of "insidious trauma," a description of the kind of trauma so often experienced by women, people of color, LGBTQIA+ people, and other marginalized communities.

Root, also a feminist psychoanalyst, argues that to understand trauma we must differentiate it from the experience of negative stressors. Negative stressors are relieved when the stressor is resolved; trauma represents "destruction of the basic organizing principles by which we come to know, self, others, and the environment; traumas wound deeply in ways that challenge the meaning of life."[24] In this way, Root moves away from the definition of trauma that rests on the *event* as an important source of diagnosis—was it violent enough? could one legitimately claim the threat of death?—to locate trauma in the experience of the traumatized person. It is the traumatized person rather than an outside observer that can determine whether or not an experience was traumatic. This feminist construction of trauma, for Root, acknowledges that feminist theory places significant value on the individual's subjective experience, depathologizes normal responses to traumatic events, considers the sociopolitical context of trauma and healing, and acknowledges the role of the spirit in wholeness.[25]

With these values in mind, Root argues for an expansion of our conventional understanding of trauma. For Root, the most commonly accepted traumas may be categorized as "direct traumas." Direct traumas include those types of trauma which form the basis of the accepted view of post-traumatic stress disorder—experiences of violence, war, natural disasters, sexual assault and abuse, etc. We expect the life of the traumatized to be in a state of upheaval after a direct trauma; it makes sense that their lives have been changed by the event. Feminist trauma theory has critiqued direct trauma when it is seen as only applicable to individuals, and has sought to expand the application of direct trauma to cultural and ethnic communities.

Indirect trauma, for Root, includes secondary trauma—witnessing trauma or being "traumatized by the trauma sustained by another, with whom one identifies in some significant way."[26] Indirect trauma, such as the internal reaction many LGBTQIA+ people described after the 2016 massacre at Pulse nightclub in Orlando where more than 50 people were murdered, many of whom identified as LGBTQIA+, is a prime example of this indirect trauma.[27] For Root, LGBTQIA+ people who experienced indirect trauma as a result of this massacre, despite not being present for the shooting itself, are often seen as reacting in an out of proportion manner to the event. Their response may be dismissed or seen as a personal failing of character rather than an instance of indirect trauma. For those watching the story unfold, imagining themselves in such a nightclub, knowing that hate crimes against LGBTQIA+ individuals are common, indirect trauma can be seen as a "normal" human response to this kind of event rather than an outsized response that suggests a characterological problem.

Finally, Root argues for a category of insidious trauma. Insidious trauma shapes the worldview of its victims, rendering the world a place that cannot be trusted, a place where psychological safety, security and survival is not guaranteed. This kind of trauma, often resulting from homophobia, racism and sexism, can also be passed down through generations.[28] Insidious trauma "results in a construction of reality in which certain dimensions of security are not very secure; as such, the individual is often alert to potential threat of destruction or death and accumulates practice in dealing with threat."[29] Insidious trauma, more than indirect or direct trauma, can result in the suspicion that if only the traumatized would "work harder" or "pull themselves up by their bootstraps," they would be able to function successfully. Rather than seeing behavior as a normal and even healthy instance of self-protection in an insecure environment, communities where insidious trauma is rare often cannot help but blame the traumatized for their situation.

In this way in particular, Root's concept of insidious trauma is helpful when thinking about people like April, and also parallels many discussions of how we might understand trauma as it relates to racism. Phyllis Sheppard, in her work, *Self, Culture and Others: A Womanist Practical Theology*, argues that where whiteness is associated with power and blackness with impotence, where blackness is the site of "badness," there is a powerful "cultural trauma" that is being perpetuated.[30] Trauma is carried not only by individuals, but, as Sheppard argues, by the entirety of the black community. To ignore the way that trauma shapes the interior life of black people results all too often in the "repetition as the abuse and violence in family life," the "identification with the values and thoughts of those who define our blackness as evil, made, base and in need of destruction," and the "cultural (re-)production of evil." For Sheppard, it is in the linking of "trauma, self, and culture within womanist psychoanalysis" that offers the potential to acknowledge the ways that trauma continues to shape the lives of black people and to breathe life into the struggle for change. To ignore trauma is to "siphon off the air supply" needed to engage in the difficult work of healing and fighting for a different future.[31]

Root argues that many times trauma does not fit in a discrete category—trauma can be indirect and insidious, and work in racial trauma reflects this fluidness. Elizabeth Alexander, reflecting on the Rodney King beating in 1991, links the abjection of the black body for centuries to the trauma of seeing another black man beaten on the television screen. She argues that in seeing the abjection of the black body over and over again for cultural consumption black people have been "forging a traumatized collective historical memory which is reinvoked at contemporary sites of conflict."[32] For these writers, trauma is larger than just what happens when one is threatened with death; trauma can be indirect or insidious, trauma is that which "severely damages an individual's sense of self *in relation to the selfobject world*."[33] From this perspective, watching Rodney King, a black man, being brutally beaten on television is not only a moment of indirect trauma, when one sees his black body and their own black body and feels as if they are one, but also a moment that reveals the traumatic way that the black worldview has been shaped by the insidious trauma of racism.

Might a story like April's, and the others we will turn to in the following chapters, parallel the trauma that is described by Sheppard, Alexander, Root, Brown and others? Is it fair to see trauma as that which severely damages our ability to understand who we are in relation to the world around us? Could trauma be best described as that which destroys our principles about how we live and move and breathe in the world around us? Is trauma not necessarily a one-time event, but rather something that shatters our beliefs about a just and safe world?[34]

LGBTQIA+ TRAUMA

Brown, developing theories about LGBTQIA+ trauma, extends Root's work to suggest that insidious trauma may be further understood in relation to the concept of betrayal trauma. Betrayal trauma is a category first proposed by Jennifer Freyd in response to the often puzzling "delayed recall of childhood abuse at the hands of caregivers."[35] How could children "forget" the abuse that they were subjected to as children, if they truly were abused? Why would they continue to love and remain in relationship with the parents that abused them even well into adulthood? Freyd argues that children cannot risk the loss of the attachment to their caregivers because of their emotional and material dependence on them. In order to preserve these attachments, the child "unknows" the betrayal, moving it out of the realm of the known in order to keep the attachment uninterrupted. This kind of unknowing, unfortunately, opens the child to further betrayals by the caregiver through a continued attached relationship.[36]

Brown argues that in the lives of LGBTQIA+ people, betrayal trauma takes the form of the frequent experience of being "rejected, shamed, and made expendable, by virtue of their sexuality and identities" in their families and church communities. LGBTQIA+ people experience both overt and covert betrayals, sometimes explicitly, like April, rejected from families and church communities, while at other times occurring in the "form of exclusion from the rituals and realities of heterosexual life."[37] Just as all humans form attachment relationships for psychological, spiritual and material security, for many LGBTQIA+ people, attachments to family and spiritual community provide needed emotional, financial and spiritual relationships. As a result, parallel to Freyd's work with abused children, LGBTQIA+ people cannot simply cut off the relationships that provide them with emotional, financial and spiritual security. Brown argues that it is in this way that many LGBTQIA+ people "unknow" the experiences they have of betrayal, because the knowing often leads to "feelings of alienation, disconnections, and conflict that may not feel resolvable and which may interfere with relationships." The process of coming out in these relationships and communities, as we will see in the stories of the participants in this study, becomes a deeply complicated process as these "unknown" moments move into the known. Relationships are necessarily ruptured, and the history of "self-silencing" in order to preserve these attachments often opens LGBTQIA+ people to the unspoken anger, rage, and sadness at the frequent and long-term betrayals enacted by people and communities they love.[38] Particularly in relation to the trauma experience of LGBTQIA+ people, Brown notes that when the messages of insidious trauma are internalized, messages that suggest queer people are bad, unholy, disgusting, evil and damned to hell, the coming out process leads to a specific trauma—now "the perpetrator and the target reside within the same skin."[39] The site of betrayal trauma, keeping this in mind, becomes even more complicated as the emerging sexual identity of the LGBTQIA+ person and their relationship and even participation in systems of oppression blurs the line between perpetrator and target of trauma.

NEW BOUNDARIES OF TRAUMA

What Sheppard, Root, Brown and others argue for is not a boundary-less theory of trauma. These critiques do not throw the door open to a definition-less understanding of trauma, but rather expand the traditional view in several important ways. Just as clinicians are moving in clinical practice toward a wider view of trauma, this view is grounded in a belief that understanding trauma does not lie in a set of symptoms, but rather in the real lives of people who are suffering in the aftermath of a variety of 'big T' and 'small t' traumas. Secondly, to name an experience as trauma, it is not the extreme nature of the event, but rather the way that the traumatized understands their life in relation to the world around them; trauma shatters the structuring of relationships and wounds in ways that compromise our understanding of meaning. Rather than using symptoms, or even an outsider's view of the traumatic event as a primary indicator, these critiques push us to see trauma as a more nebulous category, but one that still does exhibit boundaries. To allow our view of trauma to hold these critiques is not to discard any definition, but to recognize that our definition exists in a sociopolitical milieu, and that milieu is compromised by oppression, systems of power and the potential to ignore the voices of the marginalized.

What does an expanded view of trauma, drawing on these concepts of indirect and insidious trauma mean for someone like April? April's story, as well as the stories of the other people I interviewed problematize the way we think about trauma as a category in psychological circles and as pastoral caregivers. We do not begin with a set of symptoms, we begin with the stories of people who are sitting in front of us, with the ways they have adapted, survived, stumbled and thrived in response to the experiences of their lives. April's story falls outside of the ways that we traditionally view trauma, but she claims that what happened to her has destroyed the way that she had organized the world around her. Conceiving of the category of religious trauma is a helpful and necessary lens through which we, as pastoral caregivers and pastoral counselors, can care for people like April. This larger view of trauma, despite the presence of boundaries, will become most clear as the stories of participants in this study push against the traditional view of trauma. The stories shared by participants in this study are central to exploring, interrogating and potentially expanding our view of trauma to include "religious trauma" as a helpful category. The narratives of participants in this study, expanded in Chapter 4, demonstrate that the boundaries of religious trauma are unique. Their sexuality, in light of the theological beliefs of their non-accepting congregations, barred them from living a fully human life. Participants in this project anticipated that they would never experience meaningful and life-giving intimate relationships, that they would spend eternity in excruciating pain and torment, and that God no longer loved or cared for them. Not only did their sense of self collapse once they were rejected from their non-accepting congregation, but they no longer could believe with certainty that the future held anything positive for them.

Instead of hearing the stories of participants in this study and arguing that their experiences cannot be trauma, I will argue that their stories expand our view of what trauma might be, and in doing so, point us to important visions for care and healing for other LGBTQIA+ people in our communities. However, before we can enter deeply into the stories of people like April, to examine whether a category like religious trauma speaks to their experiences, we must explore the history of the concept of homosexuality within psychological and pastoral circles.

NOTES

1. Jones, S. *Trauma and Grace: Theology in a Ruptured World.* Louisville, Ky.: Westminster John Knox Press, 2009, 12.
2. Caruth, C. *Unclaimed Experience: Trauma, Narrative, and History.* Baltimore: Johns Hopkins University Press, 1996, 91.
3. Herman, J L. *Trauma and Recovery* (Rev. ed.). New York: Basic Books, 1997, 7–8.
4. Herman, *Trauma and Recovery* (Rev. ed.), 10.
5. Herman, *Trauma and Recovery* (Rev. ed.), 12.

6. Freud, S. *The aetiology of hysteria*. In J. Strachey (Ed. & Trans.), *The standard edition of the complete psychological works of Sigmund Freud* Vol. 3. 1896/1986, 197.

7. Gay, P. *Freud: A Life for Our Time* (1st ed.). New York: Norton, 1988, 93.

8. Gay, *Freud: A Life for Our Time*, 94.

9. One can begin to see this shift in Freud's (1905/1997) analysis of Dora. Though he acknowledges that she experienced "trauma" as a result of the attentions of Herr K., Freud begins to place the location of the neurosis not as a result of the sexual trauma (Dora was only 14 and Herr K was an adult male), but in Dora's fantasy about a sexual relationship with Herr K. Freud writes, "Incapacity for meeting a *real* erotic demand is one of the most essential features of neurosis. Neurotics are dominated by the opposition between reality and phantasy" (Freud, 1905/1997, p. 101).

10. Herman, *Trauma and Recovery* (Rev. ed.), 20.

11. Brock, R N. and G. Lettini. *Soul Repair: Recovering from Moral Injury after War*. Boston: Beacon Press, 2012, 107.

12. Caruth, C. *Listening to Trauma: Conversations with Leaders in the Theory and Treatment of Catastrophic Experience*. Baltimore: Johns Hopkins University Press, 2014, 274.

13. Caruth, C. *Listening to Trauma: Conversations with Leaders in the Theory and Treatment of Catastrophic Experience*, 275.

14. Caruth, C. *Listening to Trauma: Conversations with Leaders in the Theory and Treatment of Catastrophic Experience*, 278.

15. Herman, *Trauma and Recovery* (Rev. ed.), 28.

16. Freud, S. and J. Strachey. *Beyond the Pleasure Principle*. New York: Norton, 1922/1989, 19.

17. Freud, S. and J. Strachey. *Beyond the Pleasure Principle*. New York: Norton, 1922/1989, 21.

18. Brown, L. *Not Outside the Range: One Feminist Perspective on Psychic Trauma*. In C. Caruth (Ed.), Trauma: explorations in memory (pp. 100–112). Baltimore: The Johns Hopkins University Press, 1995, 101.

19. American Psychiatric Association. *Diagnostic and statistical manual of mental disorders: DSM-5*. (5th ed.). Washington, D.C.: 2013.

20. Brown, *Not Outside the Range: One Feminist Perspective on Psychic Trauma*, 101.

21. Brown, *Not Outside the Range: One Feminist Perspective on Psychic Trauma*, 102.

22. Brown, *Not Outside the Range: One Feminist Perspective on Psychic Trauma*, 102.

23. Brown, *Not Outside the Range: One Feminist Perspective on Psychic Trauma*, 105.

24. Root, M.P.P. *Reconstructing the Impact of Trauma on Personality*. In L. S. Brown & M. Ballou (Eds.), Personality and Psychopathology: Feminist Reappraisals (pp. 229–265). New York, New York: The Guilford Press, 1992, 229.

25. Root, *Reconstructing the Impact of Trauma on Personality*, 238.

26. Root, *Reconstructing the Impact of Trauma on Personality*, 239.

27. Alvarez, L. and R. Perez-Pena, "Orlando Gunman Attacks Gay Nightclub," *New York Times,* June 12, 2016, https://www.nytimes.com/2016/06/13/us/orlando-nightclub-shooting.html?_r=1; Ruiter, J. and M. Shanklin. "Groups band together to mitigate Orlando's anxiety," *Orlando Sentinel,* June 17, 2016, http://www.orlandosentinel.com/news/pulse-orlando-nightclub-shooting/survivors/os-pulse-anxiety-meditation-acupuncture-20160617-story.html.

28. Root notes the transgenerational transmission of trauma that occurs as a result of the Holocaust, Japanese-American internment camps, or refugee experiences. For further study, see Edward Wimberly's (1997) *Counseling African-American Marriages and Families*—Wimberly highlights the potential for transgenerational transmission especially as it relates to racism.

29. Root, *Reconstructing the Impact of Trauma on Personality,* 241.

30. Sheppard, P. I. *Self, Culture, and Others in Womanist Practical Theology* (1st ed.). New York: Palgrave Macmillan, 2011, 106.

31. Sheppard, *Self, Culture, and Others in Womanist Practical Theology* (1st ed.), 110.

32. Alexander, E. "Can You Be Black and Look at This?: Reading the Rodney King Video(s)." *Public Culture* 7 (1994): 78–79.

33. Sheppard, *Self, Culture, and Others in Womanist Practical Theology* (1st ed.), 132.

34. Brown, L. S. "Sexuality, Lies, and Loss: Lesbian, Gay, and Bisexual Perspectives on Trauma." *Journal of Trauma Practice* 2 (2003): 55–68.

35. Brown, "Sexuality, Lies and Loss," 60.

36. Freyd, J. J. *Betrayal Trauma: The Logic of Forgetting Childhood Abuse.* Cambridge, Mass.: Harvard University Press, 1996, 188.

37. Brown, "Sexuality, Lies and Loss," 61.

38. Brown, "Sexuality, Lies and Loss," 62.

39. Brown, "Sexuality, Lies and Loss," 59.

Chapter Two

Homosexuality in Psychology and Pastoral Theology

In 1945, an article appeared in *Crozer Quarterly,* a scholarly journal published by Crozer Theological Seminary, written by former army chaplain Bertram Crocker.[1] Crocker, after returning from duty in the South Pacific, was troubled by the assumption among most clergy that when a person approaches the pastor for counsel it is because of homosexual desires. The pastor ought "not run risks and waste time as far as your own reputation is concerned in dealing with something you know nothing about. There are no exceptions in dealing with this problem. It is just not the pastor's problem."[2] Crocker writes about the soldiers he served with in the South Pacific who would come to him filled with shame and guilt, struggling with homosexual thoughts and desires, and suggests that sending one of his "boys" to a psychiatrist was the major mistake of his career. He argues that the "Carpenter Man is still aeons ahead of Freud," and that pastors must not "dodge their responsibility" to care for the "sexually abnormal" in their midst.[3]

Crocker, writing in the 1940s, seems out of step with what we might assume was the prevailing historical view of homosexuality and how it ought to be treated in the church. Rather than treating homosexuality as an opportunity for public shaming and rebuke, Crocker suggests soldiers be allowed to say anything that they want with no fear that the chaplain will betray them. His care, and belief in the power of the relationship he has developed with soldiers, stands in stark contrast to a common vision of fire and brimstone preachers shouting from the pulpits that homosexual people will burn in hell. Despite Crocker's underlying view that homosexual people are "sexually abnormal," and that the appropriate kind of pastoral relationship will lead to the healing of homosexual desires, what Crocker reveals to us, more than half a century later, is that the relationship between pastoral care and homosexuality is much more complicated than simply fiery condemnation.

The church does not exist within a vacuum, and the relationship between homosexuality and the church reflects changes in both the psychological view of sexuality and the political world in which the church finds itself. Based on the stories of participants in this project, one might roughly divide the church into two discrete categories—those churches that bless the lives and loves of LGBTQIA+ people and welcome them into leadership, and those churches that preach and teach eternal damnation for LGBTQIA+ people. Yet, studies suggest that the clear lines between these two "types" of congregations is less starkly drawn than we might imagine. To understand how these two rough categories of churches have come to be, we can follow the development of ideas about homosexuality in both theological and psychological circles. In this chapter I will first offer a brief history of the development of the concept of homosexuality in the American church, followed by an overview of how homosexuality has moved away from a "disease" model to an identity within psychological circles. Finally, I will bring these two worlds together to examine how the Christian church still finds itself deeply divided over the view of homosexuality and its place in the Christian life.

HOMOSEXUALITY AND PASTORAL THEOLOGY: A BRIEF HISTORY

It wasn't until 1946 that the term "homosexual" appeared in an English translation of the Bible in the list of sinners "barred from inheriting the Kingdom of God" found in Paul's first letter to the Corinthians.[4] This translation, though "obvious" according to commentaries of the time, represented a departure from the general Christian view. In fact, early and mid-20th century writings of both conservative and more liberal Protestant denominations were basically silent on the topic of homosexuality. The famed Kinsey Report, a study of the sexual habits of American men in the 1930s and 1940s, suggested that "Christians, although well acquainted with the sinfulness of masturbation and premarital intercourse, knew very little about what their churches had to say about same-sex acts."[5] The debate about whether homosexuality is a sin has so shaped our understanding of sexuality and the Christian life that there is little institutional memory about how we got to such a debate in the first place; it seems as if the view that homosexuality and Christianity are incompatible has *always* been the position of the church. The contemporary acceptance of homosexuality in what are often termed "liberal" Christian circles appears incredibly modern. Heather White, in her historical survey of the rise of gay rights in the Protestant church, argues that our vision of a church forever divided over the concept of homosexuality relies on a false history. Most mainline American churches before the mid-20th century simply did not even discuss homosexuality. The cultural conversation about Christianity and homosexuality began only fairly recently. Yet, in both non-accepting and accepting denominations, mostly silent about homosexuality until the mid-20th century, the shifting perspectives on homosexuality and its place in the Christian life reflect the larger views of the relationship between theology and psychology, the interpretation of scripture and the political views of people of faith.

PASTORAL THEOLOGY AND THE RISE OF THE AGE OF PSYCHOLOGY

To follow the development of this concept, we must first examine the development of pastoral theology as a discipline. In his historical survey of the growth of pastoral theology within the North American context, E. Brooks Holifield argues that after the Second World War, parishioners were much less interested in ministers that sought to exhort and instruct, and much more interested in those that could "speak the new language" of psychology.[6] Holifield suggests that it is the rise of the "ethic of self-realization" that pushed pastoral theologians and seminaries to strengthen the relationship between psychology and theology. Military chaplains were unprepared for the variety of problems afflicting soldiers, and upon returning from the war, felt themselves to be lacking in the professional training required to counsel their parishioners.[7] Post-war America was ready for therapy to extend to the middle class, with thousands of counselors now making therapy affordable for more than just the cultural elite. America became "one nation under therapy."[8] More than 380,000 men were discharged from the military with some form of psychiatric disability, making the need for counselors even more acute.[9] Americans began turning to hypnotists, psychiatrists, counselors and other "mental healers" in record numbers.[10] *Life,* a popular magazine of the time, announced in 1957 that in America this was "the age of psychology."[11]

The rise of this "age of psychology" was not limited to secular culture. Among religious leaders, the response was varied. Many wholeheartedly adopted the language of psychology, especially the growing interest in "positive thinking" and "self-fulfillment." Religion could be understood as a parallel path to self-fulfillment, not a detriment to it. Books like *God's Psychiatry* argued that passages like the 23rd Psalm, Ten Commandments, the Lord's Prayer and the Beatitudes formed the basis of the healing of the mind; it was God's psychiatry which allowed a person to live a whole and healthy life.[12] Norman Vincent Peale, possibly the most popular author in this developing genre of Christian Psychology, in 1952 wrote *The Power of Positive Thinking,* a guide to apply Christianity to the mental techniques needed to live a healthy and successful life and to rid themselves of "guilt, pain and insolvency."[13] Yet, within theological circles not all theologians were ready to make the pulpit a tool for self-help. Though most recognized the importance of psychology for pastoral care, they argued that the cult of positive thinking oversimplified the theological anthropology of the human person. Theological language could find common ground with psychological language while still maintaining its rigor as a discipline. Seward Hiltner, one of the more prolific writers in pastoral theology of the time, though suspicious of the power of the positive thinking movement to "distort theology" in favor of the "more comfortable psychology," nonetheless argued that the modern pastor had to learn the language of psychology, because the "language of [the] century is psychological in a way not true of any previous age." If pastors neglected to learn this new language, Hiltner argued that people would begin to see "theology as irrelevant to [one's] thought and concerns."[14] This debate, whether theology was in fact simply "God's psychology," or whether theology could find common ground with the popular psychology movement, would significantly influence the education of pastors, chaplains, and those seeking to speak of and for God in the age of psychology. Though people like Seward Hiltner rejected the self-help side of this age of psychology, it was quite apparent that if pastors did not adopt these methods while growing in their ability to provide pastoral counseling, the church would become less and less attractive to people seeking answers to life's most troubling questions.

Seminaries, in response, were ready to meet this need. In 1939, few seminaries offered counseling classes, or any courses in psychological methods; by the 1950s almost all seminaries offered counseling courses, and more than 80% were offering additional courses in psychology, with at least 80% of seminaries employing a psychologist in their faculty.[15] By the mid-1950s seven universities, including the University of Chicago, with the support of grants from organizations like the National Mental Health Institute, the Lilly Endowment and others, developed graduate programs in personality and theology, pastoral psychology, pastoral counseling, or pastoral theology. Clinical Pastoral Education, a newly developed program which placed seminary students in clinical settings like mental hospitals and medical centers, became increasingly popular in seminaries, and by the mid 1950s reported training more than 4,000 Protestant clergy in clinical counseling and care.[16]

Counselors like Bertram Crocker, whose plea for pastors to "make their issue" the sexual problems brought to them by parishioners, reflect the changing view of what responsibilities and skills a pastor ought to have in the "age of psychology." Among these newly popular counselors and psychologists, clergy were facing larger and larger numbers of parishioners turning to them for counseling and expecting them to have the skills to help. In the 1950s the National Institute of Mental Health reported that 42% of people that sought help for mental problems turned to their pastor before any other mental health practitioners.[17]

As a rising number of people struggling with mental health concerns sought help from their pastors, and as more and more pastors were educated in psychological theories, it is not surprising to see these psychological theories influence the pastoral response to homosexuality. Newly educated in psychology, pastors still had to find a way to translate psychological theories into theological language. This translation of the concept of homosexuality is a fascinating window into how pastors were attempting to bridge the relationship between psychology and theology. But, what was popular psychological theory of the time saying about homosexuality? It is to this that we now turn.

PSYCHOLOGICAL THEORIES OF SEXUALITY

Just as we have seen a shifting view of homosexuality within the Christian church, we can see those similar changes within the psychological community, from the openness of Freud's work with "inverts" to the later view of homosexuality as pathology. In 1935, Freud responded to a letter from a mother seeking help for her homosexual son. Freud wrote,

> I gather from your letter that your son is a homosexual. I am most impressed by the fact that you do not mention this term yourself in your information about him. May I question you why you avoid it? Homosexuality is assuredly no advantage, but it is nothing to be ashamed of, no vice, no degradation, it cannot be classified as an illness; we consider it to be a variation of the sexual function produced by a certain arrest of sexual development. Many highly respectable individuals of ancient and modern times have been homosexuals, several of the greatest men among them (Plato, Michelangelo, Leonardo da Vinci, etc.) It is a great injustice to persecute homosexuality as a crime and cruelty too. If you do not believe me, read the books of Havelock Ellis.
>
> By asking me if I can help, you mean, I suppose, if I can abolish homosexuality and make normal heterosexuality take its place. The answer is, in a general way, we cannot promise to achieve this. In a certain number of cases we succeed in developing the blighted germs of heterosexual tendencies, which are present in every homosexual; in the majority of cases it is no longer possible. It is a question of the quality and the age of the individual. The result of treatment cannot be predicted.
>
> What analysis can do for your son runs in a different line. If he is unhappy, neurotic, torn by conflicts, inhibited in his social life, analysis may bring him harmony, peace of mind, full efficiency, whether he remains a homosexual or gets changed. If you make up your mind he should have analysis with me—I

don't expect you will—, he has to come over to Vienna. I have no intention of leaving here. However, don't neglect to give me your answer.[18]

For Freud, homosexuality was certainly "nothing to be ashamed of" and, as one examines the variety of places where Freud unfolds his theories about sexuality and mentions homosexuality specifically, his views are surprisingly modern. Most clearly, Freud deals with the question of inversion, or homosexuality, in *Three Essays on the Theory of Sexuality*. Just as Freud writes in his letter to a concerned mother, in his discussion of inversion, Freud steps away from the idea of inversion as a shameful or degenerate condition, and instead puzzles that "the nature of inversion is explained neither by the hypothesis that it is innate nor by the alternate hypothesis that it is acquired."[19] Drawing a distinction between object choice, the "person from whom sexual attraction proceeds," and object aim, the type of sexual behavior that is desired, Freud argues that it is merely in the object choice, not the object aim that inverts exhibit perversion. Homosexuality is simply a difference in the aim of sexual desire. Inversion, for Freud, is not a degenerative condition; inverts often exhibit no other "serious deviations from normal," and are often "distinguished by specifically high development and ethical culture."[20] Inversion must be a result of both constitutional factors of the invert as well as accidental factors within the environment. When confronting how homosexuality would eventually be both demonized and, in some cases criminalized, one must marvel at how Freud so easily recognizes that homosexuality is not simply the foil to heterosexuality, but another kind of sexuality on a spectrum of sexual organizations.

However, Freud's view of the cause of inversion changes over the course of his writings. In *Three Essays on the Theory of Sexuality* he argues that the perverse object choice of the invert is a result of a long and intense relationship with the mother, resulting in the taking of the mother as a first love object and the refusal to give her up. Developing love objects is normal; it is the intensity and the inability to give up the mother as the love object that leads to inversion. Freud acknowledges that the cause of inversion is likely both accidental and constitutional, but the intensity of this love leads to an overvaluing of the child's own penis (Freud deals almost exclusively with male inverts), and in response the child introjects the mother to such a degree that his ego is reorganized in her image. The invert loves men because he seeks to love what the introjected mother loves, the penis.[21]

Freud offers several correctives and expansions of this theory, most importantly in his case study of *Little Hans*. Here he argues that inversion is a result of the realization that the mother does not have a penis, which heightens castration anxiety within the child. Horrified and disgusted at viewing the mother's "castrated" body, a body missing a penis, the child is unable to internalize this vision during latency as with "normal" heterosexual development and as a result cannot continue development into the oedipal complex; instead he regresses to the earlier anal stage. He eventually takes on himself as a narcissistic love object in order to reject this horribly castrated mother. This internal narcissism leads the child to fetishism, the constant search for a mother with a penis, or to homosexuality, seeking a feminized man, or what one can argue is the eternally uncastrated mother.[22]

Freud did not believe that homosexuality is a pathological condition; he argued that many inverts are able to live, love and work with great joy. At the same time, Freud's work opens the door to the possibility of pathology. If inversion is a result of the reorganization of the ego as a response to the introjected or rejected mother, what is left is a biologically inappropriate ego for a boy. A regression to the anal stage and narcissistic love for the self in object choice suggests the possibility of pathological narcissistic organization. Though Freud wonders at the "high intellectual development and ethical culture" of inverts, he still frames his understanding of inversion as other than "normal."

HOMOSEXUALITY AFTER FREUD

Theorists who followed Freud would slowly move toward a more pathological view of homosexuality. Melanie Klein situated the beginnings of homosexuality in the period prior to the oedipal complex, what she called the paranoid schizoid position in infancy. During this period, the infant "splits" the world into good and bad, and in the case of homosexuals, overly idealizes the "good penis" as a protector against the "bad penis" which persecutes and seeks to do harm. Stuck in this preoedipal stage of development, a homosexual overly idealizes this good penis leading to later seeking a protective penis.[23] In Klein's view, homosexuals do not exhibit the proper ego organization required to enter into later stages of development; they are frozen in this paranoid schizoid position. Theorists following Klein would locate the beginning of homosexuality even further back in development, suggesting that it is not just a frozen stage of preoedipal development, but appears as early as the prenatal stage. Homosexuals failed to develop properly, and their "illness" left them unable to mature normally.

Edmund Bergler, writing largely in the 1940s and 50s, positioned himself as a "specialist" in the psychoanalysis of homosexuals. Bergler is particularly interesting because he exemplifies the prevailing view of homosexuality within psychological circles at the time. Bergler writes in *Homosexuality: Disease or Way of Life?*

> I can say with some justification that I have no bias against homosexuality; for me they are sick people requiring medical help ... Still, though I have no bias, if I were asked what kind of a person the homosexual is I would say: Homosexuals are essentially disagreeable people ... the shell is a mixture of superciliousness, fake aggression and whimpering ... They are subservient when confronted with a stronger person, merciless when in power, unscrupulous about trampling on a weaker person. The only language their unconscious understands is brute force."[24]

Bergler, departing from Freud, categorized homosexuality not as inversion, but as a perversion, and locates it in the oral stage of development. In using inversion to describe homosexuality, Freud moved away from the pathological to the anthropological, suggesting that inversion is a sexual object choice of the same sex.[25] A homosexual seeks a love object like themselves, so the choice is inverted, or turned in to the self. Bergler, in arguing for perversion, took on a decidedly pathological view of homosexuality; it is not simply an "inverted" sexual object choice but rather a perverse or pathological object aim. The perverse homosexual, according to Bergler, suffers from "weaning shock" and in the rage against the mother "they discard the whole disappointing sex: women."[26] In many ways, Bergler merely shifts the view of Klein, but what is truly surprising is his deep disdain and dislike for "the homosexual." Throughout his writing he refers to homosexuals as "sick persons" with a great percentage being "swindlers, pseudologues, forgers, law-breakers of all sorts, drug purveyors, gamblers, pimps, spies, brothel owners, etc."[27] Gone from Bergler's writings, along with many of those of his colleagues, is the Freudian assertion that "highly respected" people have been homosexual. For Bergler "there are no happy homosexuals, even assuming that the outer world would leave them in peace."[28] What makes Bergler an important analyst is not just his own claimed "expertise" in the study of homosexuals, but the general view within the psychological world that his claims and his attitude toward homosexuals were worthy of acceptance.

This shift, subtly beginning in the work of Freud, and gathering strength as time passed, changed the view of homosexuality. In Freud's earliest work homosexuality was merely a sexual variant among many potential sexual variants. Bergler and others argued that homosexuality was a sickness or a disease that needed a cure. For Bergler, one could make sweeping generalizations about homosexuals, arguing that homosexuals were, at their core, all the same—bad people.

HOMOSEXUALITY: IDENTITY OR THREAT?

Kenneth Lewes, in his historical survey of homosexuality and psychoanalysis, argues that the move toward pathologizing homosexuality after Freud is related to both social and political factors as well as trends within psychoanalysis itself. Following World War II, homosexuality was often compared to Nazism; the "solution to the problem of homosexuality" was the "traditional" family as a center for patriotism and American values.[29] The homosexual was a threat to what Americans held dear, and the "solution" required not just a psychoanalytic cure, but laws to protect the larger culture from the threat of homosexuality.

This threat, and the desire to cure it, was central to the psychoanalytic treatment of homosexuals. Male homosexuals were the greatest danger to both social and moral living, reflecting a "gynecophobic stance" in treatment; male homosexuals were defective because they acted like women. Homosexuality became the cause and singular issue in treatment, not simply one aspect of the entirety of personality structure. Lewes argues that unexamined countertransference issues in the therapeutic encounter are at least partially to blame for this extreme animosity toward homosexuality in psychoanalysis. For Lewes this period in psychoanalytic history reflects "an attack on homosexuals conducted with intemperance, ferocity and a lack of empathy that is simply appalling in a discipline devoted to understanding and healing."[30]

It wouldn't be until 1973 that the American Psychiatric Association would remove homosexuality from their official list of psychiatric disorders.[31] Like Freud, a number of theorists simply could not reconcile how "a significant portion of homosexuals were satisfied with their homosexuality, showed no significant signs of pathology, and could function well" with the view that homosexuals were innately defective and prone to immoral living.[32] The rise of the "homophile movement," most clearly represented by the Stonewall Riot in New York, when patrons of Stonewall, a gay bar, responded in violent protest to a police raid, forced into public view the gay liberation movement.[33] The assumption of people like Bergler, that homosexuals were inherently unhappy, sick and pathological, fell flat in the face of homosexuals who were living well-adjusted lives while refusing to remain in the cultural shadows. Particularly important to the changing view of homosexuals is Robert Stoller, a researcher on gender at UCLA. Stoller questioned the positioning of heterosexuality as "normal," thus making homosexuality perverse. He argued that "perversion" indicated not object choice or object aim, but eroticized hatred. This hatred was exhibited in either sexual performance or fantasy involving "hostility, revenge, triumph and the dehumanized object."[34] Stoller argued for two forms of sexual aberration, perversions characterized by eroticized hatred, and variants, which vary from the statistical average but do not involve rage or desire to hurt. Homosexuality was, for Stoller, not a perversion, but a sexual variant.

Stoller's work was the first to acknowledge the unspoken assumption that heterosexuality was "normal." The claim that homosexuality did not reflect rage or desire to hurt was central to the argument to remove homosexuality from the list of pathological disorders. However, proponents on either side were not ready to give up their views of "the homosexual." Conferences were plagued with angry analysts, often resulting in "circuslike disruptions . . . wherein [one analyst supporting a pathological diagnosis] was called a 'motherfucker' and one psychiatrist of a behavior modification bent was accused of having done his residency at Auschwitz."[35]

The removal of homosexuality as a diagnosis, given the hardened views of many within the psychological community, did not automatically change the view of homosexuals as inherently capable of loving relationships and success in adapting to life challenges. However, the removal of homosexuality as a category of pathology did increase the study of the questions raised by theorists like Stoller. Nancy Chodorow, for instance, argues that "psychoanalysis does not have a developmental account of what we think of as 'normal' heterosexuality (which is, of course, a wide variety of heterosexualities) that compares in richness and specificity to accounts we have of the development of the various homosexualities and what are called perversions."[36] For Chodorow, there is a cultural and individual story behind the development of both heterosexuals and homosexuals; if no such story existed, then any man would do for any woman. This developmental story goes well beyond simply a binary between heterosexual or homosexual, and includes the reasons for the selection of love objects that have "both cultural and individual psychological resonance." Echoing Freud's *Three Essays on the Theory of Sexuality*, Chodorow pushes theorists to think beyond simple sexual attraction, and to recognize the complexity of sexual development. She argues that it is the heteronormative cultural assumptions that foreclose on the complexity of the individual story of sexual development by becoming overly attuned to the question of heterosexual versus homosexual identification. For Chodorow, there is no "normal" sexuality; individual sexuality is a result of a variety of forces, "fantasy, conflict, defenses, regressions, making and breaking relationships internally and externally, and trying to constitute a stable self and maintain self-esteem."[37] Chodorow extends Stoller's argument, pushing us to look beyond what is and is not pathological about sexuality in order to see the ways that all sexuality is complex and varied.

PSYCHOLOGY, THE CHURCH AND A BATTLE FOR SCRIPTURE

The post-war period in particular created a sense of a cultural excitement about the connections between psychology and theology. The intersection between these fields is a major influence on the development of theological views of homosexuality. All participants in this study began their faith lives in congregations that were either explicitly anti-LGBTQIA+, or, through silence, abundantly clear about their anti-LGBTQIA+ stance. Oliver, a member of a church largely silent on the topic of homosexuality says,

> The church never, it isn't like some of the Baptist churches that were like, homosexuality is wrong you are going to hell, I didn't hear sermons like that, it was never talked about and it was secretly known that it was bad. And here is a weird thing, later in life when I came out, I found out that some of my mother's friends that weren't from our church or anything were actually lesbians. But nobody, for like 25 years, had said anything about it, told me anything about it.

This study deals with two very different Christian communities: those that are "conservative" and non-accepting through explicit or implicit anti-LGBTQIA+ messages, and those that are "progressive" or accepting and have adopted denominational or congregational statements of support for LGBTQIA+ people. Some may suggest that categorizing churches into these two somewhat strict categories does not address the lived reality of many churches. Though participants often felt no one in the non-accepting faith community supported their sexual identity, certainly there could have been members of their community who were uncertain or disagreed with the negative views of homosexuality in the non-accepting church. This project can only speak to the experience of the participants as they lived it in their congregations, and many participants remain hopeful that someday these non-accepting churches might become more open to LGBTQIA+ people. There are signs that change within the non-accepting church is not completely out of the realm of possibility; a qualitative study of the current climate in non-accepting evangelical communities suggests that there are three groups present in the non-accepting evangelical church: "a strengthening progressive faction, conservatives resisting the change, and those caught in the middle parsing through mixed feelings."[38] Other signs point to potential changes within the evangelical Christian community, especially among younger evangelicals. Support for same-sex marriage among young evangelicals jumped from 20% in 2003 to 42% in 2014.[39] This study, however, recognizes that despite changes in some communities there still exist a number of non-accepting congregations that are decidedly anti-LGBTQIA+, and those congregations are still affecting the lives of LGBTQIA+ people in their midst.

Living in a time where non-accepting and accepting congregations are not always ideologically or theologically pure, the current debate about homosexuality and Christianity still reflects the intertwined relationship of psychology and theology. Non-accepting congregations, according to participants in this project, exhibit a clear "disease model" of homosexuality, both homosexual desires and actions can be "cured" through prayer, counsel and attention to scripture. Accepting congregations recognize homosexuality as an identity, often talking about it as a "variant" in sexual identity within the Christian life. The disease model reflects a simplistic view of sexuality. In this model, homosexuality is an immoral choice, but also has the potential to infect those who are not vigilant in resisting the disease. Viewing homosexuality as a sexual identity is a much more complex view of how sexuality is lived out in both public and private spheres. Both accepting and non-accepting congregations understand themselves to correctly interpret scripture, tradition and Christian values. Yet their interpretations result in widely divergent values around sexuality. As a result, we must bring together the history of homosexuality within psychological circles and the growing pastoral care movement to understand how these two kinds of Christian communities exist in our modern world.

As Stoller argues in his opposition to homosexuality as a pathology, throughout the history of psychology heterosexuality was assumed to be the normal path of development. Whatever veered from normal suggested that something, whether it was an overly intense relationship with the mother or early sexual experience, had gone awry. This view, particularly important to the post-WWII psychologists as well as the newly translated biblical condemnation of homosexuality in the late 1940s, resulted in "the opposition between healthy heterosexuality and unhealthy homosexuality [taking] up the patina of long-standing tradition as Christians implanted these assumptions into their texts and teachings and thus into a retroactive sense of the past."[40] The post-WWII era was the perfect storm of rising interest in psychology, growing suspicion of homosexuality as a prime example of "communist values," and the interpretation of biblical texts as directly applicable to the sexual life of Christians. Homosexuality was a disease that threatened both American and Christian values, but it was a disease that could be cured.

It is precisely this disease model that was quickly adopted by both progressive and conservative Christian communities in this post-WWII era. Homosexuality was the exact opposite of healthy sexuality, and healthy sexuality was a part of the Christian life. Authorities like Seward Hiltner interpreted the Kinsey reports on sexuality through what he argued was a thoroughly Christian lens, reminding readers that "it is clear that sex is created by God, that man's body is not peripheral to his nature . . . that sex life itself is to the glory of God . . . "[41] People like Norman Vincent Peale, father of the power of positive thinking movement and a well-known and highly regarded pastor, "defined marriage as the apex of social and spiritual maturity-and thus worried that homosexuality constituted a stubborn impediment to both psychological health and moral progress."[42] These congregations, both progressive and conservative, focused their energy on "healing" what had broken within homosexuals in order to restore them to the highest form of Christian living, the heterosexual married life.

Yet, just as many psychologists were recognizing homosexuality as a variant rather than a pathological condition, within Christian circles a new public voice was loudly proclaiming the absolute incompatibility of Christianity and homosexuality. Loudest of these voices was arguably Anita Bryant, a popular singer and spokesperson for the Florida Citrus Commission. Bryant founded the organization Save Our Children with an explicit mission to defeat a motion in Dade County, Florida, to protect gay and lesbian people from discrimination.[43] Bryant employed the rhetoric of disease to describe the risks to children in Dade County, proclaiming that "God gave mothers the divine right to reproduce and a divine commission to protect our children, in our homes, business, and especially our schools . . . homosexuals cannot reproduce—so they must recruit. And to freshen their ranks, they must recruit the youth of America."[44] Homosexuality, for Bryant, was not an identity but a disease that could spread through human contact. Homosexuals were seeking to infect the youth of Dade County, and it was the job of Christians to rise up and demand "family values politics" in their communities.[45] Bryant, who epitomized the membership of Save Our Children—white women active in churches who self-consciously identified as parents—was known as a "wholesome, religious, and maternal" celebrity who sang alongside Billy Graham's preaching at an Evangelical Youth Crusade.[46] Bryant and the Save the Children movement explicitly connected anti-homosexual and "moral" politics to the Evangelical Christian Church. Homosexuality was a threat to the Christian family, and both church and politics had to protect the heterosexual "normal" family at all costs. The Dade County Coalition for the Humanistic Rights of Gays argued that the removal of homosexuality as a psychiatric disorder by the American Psychiatric Association made clear that "no child or person can be recruited into a homosexual lifestyle," but the Save our Children movement only continued to gain strength.[47] Conservative pastor Jerry Falwell held the "Christians for God and Decency Rally" in Miami in 1977, a rally that cemented the relationship between the Moral Majority movement in politics, Christian Evangelicals and anti-gay rhetoric. Bryant would even call the overwhelming number of voters who turned out to vote against the gay rights ordinance the "normal majority," a name which would eventually become the

Moral Majority.[48] The Moral Majority, a well-known political action committee throughout the 1980s, would gain significant political and social power.

This pairing of Christian "values" with morality and normalcy is the foundation of the difference between the progressive Christian church and the conservative church. The progressive church, before actively welcoming LGBTQIA+ individuals, viewed homosexuality as a disease that could be cured through pastoral relationship. People like Bertram Crocker, with whom we began our chapter, reflect a compassionate and hopeful view of how homosexuals might find a place in the Christian church. However, the 1970s and 1980s would usher in a moment in history when the conservative church gained political and cultural strength as the "true" representative of Christian values, while the progressive church was plagued by internal dissent over issues like homosexuality, women's ordination and sexuality education. This internal dissent resulted in the attempt to both adopt statements prohibiting the ordination of LGBTQIA+ people in their denominational bodies and at the same time support the political and civil rights of LGBTQIA+ people outside of the church. This ambiguous stance on sexuality in particular would eventually allow the conservative church to represent, culturally, the "real" Christian voice, while also painting the progressive church as adapting to culture and becoming "less" Christian as their denominations became more and more supportive of gay rights.[49]

What we can see now, as we look back over the history of both of these movements, is the reality that at one time both the conservative and progressive church held the same frame for homosexuality; it was a disease, but a curable and preventable one. In the 1970s and 1980s what would become the progressive church moved away from a disease model, while the conservative church reinforced it. The publication of the New International Version of the Bible, with its clear use of homosexual as the "plain meaning" of biblical texts, further reinforced the move toward literalism in the conservative church. "In addition to avowed fidelity to biblical authority, the practice of literalism also conveyed a personal and affective relationship to the text and its divine author—the Bible not only speaks authoritatively but speaks *to me*."[50] Conservative Christians, united around biblical literalism, political action, and the threat of homosexuality, popularized movements to use psychology and "conversion therapy" to cure homosexuality.

Today, we find this distance between accepting and non-accepting churches wider than ever. As many mainline denominations including the Evangelical Lutheran Church in America, the Presbyterian Church USA, the Episcopal Church and many others have adopted statements of welcome for LGBTQIA+ people in leadership and membership, non-accepting churches have continued to argue that homosexuality is incompatible with Christian moral values. The psychological community has not only accepted homosexuality as a normal variant in human sexuality, but has condemned the practice of conversion therapy, a system of "converting" a homosexual person to a heterosexual person, relying strongly on the view of homosexuality as a disease that can be cured through intense therapeutic work.

Simply recognizing that there is a gap between non-accepting and accepting churches around the issue of homosexuality does not do justice to the experiences of participants in this study. Participants were treated like they had a communicable disease; a disease which would condemn them for all eternity to a place of unimaginable suffering. Their stories require us to think about how the accepting church can be a place of refuge and healing for those who have been cast out and shattered by their community of faith. Though many visible leaders in non-accepting traditions have changed or softened their views of homosexuality, participants in this study noted that the lived reality within their non-accepting communities was radically different. In 2013 mega-church pastor Rob Bell publicly affirmed same-sex marriage. Jim Wallis, founder of Sojourners, a popular evangelical organization and magazine, soon followed. Tony Campolo, another well-known evangelical preacher, admitted that his feelings about homosexuality had become "shaky."[51] These changes are slow, but they provide some level of hope. Yet, even as views within parts of the Evangelical church shift, there still remain numerous congregations that will not tolerate LGBTQIA+ people in their midst, holding fast to a theology of condemnation for LGBTQIA+ people.

Despite these changes, slow though they are, participants in this study describe experiences of trauma that were healed only when they were able to live out their identity in a progressive church community. As will be expanded in Chapter 3, the non-accepting communities described by participants in this study often exhibited key theological similarities including a commitment to biblical literalism—a belief in scripture as an ultimate source of guidance. Scripture, in these non-accepting communities, was directly applicable to living one's best life, and provided a clear system of ethics. Though these non-accepting communities differed in denomination, style of worship and location, their commitment to the incompatibility of homosexuality and the Christian life made it impossible for participants in this study, once they acknowledged their sexual identity, to see themselves as acceptable to God. These stories highlight the real lived cost of this debate, and force us to ask ourselves what can be done to help those who have been victims of religious trauma.

NOTES

1. I first encountered this passage from Bertram Crocker's letter while reading White's *Reforming Sodom: Protestants and the Rise of Gay Rights,* an excellent text which offers a particularly detailed history of the Gay Rights movement within the Christian church.
2. Crocker, B. "Pastoral aid for the abnormal." *Crozer Quarterly* (1945): 242–245.
3. Crocker, "Pastoral aid," 245.
4. White, H. R. *Reforming Sodom: Protestants and the Rise of Gay Rights* (1st edition) Chapel Hill: University of North Carolina Press, 2015, 1.
5. White, *Reforming Sodom: Protestants and the Rise of Gay Rights,* 3.
6. Holifield, E. B. *A History of Pastoral Care in America: From Salvation to Self-Realization.* Nashville: Abingdon Press, 1983, 259.
7. Holifield, *A History of Pastoral Care in America: From Salvation to Self-Realization,* 271.
8. Muravchik, S. *American Protestantism in the Age of Psychology.* Cambridge; New York: Cambridge University Press, 2011, 2.
9. Snodgrass, J. "From Rogers to Clinebell: Exploring the history of pastoral psychology." *Pastoral Psychology* 55 (2007): 513–525.
10. Holifield, *A History of Pastoral Care in America: From Salvation to Self-Realization,* 263.
11. Havemann, E. "The age of psychology in the U.S." *Life* 11: 68–82.
12. Allen, C. L. *God's Psychiatry: The Twenty-third Psalm, the Ten Commandments, the Lord's Prayer, the Beatitudes.* Westwood, N.J.: F. H. Revell Co, 1953/2015, 11–12
13. (Davis, 2011, p. 347). Davis, R L. *"My homosexuality is getting worse everyday": Norman Vincent Peale, Psychiatry, and the Liberal Protestant Response to Same-Sex Desires in Mid-Twentieth-Century America.* In C. A. Brekus and W. C. Gilpin (Ed.), American Christianities: A History of Dominance and Diversity. Chapel Hill: The University of North Carolina Press, 2011, 347.
14. Hiltner, S. *Preface to pastoral theology.* New York: Abingdon Press, 1958, 26.
15. Holifield, *A History of Pastoral Care in America: From Salvation to Self-Realization,* 271.
16. Holifield, *A History of Pastoral Care in America: From Salvation to Self-Realization,* 271.
17. Holifield, *A History of Pastoral Care in America: From Salvation to Self-Realization,* 274.
18. Freud, S. "Historical notes." *American Journal of Psychiatry* 107 (1951): 786–787.
19. Freud, S. and J. Strachey. *Three essays on the theory of sexuality.* New York: Basic Books, 1910/2000, 6.
20. Freud, *Three essays on the theory of sexuality,* 4–6.
21. Freud, *Three essays on the theory of sexuality,* 11.

22. Freud, S. *Analysis of a Phobia in a Five-year-old Boy.* In J. Strachey (Ed. & Trans.), The standard edition of the complete psychological works of Sigmund Freud (Vol. 10), 1909/1986, 27.

23. Klein, M. *The Psychoanalysis of Children.* New York,: Grove Press, 1960, 345.

24. Bergler, E. *Homosexuality, Disease or Way of Life?* New York: Hill and Wang, 1956, 28–29.

25. Freud, *Three essays on the theory of sexuality,* 5.

26. Bergler, E. "Differential Diagnosis between Spurious Homosexuality and Perversion Homosexuality." *Psychiatric Quarterly* 21 (1947): 399–409.

27. Bergler, "Differential Diagnosis," 403.

28. Bergler, "Differential Diagnosis," 405.

29. Lewes, K. *Psychoanalysis and Male Homosexuality* (1st softcover ed.). Northvale, N.J.: J. Aronson, 1995, 220.

30. Lewes, *Psychoanalysis and Male Homosexuality,* 225–227.

31. Lewes, *Psychoanalysis and Male Homosexuality,* 172.

32. Lewes, *Psychoanalysis and Male Homosexuality,* 202.

33. White, *Reforming Sodom: Protestants and the Rise of Gay,* 138–139.

34. Stoller, R. J. "The Samuel Novey lecture: Does sexual perversion exist?" *The Johns Hopkins Medical Journal,* 134 (1), (1974): 43–57.

35. Lewes, *Psychoanalysis and Male Homosexuality,* 208.

36. Chodorow, N. "Heterosexuality as a Compromise Formation: Reflections on the Psychoanalytic Theory of Sexual Development." *Psychoanalysis and Contemporary Thought,* 15, (1992): 267–304

37. Chodorow, "Heterosexuality as Compromise Formation," 267–304.

38. Lee, D. J. *Rescuing Jesus: How People of Color, Women, & Queer Christians are Reclaiming Evangelicalism.* Boston: Beacon Press, 2015, 153–154.

39. Dias, E. "A Change of Heart." *Time,* 185(2), (2015): 44–48.

40. White, *Reforming Sodom: Protestants and the Rise of Gay Rights,* 174.

41. Hiltner, S. *Sex Ethics and the Kinsey Reports.* New York: Association Press, 1953, 17.

42. Davis, "My homosexuality is getting worse everyday," 348.

43. Frank, G. "The Civil Rights of Parents: Race and Conservative Politics in Anita Bryant's Campaign Against Gay Rights in 1970s Florida." *Journal of the History of Sexuality* 22 (2013): 126–160.

44. Frank, "The Civil Rights of Parents," 127.

45. Frank, "The Civil Rights of Parents," 129.

46. Frank, "The Civil Rights of Parents," 142–143.

47. Frank, "The Civil Rights of Parents," 150.

48. Frank, "The Civil Rights of Parents," 157.

49. White, *Reforming Sodom: Protestants and the Rise of Gay Rights,* 178.

50. White, *Reforming Sodom: Protestants and the Rise of Gay Rights,* 182.

51. Lee, *Rescuing Jesus,* 241.

Chapter Three

What Was Lost: Describing the Attachment to Religious Community as Selfobject

In order to understand what shattered a "predictable" world, we must first understand how that world was ordered. For participants in this study, religion played a major role in their life growing up; for many it was the central place around which their entire family organized their lives. Jorge, a Latino man now in his early thirties, first started attending a Baptist Church when approached by some congregants who took a bus through his neighborhood recruiting people. He says,

> I started going when I was in fourth grade, so ever since then I was going to the same church, ever since fourth grade it played a huge role where I then went to their school, graduated from their schools, went to their college, graduated from their college, went on to teach at their schools, taught at their schools, was the choir director for the church, so it was pretty much my life. I only had a couple hours to myself pretty much. But it was very much 24/7 for a good, probably since fourth grade . . . So we got picked up sometimes Sunday morning while they did the rest of the route, picked up people, and then we would get on the expressway and drive and have a program on the bus all the way up to the church and then we would have a Sunday School and then we would break off into church service, and then we would get back on the bus go home until I was probably in Junior High, that is when I started going to the evening service as well, so I would get back on the bus drive back for the evening service, I would get home to eat and then get back on the bus and come back home around 10 at night on Sunday nights.

But for Jorge, it was not just sheer number of hours that made the church a central part of his life; it was also a response to his "acting out" in public school. Soon after, his entire family started attending the same church regularly, so towards my junior year in high school my parents started seeing a huge change, by this time, my brother, my sister and my other brother were going with me as well. And they then started going to church every Sunday with us, they started getting in a car instead of the bus, we would all go to our separate services, the adults would go to separate services, and then meet up after church, go to lunch, and then I would then, by that time, I would stay in afternoon programs instead of going all the way [home], there was a program for teenagers, in between services where we got taught different characters, how to live, how to work, inner city kind of relationship building, and then we would go to service after that. And that's, I guess that hour and a half, two maybe three hours of break we learned sports, we learned music, that is actually where I got my love for music, and then, they taught us how to be preacher boys (laughs) and go on to serve God.

Jorge was raised in the halls of the church, his friends were Baptist, his community was Baptist, and being a member of the Baptist church taught him how to be a "god-loving man," which meant,

> we had a whole Christian manhood class, on how to look like a man, and how to carry your bible and how to walk and how to protect a lady, how to look after the home, you're the authority in the house, this is how you should be when you are a man going on to college and so on and so forth, and I remember [the pastor] pointing out people that they were a little effeminate and making fun of them.

For Jorge, the church was a place you learned how to be a man, how to be a good person, and how to stay out of trouble. In Jorge's experience, the church was a place where you learned what it meant to live a "godly life."

Alex, a white genderqueer person in their late twenties, had a similar upbringing, but in the Lutheran Church Missouri Synod, a much more traditionally liturgical congregation.[1]

> We had Matins before divine liturgy, so we would get there at like 8am on Sunday, do a full matins service and then go to divine liturgy. There is a little, kind of mini-lunch afterwards and then formation. It is like 8 until probably 1 or 2. It was a whole, that was like, it was a big deal. And we never missed. And then there is also midweek services, so we would go for, depending on the time of year, either divine liturgy or vespers service and a meal and then also formation every Wednesday. So it was, big involvement. And then I, so that was my involvement as an acolyte and with music and all of that.

Alex's family was one of "three core families" in the congregation, and their interest in both music and the priesthood made church a place where they spent most of their time.

This church was also very high church liturgically speaking, so we had incense, and processional crucifixes, and 20 acolytes and all this stuff. So I was involved with that, and then also with music from an early age. And just, the parish didn't have money at the beginning for quite awhile to pay a permanent musician so what they would do was pay somebody to come in and record on the organ and then I would be back there pushing play, and then eventually I learned how to play so I became the musical part of the place, and started conducting a choir when I was thirteen there.

Alex describes that the whole family, as well as the pastor at their church all anticipated that they would become a priest theirself. Church was where they felt most at home,

And also just being so involved in the church growing up, I felt like I experienced God in the liturgy growing up, as a kid, I was enthralled, I loved it. I was the one who would go and wake up the entire family to go to church. To get everybody up, wake them up, I was the one who was the first in the door and the last one out. I loved it. I couldn't get enough of it.

For April, a white woman in her late twenties, church was not just a place where she spent most of her time, it was additionally complicated by the fact that her father was the pastor.

And, I am sure you know a lot about the Southern Baptists, but they are way over in the no drinking, no dancing, not even like waltzing, and with my dad with being a minister there was, but also for most families in the church, Sunday night, Wednesday night, usually an activity on Saturday. Because it was pretty much you did school and you did church and there wasn't really that much other stuff. So it was a big part of that.

April, as a pastor's daughter, felt the intense pressure to believe everything she was hearing, despite the growing doubts she had about the theology taught in her Southern Baptist home and congregation.

When I was little I took my naps on the pews, I read a lot of theology books I didn't really understand because I was bored. I liked it when I was very small, but once I got to be about, maybe 8 or 9, I started realizing that this doesn't actually make any sense, because they are super super super literal. All of the youth classes were sort of like using "scientific" facts to defend the parting of the Red Sea and resurrection and in intense detail like there were workbooks and video and it was very intense. And at first I was like, oh, hey, this doesn't make any sense but then I kept getting so much negative feedback, so then I started not liking it, but then I started to get very very terrified I was going to hell, because that is like a real serious thing for them. We heard lots of sermons about what hell would be like, so probably from age 10 or 11 until about early 20's, I would alternate between thinking this is so stupid there probably isn't even God and repenting frantically . . . But I got a lot of flack from my mom, that no one in the church would respect them and my dad would lose his job and we wouldn't have anywhere to live if people thought I was a bad kid. So most of the other kids in the church were either home schooled or went to a private Christian school, my parents couldn't afford it so they sent me to the public school where I was taught things like evolution . . . Yeah, you know actual facts. So, there was a lot of pressure to always be like very good because otherwise you will ruin the family both in name and like actually.

April recalls standing on street corners and handing out tracts describing the future that lay ahead for people who did not let Jesus into their lives. She felt like anything outside of her Southern Baptist way of life was a "whole other planet," and couldn't imagine that it was even possible to live any other way. In April's community there was significant pressure to convert others in order to save them from eternal damnation. Even when leaving for college, finally getting out of her small southern town required

> prayer sessions and hands laying on sessions that I would be this strong Christian woman who would go and convert the Yankee heathens. That's a direct quote. They were like, you have the strength to stand up to this, it is going to be really hard, but you can go and be a light in the darkness.

What she was supposed to stand up to is hard to pinpoint, but the message was clear to April, being outside of the church was bad, being inside was where the world was safe and made sense.

Oliver, a white man in his early thirties, also recalled church being a huge part of his upbringing.

> Well, I went to the Christian Reformed School—kindergarten through eighth grade and then again for high school. We went to church every Sunday, some Sundays twice in the morning and the evening, so it was a very church religious background . . . You had to go, you didn't have a choice. And I never, in that church, I never felt like I really had friends, you had to go because that is where you parents went and they told you you had to.

Like April, Oliver was surrounded by a community that was connected through his local congregation,

> Well, to be honest, most of the people I knew growing up went to the same church or school, and if they didn't go to our church they went to the First Christian Reformed Church down the street, or they went to the one the next town over . . . I mean, I can probably count on my hand the number of my

mom's friends or something that weren't from church or the denomination, and usually they went to the same church.

Oliver wanted to the "perfect little Christian Reformed person you could be," which meant making a church a major part of your life, even if it felt routine.

> You go there, you do this and then you leave. Check in and check out. God was like this big person in the sky, and made sure you did everything right, you know . . . like to be the right Christian, you had to do things to fit in.

For Oliver, April, Alex and Jorge, church was not just a place for them, it was a place where their families participated in rituals that defined who they were as a family. Church was something they "always did"; it was a part of their identity. For all of these participants, participation in worship and their presence in church made them part of the "core leadership" of the church; if their family did not attend worship their absence was noted. It was not just the sheer number of hours that they spent attending worship or participating in community events; these communities were where they connected with the people who were important in their lives. April remembers,

> Sunday night church was always, or just in the summer, I can't remember, but at least in the summer we would do we call it covered dish, but it is like potluck dinners, and everybody would bring food, and that was a really nice social time. Because when I was really small there were probably like 200 people there, but really a core of about 50. So everyone would get together, and Miss Bertha would always bring her macaroni salad and it was always so good and Miss Carol would make her jello . . . every Sunday night you would eat together, and in the fall we would do soup suppers every Wednesday night as well. So it was really very communal in a lot of ways, and I kind of miss that.

Yet, April, Oliver, Alex and Jorge also internalized the fear of what happened outside of the church, in a world that was often thought of as scary or immoral. Concepts like safety, morality, and perfection were part of what kept them returning to this church community over and over again, because the world outside of the church was unknown and threatening. Several participants noted that even denominations outside of their own were considered suspect, Beth says, "I really questioned anyone who was a Methodist, anyone who was a Catholic definitely . . . And Mormons absolutely. Absolutely not. I mean, that's just kind of how indoctrinated, you know, your way, this way, is the only true way."

But not all participants experienced church as a source of family stability like Oliver, April, Alex, and Jorge. For Beth, a white woman in her early fifties, going to worship was a reaction to what she described in general terms as the growing instability at home.

> I never went to church with my parents, I went with my neighbor Sally who always invited me, each summer to vacation bible school. And my parents never went to church. And my aunt and uncle, my mom's sister and her husband they were very much active in a Free Will Baptist Church. Free Will Baptist is more of a charismatic, they would never use that word, but that's the type of church it was. Like all the men sat on one side all the women sat on one side, you couldn't sit together. The pastor in my earliest memories of a pastor was [Bobby White], [Rev. Bobby White] . . . he would walk up and down the aisle and the Lord would say, and spitting, and I was terrified. I was terrified of this God . . . I was young, too, I was like four years old. So every once and awhile we'd go with them, and that was just terrifying to watch him. But [Batesville] Baptist wasn't like that, men and women sat together, there was a children's choir and vacation bible school was how I knew that church. And so, I grow up, and I was probably about seventeen, I don't know if it was teenage angst or whatever, I mean things at home, my family life wasn't so good, and I just needed wanted something different. I just needed something. So one day I woke up, and I said to my mom, "I'm going to go to church," and she was like "okay." And I did, I drove to church and I went to church, and that was the Sunday I accepted Christ . . . I mean it's right down the road from where I grew up, probably two miles from my house if that, and I just did it, I completely went hook line and sinker. I was like okay God, I need you to help me figure this stuff out . . . I just woke up and said this is what I am doing, something's gotta give. Something's gotta mean something, something's got to matter in this world. I don't know. Things at home were just not good, not good at all.

Beth quickly became a leader in her new church, and continued her leadership roles in college, involving herself in a number of Christian groups at school, and finally enrolled in a Southern Baptist seminary. Being an active young leader in the Southern Baptist Church, despite the more traditional views of women's roles, "opened a lot of doors" that Beth thinks would not have been available to her if she wasn't active in a church. She recalls with great fondness "being immersed in that group, travelling with that group, you know, loving classes on religion, and having a teacher, one of my professors, being like, 'you know, have you thought about this . . . going to seminary . . . ' and you know, it was good. It was a good group, and it was a good exposure, I met a lot of good people." Beth spent most of her time at church, "Oh, Sunday, Wednesday night, Sunday morning, Sunday night. And if anything else fell in there, I was there. I was there every time it was open. And I was wearing dresses, and trying so hard. And now I can't stand dresses, I hated them even then."

Jasmine, a black woman in her mid-forties, was primarily exposed to church through various relatives after her parents divorced.

> So my first church visit that I remember I was around 8 or 9, my grandma was Catholic so I went with her for a number of years, and then I started going with my aunt she was, what is it called again, Pentecostal, so that was a huge switch . . . Yeah, and then I would visit other aunts on my dad's side and they were Baptist . . . So I was exposed to a lot of different denominations within the faith, made me super confused. (Laughing) I didn't know if I was coming or going, I remember being on my knees at Mass and then having my grandma talk about confession, I remember not liking the idea of telling my secrets to a guy behind a screen.

Jasmine continued to attend a variety of churches with various family members, and even tried a Unitarian congregation on her own. When looking back, she felt like she was looking for a connection, and that "going to church was where you found God." She felt like she was desperate for a connection with God in response to the emotional distance and abandonment she felt in relation to her parents.

> That idea of God comforting me when my parents couldn't be there for whatever reason. My mom, she had postpartum, and she was taking care of my two-week-old sister, and seeing her sad all the time took a toll, and me wanting to fix it. And then my dad, literally not physically being there and leaving me with my grandma. I wanted to have some type of connection with that family, and through that process feeling like there was some kind of presence with me, looking back I would say it was God, but I couldn't name it . . .

Church, in her wandering from denomination to denomination, was a place of solace for Jasmine, and a location for a connection to something bigger than herself. After a short break from church she felt,

> then I had a crisis when I was in my early to mid-30's, I was just in a bad place. I didn't know where I was going in life, I didn't like what I was doing, I was just being like an administrative assistant. I had dropped out of college, it was a lot of stuff going on, I started seeking counseling, and throughout that time of counseling in particular I realized that my faith was the one thing that was missing . . . eventually I took [my therapist's] advice and I went to a Vineyard Church that a colleague of mine attended. And I participated for two or three months, people were very welcoming, it was a small congregation. I was still kind of self destructive at the time, overeating, I was self harming at the time. And I confessed that to the pastor because I just wanted to feel better . . .

Jasmine felt that church was a place you went not just for a connection, but for healing when the world around you was falling apart.

Lucas, a white man in his late thirties, like Jasmine and Beth, had more than one denominational home,

> I was raised basically Methodist. However, I spent my summers with grandparents who were in that firebrandy Missionary Baptist kind of background. I wish I could remember the name of the . . . it is a particular denomination but I can't remember what it is called, but it is like Southern Baptist. So, that is just the beginning of how when I was very, very young my formative relationship with God, with religion was, even though I went to a Methodist church and my parents identified as Methodist, in a weird way what more stuck with me was they would send me to my grandparents who would then send me to these more extreme ten hour long church services, even though I went to a more standard mainline Protestant denomination when I was with my family, I spent so much more intense time when I was at these camps and stuff when I was at my grandparents' that they had a more lasting impact on me, I think.

Lucas was sexually abused by an adopted sister as an infant and young child. Lucas felt protected from having to think about both the sexual abuse and his developing sexuality by a theology that allowed him to believe all sexuality as bad. He eventually settled in a Southern Baptist Church, which he felt provided this important mental protection.

> Yeah, so a few years after that I started to get really depressed and started to not want to go to school. And now I can identify that I was probably starting puberty and not wanting to deal with those feelings. But what I experienced at the time was profound depression and I did not want to go to school. And I was very confused. What happened is, I don't know what I encountered specifically, but at that point in my life I then basically somehow connected with the local Southern Baptist Church in Texas where I grew up, and their youth group or whatever, and I "got saved" whatever that means. And then I became very involved with them, and it has taken a lot of therapy and a lot of stuff to understand this whole process, but what I understand now it to be is that, is that I felt lost and I felt confused, and that whole, that becoming born again thing stuck with me for a good while that lifestyle, and I really think that I used that as a way to cope with the sexual abuse. Because I was then old enough to remember it and think about it, and have confusing feelings and stuff like that, so now I understand that I used that in a way to be like, yeah, sex is bad!

The church functioned as a "home" for Lucas when he felt lost and confused, and provided needed internal structure to allow him to set aside the chaos of sexual abuse. The church was safe; what was going on in his mind and in his home was not.

Sarah, a white woman in her late twenties, left church when she was 13, only to return again at age 18.

> So when I was a kid [church] was something you did on Sundays, I grew up in the bible belt, so where you went mattered for social status, and it plays into in the South everyone assumes you are Christian, there is no spoken, it is just an assumption that everyone makes. It was just something you did. And when I was about thirteen, it actually had nothing to do with me, but the other girls in my group were really bullying this one kid, she would like cry in the bathroom, and I told my mom I didn't want to be a part of that anymore. So I kind of left the church when I was thirteen, had nothing to do with any kind of issues with the church but I went back when I was about eighteen in college to a non-denominational evangelical Southern church.

As a freshman in college, looking for a place to connect with something bigger than herself, Sarah joined a new local mega-church,

> It would be considered a hip Southern church. It was pretty weird, and when I talk about it, man, it was kind of cultish . . . You know always being there, we had Wednesday night college ministries, and at our largest would get like 200 people. Yeah, it was just a really dynamic leader, it was just really kind of hip. They would just talk about life.

After graduating from college she moved to a larger city and began attending a non-denominational church. Despite growing up in a home that she describes as inclusive and welcoming, she found herself joining and dedicating a large amount of time to these congregations,

> I think it is one of those things, when I think about it, you like the people, and I think a lot of people do this with churches too, I feel like the people, I just hang out with these people and I go there on Sundays but it is not really affecting my day to day, and then you kind of stop thinking about what do they actually believe? And when you sit down and actually think about it, you are like, oh, this is horrifying. But there is that aspect of just wanting to belong to a group, and especially that group in college, it was such a dynamic group of people and really all about going out there and doing things, really charismatic leaders and they were young, and they just were, you were just like, I want to be a part of something, and I will just keep my mouth shut about these because it is not like they are really demanding that I, or digging into what my beliefs are, and normally I have always had a flight response to when things get too weird, I take comfort that I left those places eventually . . . because you look back and I am like, yeah that was terrible that I was going there, especially that church in college I would have invited people there! I would never invite people to belong to the [non-denominational] church here, and that church was always asking why I

never invited people, and I was embarrassed saying I am not going to invite anyone here, but it was also one of those things, like I was too embarrassed to leave.

All of the participants, whether the non-accepting church was a central part of their family experience, or whether they came to it on their own, recalled these churches shaping who they were as people. They learned what it meant to be "good" people in these congregations. For many, the church was a safe space from the internal and relational chaos they faced outside of its walls. The church was a refuge from either a dangerous world, or an unstable home.

What might this demonstrate to us about the appeal of these congregations? What was pulling these seven participants toward these gatherings of people, given that they were both an aspect of their family organization for some, and a reaction to chaos for others? What is the appeal of religion and religious community?

IDEALIZATION AND SELFOBJECT RELATIONSHIPS

Freud argues against the necessity of religion in several of his writings. He suggests religion rose out of the need to on the one hand, "defend oneself against the crushingly superior forces of nature," the natural disasters that remind us how miniscule we are in the vastness of space and time, while also, on the other hand, to create a "moral world order" to protect us against the internal desire we all have to kill, steal and destroy.[2] Religion acts as a buffer against natural fears, but it is an insufficient buffer; religion is the result of an infantile wish that the world would be ordered and free from chaos. Heinz Kohut, expanding upon Freud, argues that Freud saw religion as "poor science," with the assumption that true science was based in what could be proven and observed in reality. For Kohut, religion may be poor science, but it is an "understandable attempt to find explanations for things." Kohut argues religion, in its complexity, is a supportive selfobject, an institution which functions to support the self-concept.[3] Religion puts into words what is "in people," what is beyond science. For Kohut, Freud focused too specifically on the failure of religion to hold up to scientific rigor.[4]

The search for and function of selfobjects forms much of the theory of self psychology, first articulated by Kohut in the 1960s and 1970s. As a psychoanalyst, Kohut grew dissatisfied with the Freudian psychoanalytic focus on biological drives as the primary motivators in human life. For Freud, to put it in somewhat simple terms, the biological drives within the human person are the basis for human action. People are driven to seek after pleasure or destruction. Kohut argued that drives were best understood as "disintegration products," or a response to failures in the primary selfobject matrix.[5] Drives were not central to our behavior, but a result of things that were missing from primary selfobject relationships. But what are these selfobjects? Objects, broadly, are things outside of ourselves in which humans have interest. Objects are not just other people, but "animals, pets, interests in things ones pursues, such as art, music, or whatever it may be."[6] Selfobjects are objects that "maintain and enhance an individual's self-esteem, creativity and self-efficacy and in which the individual can invest their energy." We internalize selfobjects naturally, we invest our emotional energy in objects we can idealize, objects that mirror back to us our achievements, and objects that provide us a sense of belonging.[7] But how does internalization happen?

This process of internalization begins when we enter into relationship with objects that love, support and care for us. A baby has someone who keeps them warm, feeds them when they are hungry, but, also, when the baby is anxious, picks up the child, rocks them and sings, including the child "in her larger calmness" so that the baby could feel attached and "become calm in the process." Kohut argues, "it is on the basis of first having had this from the outside, and then very gradually losing it, that [the baby] gradually acquired the ability to take it over [itself] like any other skill." Selfobjects are like the "building blocks" of the internal self structure we need.[8]

Kohut recognizes that the foundation of health is the ability to love and be in relationship with objects; normal development is a movement from "self-preoccupation to preoccupation with objects, from self-concern to concern with others, and more simply from egoism to altruism."[9] Narcissism, in contrast, is typically seen as a failure in development; to be narcissistic is to be overly concerned with the self, to be stuck in egoism and unable to move toward altruism, to be preoccupied with the self instead of able to love objects. Kohut, however, in moving away from drives, moves toward the centrality of narcissism in human development. All humans move from primitive narcissism to "mature, adaptive and culturally valuable" narcissism.[10] All humans begin with narcissistic needs to be loved and valued, just as "you are constructed to be born in a world of oxygen." Kohut argues that a baby is "constructed psychologically to be born into a matrix of responsive selfobjects." Put simply, a baby is born into a world of relationships.[11] In optimal situations, this relational matrix provides not just for the physical needs of the baby, that it be changed, fed, and clothed, but this relational web provides for the psychological needs of the child. Selfobjects satisfy these primary narcissistic needs, for empathic mirroring, twinship and idealization. Throughout life selfobjects help maintain the "cohesion, vitality, strength and harmony of the self.[12] But how?

For the baby, there is no concept of I-You; everything is I. An infant cannot experience the mother as separate, but rather experiences the mother as an extension of self. As psychological or physical needs are unmet, the diaper remains wet, the cries for hunger and not immediately satisfied by the breast, the gaze of the mother does not hold the emotional energy the child seeks, the infant begins to naturally sense that there are "shortcomings in this narcissistic paradise."[13] These shortcomings lead to two distinct thoughts and attendant needs. First, that the child is all good, but something bad exists outside of it, otherwise known as the concept of the *grandiose self.* Second, that something bad exists within the child, and so the parent must be all good, and makes the child good again by allowing the child to attach to the parent's greatness, or an *idealized parent imago.* For Kohut, the nuclear self, the most central and basic self, is a result of the grandiose self and the idealized parent imago.[14]

Kohut argues that throughout life, we require selfobject relationships. We need relational experiences that "joyfully respond to us," and are a "source of idealized strength and calmness, silently present but in essence like [us] and able to grasp [our] inner life more or less accurately so that their responses are attuned to [our] needs and allow [us] to grasp their inner life when [we are] in need of such sustenance."[15] Our nuclear self allows us to function at our best, to be creative and courageous. We build this strong nuclear self when from the earliest stage on we are surrounded by a matrix of relationships that are attuned to our needs and also hold our need to idealize something as greater than ourselves. Our relationships with selfobjects create the internal "psychic structures" that make us who we are. Primitive narcissism, like the narcissism of the baby, cannot tolerate the disappointments of selfobjects, because the baby has not yet been able to build up the internal psychological structure. Mature narcissism suggests that one has developed a healthy nuclear self, a self that, when faced with the early disappointments of selfobjects, was able to build up, internally, the self structure needed to remain in relationship with those selfobjects and to select selfobjects that are appropriate and healthy for us.[16] Mature narcissism is a direct result of slow and non-traumatic disappointments in the selfobject milieu. When disappointments are gradual, the experience of the selfobject becomes more realistic, and the idealization provided by the selfobject is slowly internalized. For Kohut, there is "not one kind of healthy self" which results from these gradual disappointments, but when one exhibits a healthy nuclear self one is able to lead a creative and meaningful life. This kind of health is not achieved by being entirely autonomous, but by remaining in healthy relationships with necessary selfobjects.[17]

How does this connect to the religious communities of these participants? Kohut argues that throughout our lives, this need for selfobjects, for things that both reflect back to us our own grandiosity and also allow us to come alongside their own greatness, are part of how we exist in the world. Kohut calls these basic needs mirroring and idealization. On the spectrum from pathology to health, the needs remain the same; all humans need to be mirrored and to idealize, but the way we satisfy those needs demonstrates whether we have adequately internalized the structure needed to live full and meaningful lives.

This natural need for idealization, according to psychologist of religion James Jones, is at the core of our relationship with religious institutions. Idealization can be satisfied in religious communities as we are taken into a world of the sacred—God is ultimately good, and God calls us God's children. Freud, responding to a letter from a friend, notes that for many believers the sacred brings about a "sensation of 'eternity,' a feeling of something limitless, unbounded—as it were, 'oceanic,'" a feeling which harkens back to the intimate and total connection a baby feels with the mother.[18] This state of ultimate bliss, primary narcissism in Kohut's theory, "reverberates unconsciously" when we encounter a similar feeling selfobject later in life. For many, the idealization of God as a selfobject leaves us with an oceanic feeling, "the old uplifting experience of being picked up by our strong and admired mother and having been allowed to merge with her greatness, calmness and security . . . the unconscious undertones of joy we are experiencing as adults."[19]

This need for idealization, as Kohut notes, can be mature, and can be lived out in appropriately chosen selfobject relationships, or it can reflect a hunger that has been unmet since childhood. A traumatic loss or unavailability of idealizable or mirroring selfobjects can lead to a variety of unhealthy patterns in relationships—rage at the experience of a slight, intense feelings of guilt and shame, an inability to remain in relationships with people or ideas when they lose their originally perceived perfection.

IDEALIZED SELFOBJECTS AND NON-ACCEPTING CHRISTIAN COMMUNITIES

Alex, Oliver, and April grew up in the halls of the church; it was central to the structure of their families. Kohut argues that our primary idealized selfobjects are our parents; it is the "greatness, calmness and security" of our mothers which reverberates when we are in similar selfobject relationships later. Yet, for Alex, Oliver, and April, the greatness of the parent was pale in comparison to the greatness of God. For their families, the ultimate source of life was God; God was the greatest of all beings, the ultimate idealized selfobject. It is hardly surprising that for these three participants, the church and the God that lived there, became a central part of their lives. God was the source of love, of mercy, and of judgment. God was far beyond their parents, and in seeing their parents submit to God, to kneel and pray, further reinforced the centrality and importance of God as the ultimate example of "greatness, calmness, and security." Multiple times a week, Alex, Oliver, and April sensed that "the natural order of things [included] the existence of this being to whom all adults [came] with weekly solemnity or at least at times of major events—weddings, births, deaths—in order to submit to his wishes."[20]

Beth, Jasmine, and Lucas came to religion by a different path, but still exhibited the draw toward this idealizable selfobject. For Beth, Jasmine and Lucas, home was a place of chaos. Even with some idealizable selfobjects for these participants, these potential selfobjects also failed, either to keep the home safe in the case of Beth, to protect from sexual abuse in the case of Lucas, or to be present physically in the case of Jasmine. The search for a religious figure to respond to their need for "greatness, calmness, and security" is not surprising. God was the one who could provide the mental and physical safety they yearned for. The church, and the God within it, became a safe space where they could trust that they would be loved by the most ultimate of beings.

Neither Jorge nor Sarah fit nicely into these two groups; both came to these non-accepting religious communities before their families, and neither felt that their homes were unsupportive or unsafe. Jorge describes his relationship with his mother as "great" and "all he needed" when he was in crisis. Sarah also speaks of her parents in glowing terms, describing her home as "loving" and as a refuge from much of the racism and homophobia in the South. Jorge eventually led his parents and the rest of his siblings to church, but clearly learned from the other adults in this Baptist community that God was the most important part of your life. Jorge remembers thinking, "God was a friend, God was someone I could always relate to in my good times and bad times, I would get in a car, and having a bad day, and I remember praying—I may not know the answers you just send me my way." Not only was God a constant presence to Jorge, a friend who was always with him and who had all the answers, but the pastors in the congregation were direct lines to God who embodied this holiness. He describes his youth pastor as follows:

> I mimicked him for the longest time, I would try to dress like him, to step up to him, and later on I became his right hand man for after program and the youth department, one of his Sunday School teachers and ran the Junior High Department for him and everything. So I became one of his leading men.

Every Sunday, Jorge estimates that 30,000 people attended worship in some capacity, so the energy directed toward these leaders and to God was intense. The church captivated him, and the desire to be a "godly man," to be like God in all ways, was embodied by these pastors. Jorge felt special and loved in the presence of these leaders, and in his relationship with God.

Sarah grew up in the South, and felt that church was important culturally because "where you went mattered for social status." Though she left her Methodist congregation at thirteen when she encountered a group of adolescents bullying another student, she returned as a freshman in college, recalling

> In college I was always kind of the good kid, so I hung out with a lot of the Christians, and then in college, I got really into it, helped to start a lot of the college youth group of this start up church . . .
>
> I don't know, I think I have always had this underlying draw to religion and faith, but for the most part, their values, when you really look at them, they see women shouldn't be in leadership roles, and I grew up in a house with a mom who always worked, and really different life from them. They thought something was wrong when the mom wasn't in the house all the time. And the fact that I stayed in that church for college, I was in college for 5 years because I took an extra year, so a good four and half, the fact that I think back on it, and I let those values define my life in college, even relationships, at that point I was only dating guys, but to think that's how I did it. I also wanted to belong to something, so that something cool came along I think had a role in it, I think what drew me to it was wanting to experience something new and different and this was new and different. And I guess I just ignored the parts that I didn't agree with.

Church was a central place where she met her friends and connected with a needed social group in her new college setting.

> I have close friends that I went to it with, but it is just not, it is weird to look back and see how involved I was and how I never really questioned, because there was this thing when you become a member you have to take this test kind of, and find a person to sponsor you, and I remember this is actually really weird, like Jesus wanted everyone, his table is open to everyone.

For Sarah, church, small groups, and bible studies were a central organizing feature in her college life. Being a Christian was something she could "really get into."

For all of these participants, God was the ultimate idealized selfobject. God was omnipotent, omniscient, and supreme to all other relationships. God was the organizing center, and as a result, the way that God felt about them was of utmost importance. God cared about sexuality, and to disobey God's will meant living outside of God's love. God could not be questioned; doubt was unacceptable. Drawing on Kohut, the selfobject relationship had to remain archaic because there was no space for imperfection.

Chapter Three

HOMOSEXUALITY, SEXUALITY AND HELL

Messages about homosexuality specifically and sexuality in general were loud and clear to the participants in this study. For some, the messages were explicit, and leadership within the congregation spoke specifically on the incompatibility of homosexuality and Christianity. Sarah remembers,

> There was only one message ever, so they would do things that were tied to the modern world, sermons on movies and then tie back, but they were always movies with Christian undertones, and then in one series they had, it is kind of like the Reddit ask me anything thing, you would write in your questions anonymously and they would answer any question. So they were going through a bunch of them, it was like a series, and there was one Sunday, probably toward the end of my college career, so I was kind of on the outskirts, getting kind of burned out, and someone asked if you could be Christian and gay, and the pastor in the big campus on the screen, was like, you know what, I never thought I would get these questions, you know I wasn't going to answer it, but then I was shocked I got so many, and I can't believe anyone in the congregation ever thought it would be appropriate to ask this question. He said, I am only going to say one thing about this, and then I don't want anyone to ask me ever again, and it was like seven words, you cannot be Christian and be gay. That is it, we are never going to talk about it again, that is a silly subject . . .

Jasmine also recalled a similar reaction to questions about homosexuality, but with a warning about what happened to homosexual people.

> You are going to hell. That was the worst. That was like up there with murdering. And you have to, well, the message that I got, was that if you are you confess your sins and you hope that He changes you. You don't date. You keep it secret, family really doesn't want to know so you keep that between you and God.

For Jasmine, the message internalized was one of secrecy and shame. If you were queer, it was something you spoke about to no one. At the same time, the theology of God's ultimate power to change you did not feel like freedom to Jasmine, but rather another force to keep her questions about sexuality secret. She was to turn to God in prayer in order to heal what was broken inside.

Beth had a similar feeling about what God could do for homosexuals. Though she was clear that homosexuals were "going to hell," she also believed that God was powerful enough to change people.

> It was really painful. And so then I spent the next was that 12 years, trying everything in my power and asking God to take this from me . . . It was more like, okay, God please just take this away. Because also that was another thing, you know, like God could do anything. God answers your prayers, God can

change things, God can move mountains if you have faith the size of a mustard seed. And it's like, okay, okay.

Beth believes her dedication to the church was a way of warding off her fear that she was going to hell. She also hoped that with enough fervent prayers and attention to God, God might change her.

Jorge was also clear about the eternal damnation saved for homosexuals. In Jorge's congregation, the messages about the sin of homosexuality were frequent,

> If it wasn't every week it was probably every other week . . . Homosexuality from the pulpit was demonized, it was you are going to hell if you think of, generally was, you are going to hell if you think of sex, even touching opposite sex we got in trouble, at school we were not allowed to touch a girl, we were not able, until I got married that was the first time I kissed my wife, back then, [now] my ex-wife. But we were not able, we would get demerits, if we were caught kissing we would get spankings and so on so forth. But it was at a very young age I heard sexuality, or being gay or homosexual was a sin, and demonic, and that I would go to hell.

In Jorge's congregation, sexuality was something to be protected, and this meant even refraining from sexual acts with people of the opposite sex until marriage. April had a similar experience, while also recognizing that the opposition to homosexuality was part of what bound the congregation together.

> Every time there would be a news story about it, or a state accepting it, where was it first Vermont? Massachusetts? It was a big thing—I can't believe this, it is the start of the end times, like the world was ending literally. But no one ever said you shouldn't be gay, because it was like so far beyond the pale. Like it happened to them over there, and you kind of feel sorry for them because they are all going to die of AIDS anyway.

In April's congregation, the feelings about homosexuality extended to the way members of the church were supposed to interact with groups outside of their denomination. Homosexuals were not just bad people, but they actively tried to recruit children into their lifestyle, and so Christians had to be aware in order to resist. She says,

> I don't remember there ever being a sermon on the topic. I remember that there was, I must have been like six, because my cousin was just born, and the Southern Baptist conference was in New Orleans that year and they decided to boycott Disney, and my parents sat me down and explained why I couldn't watch Disney movies anymore and it was because Disney World was having a Gay Pride Parade, and I was just six so I was like "what is that?" And they

started telling me, I think they said "really messed up people" sometimes they go out and they start to want to be having sex with people who are the same, like men and men, and that's really really evil, and so we have to go out and make sure people know that this is really really bad. And it was presented like we have to go out and make sure that people know so they don't get fooled into doing it . . . to convert you they recruit children, I don't remember how I knew that, but I knew that happened.

The concern the church showed about homosexuality also extended to heterosexuality. Engaging in any kind of sexual activity outside of marriage mattered to God as well as your potential future spouse.

Yeah, and it definitely came up when reading and my dad would do sermons like on Paul's letters, the good people will inherit the earth and the pedophiles and the homosexuals and those people will go to hell. And it was always sort of a footnote, because the sermons were usually about being faithful and chaste, and their version of faithful and chaste was like really really strict, you don't look at another person with lust in your heart because that is the same as having an affair . . . we did a whole True Love Waits program, when I was 14, 15 somewhere in there, and it was like a multi month course we did in the youth Sunday school. And one of the hands on activities that was one of the students in the class went up and we wrapped them up you know, kind of fun like the mummy game you do at Halloween, and we wrapped up with toilet paper, and we put stickers all over the toilet paper and ribbon and no one knew what we were doing. And then the teacher had us each come up and rip a piece off, and they were talking about how now imagine that this is your wife, that this student was going to be your wife, would you still want her when everyone had taken a chunk off, and they were referring to her virginity as a present with bows and things, and if you ever kiss somebody that is like unraveling the bow, and if you ever make out with somebody that is like smudging the wrapping paper. So it is not only like not only your vaginal virginity, but it is a package deal.

For April, sexuality was always at risk, either from homosexuals who would try to convert or trick you into adopting their lifestyle, or from the temptation to engage in sexual acts outside of marriage. Sexuality was something to be feared.

Alex also remembers the influence of current events on what was preached about homosexuality in their congregation:

[The pastor] would talk about, depending on what the lectionary was, and depending on current event things, that is also when I think it was around that time when Massachusetts had passed civil unions, it was somewhere around there, and I remember very clearly that, a sermon on that, so 45 minutes of like man, woman, period, that kind of stuff. So I remember that but there, so there was, for those later years of my time there.

For Oliver, the messages about homosexuality were less explicit, but no less clear. As April recalled it being "so beyond the pale" for a homosexual person to be a member of the congregation, Oliver also recognized that the silence about homosexuality was a message about how bad homosexuality was. Additionally, for Oliver, the past excommunication of a homosexual member of the congregation inspired fear about the threat of homosexuals in church.

> It is weird because we, I knew it was, okay, when I was young, like in the 80's I remember them excommunicating someone for being gay . . . But at the time I didn't understand what being gay meant so I didn't, they used the word homosexual and I thought does that mean they have sex at home? I don't understand what is wrong with that, isn't that where you are supposed to have sex? (both laugh) I didn't get it and my parents never explained it. The church never, it isn't like some of the Baptist churches that were like, homosexuality is wrong you are going to hell, I didn't hear sermons like that, it was never talked about and it was secretly known that it was bad. And here is a weird thing, later in life when I came out, I found out that some of my mother's friends that weren't from our church or anything were actually lesbians. But nobody, for like 25 years, had said anything about it, told me anything about it. There was like an undertone, like, well, I think in church in general you didn't talk about sex at all. Whether it being good or bad, same thing with homosexuality and stuff. Yet you knew it was wrong, or whatever, and like I said, there was someone who had been excommunicated from the church . . . I was young and I didn't get it, it wasn't until later that I was able to piece things back, because a lot of people would say that to me, in your church did people preach against it, like some denominations? And I'm like, no, they really didn't say anything about it, it was all hush hush, you weren't supposed to talk about it, you weren't supposed to do it, but there weren't the fire and brimstone sermon or anything.

Lucas, who recognizes how the church helped him to compartmentalize his own sexuality and early sexual abuse through their view of the sinfulness of sexuality, also felt the power of the silence around homosexuality and sexuality in general.

> Well, on the one side the younger side, the more Baptist kind of side, is the, we don't talk about it, it is the . . . like cover yourself, hide yourself, a portion of my family is in this church and the women don't even cut their hair and wear long skirts. So, it is something that is not talked about, and something to be feared.

These themes, of condemnation, fear, punishment, and silence were powerful memories for participants in this study. God, an idealized selfobject, did not approve of homosexuality, and all participants in this study recalled that homosexuality was incompatible with Christianity. Homosexuals were going to hell and fell outside of God's love. To hear that homosexual acts were tantamount to murder was unsurprising to participants in this study. The "choice" to be homosexual meant the relinquishing of a selfobject relationship; this relationship could not withstand anything but absolute adherence to God's laws. The messages about homosexuality assured the participants in this study that there was no middle ground; God was all holy and homosexuality was deeply sinful. God was unchanging, and in order to maintain a relationship with God, one could not be homosexual.

James Jones argues that this unchanging nature of God harkens back to the archaic selfobject relationship the infant first experiences. " . . . if a religious institution insists it is pure and without error; if expositors insist that a text is infallible; if a teacher or master insists he or she is perfect, then the devotees will be kept in a state of developmental arrest, no matter how deeply they love that institution, or that text, or that teacher, or how powerful that emotions are that are evoked."[21] In order to enter into a mature selfobject relationship the infant has to experience the internalization of the imperfection of the selfobject. Kohut calls this "transmuting internalization," a process by which the infant slowly recognizes that the selfobject is not all perfect, and is able to transmute the need for idealized perfection in the selfobject into psychic structure within the self. As this internal psychic structure is built, the external relationship with a selfobject matures; the selfobject still provides some of the needed experience of greatness, but the individual also now carries greatness inside themselves. They are able to tolerate a realistic experience of the idealized selfobject, and, in turn, accept a realistic view of themselves. In situations like those described by participants in this study, the selfobject relationship remains archaic. This ultimate idealized selfobject placed them in an untenable position, their need for God was intense and dependent, and at the same time, the relationship with God could not tolerate any question or doubt. Religion, in the view of their communities, meant unquestioned allegiance to God, with no space for complexity.

The God described by these participants in their early religious lives could not tolerate any imperfection. God was absolutely perfect, and required constant striving for perfection in God's followers. The bible was infallible, the church itself was without error. The world outside of the church, however, was a place rife with sin and required saving by those within the church itself. Even questioning God's Word was a sin. April recalls, "it is very much an all or nothing community," and that the community provided her with "this entire notion of like absolute truth, and you know what the truth is, you know the right thing and the wrong thing and there is a rule for everything." When April tried to question the doctrines of the church, even in a causal way, she was grounded or her questions dismissed. Being "all in" was the only way you could remain a member of this community,

> there is a lot of stuff I had accepted in the background that I never really thought about, like evolution. Like, hey, so that is probably a thing, too, isn't it? Turns out it is. Climate change. Abortion. Women working outside the home. All of those things, like now it sounds kind of silly even to me, but all of those things were part and parcel, like you have to take the whole thing, you have to be all in, and if you take away a piece of that you are not all in and therefore you are not in at all.

Similarly, Beth says, "when I go back to the South if religion comes up and I offer a different thought, or option or opinion, and I remember feeling this way, too, when someone did that. You see fear. And you see pulling, there is like this instinct within you, like, be careful, this could be the devil. Does that make sense?" In a number of these communities, the devil was a very real presence, and when one questioned the values of the church, there was a possibility that this was the devil tempting people away from what was holy.

What these participants describe is a culture of intense idealization of both God and the church, a strong fear of people and culture outside of the church, and a belief that questioning or doubting would cast the questioner out of the safety of the church and into eternal damnation. God cared deeply about sexuality and saw homosexuals as a threat to what was holy, and God did not change. For these participants the realization that they themselves were homosexual would radically reorient the way that they understood their place in the church and in God's love. Their trauma hinges on this conflict, on the one hand, a church and God that forced them into a dependent, archaic selfobject relationship, and on the other, a growing realization that their sexuality was unacceptable to this God.

IDENTITY IN CONFLICT WITH SELFOBJECT RELATIONSHIPS

For many LGBTQIA+ people, the experience of coming out, or publicly acknowledging one's identity within this group, marks a major milestone in development. Since homosexuality is no longer considered a category of pathology, the question of identity development, "or the process by which [LGBTQIA+] people come to know and value more fully who they are," requires additional analysis.[22] For participants in this study, openly identifying as LGBTQIA+ meant risking not just their place in their families and their church communities, but their eternal salvation.

To assume that all LGBTQIA+ people develop and accept their queer identities in the same way, or in a linear progression, ignores the very specific nature of identity development and the impact of sociocultural factors. While acknowledging the uniqueness of individual stories, it is also possible to recognize that LGBTQIA+ identity is not simply a moment of "coming out," but is rather an "emergent, continuous life process."[23] As participants in this study exemplify, coming out "consists of a series of complex cognitive, affective, and behavioral changes, [including] an awareness of same-sex sexual feelings; initial same-sex sexual encounters; participation in the gay, lesbian, and bisexual subculture; labeling of self as *gay* or *lesbian*; and disclosing a gay or lesbian identity."[24] For many participants in this study, the coming out process began with internal awareness of same-sex sexual attraction, but was immediately followed by an attempt to silence or pray away this growing realization. Though this particular reaction may be unique to LGBTQIA+ people who are in non-accepting religious communities, the process of integrating an LGBTQIA+ identity often includes some initial identity confusion.

Vivienne Cass argues for an active role in homosexual identity formation, suggesting seven stages of homosexual identity development: Identity Confusion (Who am I?), Identity Comparison (I'm different), Identity Tolerance (I probably am a homosexual), Identity Acceptance (Selective disclosure), Identity Pride (Gay is good, I am gay and proud), and Identity Synthesis (I am both similar to and different from other homosexuals and heterosexuals). Though Cass developed these stages in the late 1970's when homosexuality was slightly less openly mainstream than today, the seven-stage model still offers a helpful format for considering how a LGBTQIA+ person might work through the integration of their identity. Particularly helpful in Cass' model is the recognition that LGBTQIA+ people are active participants in identity formation.[25] A LGBTQIA+ person can foreclose further development at any of the stages. For many of the participants in this study, the power of the religious idealized selfobject relationship as well as the family system itself caused significant distress at a number of stages, and at times led to the refusal to integrate a homosexual identity at all.

Beth recalls driving to school soon after she had accepted Christ and made a profession of faith at the Baptist Church.

> So I drove myself to school my senior year because I had my car, and it was driving there one morning, I don't know, I knew I'm am one of those people and I can't be one of those people. I was devastated that God wouldn't love me, that I'd be cast out and go to hell. I mean, devastated. It was really painful. And so then I spent the next was that 12 years, trying everything in my power and asking God to take this from me.

She continued to attend church and felt, "Angst, yeah. Like, God please, please take this cup. So I was, yeah, pretty much known as a straight woman." Beth desperately wanted to believe that God could take away from her the feelings she was having, and did everything in her power to convince the world that she was heterosexual.

> This is how closeted I was . . . and this is true, and this is how hard I tried, I tried so hard to be straight. One of my closest friends at seminary, we moved together, and he was in the process of coming out, and when we got here he basically came out, and I was in the process of dating men, and his name was [Jason], he's passed away, and we were roommates and we were in the kitchen and he's like, "you know, I think you could try sleeping with a woman, but you just like dick too much." And that was his, you know, it devastated me, because I was like, he has no idea, like I was so . . . the only reason I am telling you that story is, I was that closeted.

Beth felt the pressure to be "normal," she dated men and even considered getting married.

> And it is terrifying, to think that I could have chosen that. Cause I was, I was so buried under all that. I was truly truly terrified of being lesbian. And if I was out or around and ran into someone that I thought was gay or lesbian it would cause so much anxiety. I used to be, really super skinny. I think it was because of all of the stress, trying to hide constantly . . . I was pushing down, pushing down, pushing down.

Beth decided to applied to a Baptist seminary, and was denied entrance on her first application, a denial she attributes to her ambivalence about attending as she still struggled internally with her own questions about sexuality. After another application she was accepted, and remembers thinking at some level that though it was not allowed, she might become the first female Southern Baptist minister. Yet, these questions of sexual identity still plagued her.

> At a point yeah, but there really was an ambivalence as well that I can't put my finger on, I think because of the sexuality. It's like being a fractured person. I was putting a lot of energy, so much energy into hiding. That I don't think I had it, it's like all these people were seeing it in me so it must be. But really my chance to go inward and reflect, all that energy, was being, pushing it down, keeping it in, this thing I can't be. And if people know this, what will they do? This can't be real. So I have to figure out a way to make, that I like this guy, that this is really going to work, and I really don't, I mean, you have to kiss 'em, you have to . . . So think about repressing that, putting all that aside, and saying I have to have sex with this guy, I have to do it, I have to make this happen . . . And that was really hard, and I hurt all those relationships, because they could

64   *Chapter Three*

> clearly tell, I wasn't, I wasn't in . . . Something was wrong, they don't know what it is. She must not like me, I was cold, I mean, because I couldn't, I tried hard, but it was just so exhausting. And I didn't want to talk to them everyday. And I didn't need to see them everyday, and I didn't need to do, and I would look at other couples and think, God, really? That seems like so much. But, now I get it. Like, yeah, if you actually do find yourself attracted to a person . . . Yeah, you do want to be around them, it's not like, oh, God, I have to hold their hand, really?

As Beth continued to try and "be straight," the cost of maintaining this exterior identity was high.

> Yeah, anxiety was horrible. It was constant. And I don't think I really knew it. It was such a part of my daily life. And I was super skinny, and I didn't really eat. And it just took a lot of energy, not being real, not being who you really are, not feeling safe. . . . Yeah, not feeling safe anywhere. And trying so hard to be this person that I think everyone needs me to be.

April also remembers the first time she realized she might be attracted to other women,

> Well, the very first time it ever, ever occurred to me, I remember exactly when it happened, the Rent movie had just come out and it was my Freshman year, and one of my friends, my female friend, we had the soundtrack to Rent playing and she was dancing around and I thought, wow, she's really hot. And then, basically, oh, fuck, oh, fuck, oh, fuck for the next year or so. At first I was like, okay, that's just a weird thought, shit happens, it is fine, but once that door was opened I was like, wow. And I suddenly realized that a lot of the women I knew I thought were attractive. And I never dated in high school, I never thought any of the boys were cute, I had some really intense female friendships that I totally had crushes on them but I had no idea. Like, whenever I had sleepovers from like 13, 14 on, when you are too old for sleeping bags, and you like share your friend's double bed, I never could sleep because I would get very anxious like palm sweaty, and in retrospect it's like, huh, so I started having a lot of those feelings. I started to get really really depressed because I thought like I was really broken and I needed like treatment, but I couldn't bring myself to go there. Because even the idea of showing up and saying hey I have this problem was just too much.

April felt intensely depressed about the possibility that she might be gay, and eventually brought her thoughts up to a small group at her non-denominational church.

> Like 7, 8 months later I finally told a small group that I was attending sporadically with the Vineyard church and they were like, oh, hey, that's totally fine.

And I was like, wait, it is? And they are like yeah, it's great, turns out that they have a twelve step program for recovering gay people. Which really pisses me off now that I think about it. And they attracted like a lot of gay artists and musicians, because the church was really artsy, so they had like ex-queer people. So they were like, oh, we have a program for that, and you are going to be okay and it's going to be fine-look at Bob, Bob is doing great now! And I was just like . . . It just kind of happened one day. Because the small group is really intense, they'd do like a lot of hands on prophecy, and it sounds really weird, and it is kind of weird, like, six or seven of us, there would be a group and you would talk and you would eat and there would be a bible study lesson. And then you would pray and some people would chant, or sing, and everybody would be touching this one person, and if you got what you felt like was a prophetic image you'd start talking about it, and it was my turn, and people were like, oh you look really stressed, what is going on? And I had no intention of being like, oh, I'm gay, but then it just sort of happened. And I was like, freaking out, and they were like, no, it's fine. No big deal. Makes sense that you are stressed about that, and I am like, oh, okay. And they are like, no, just sign up for this twelve step program. And I am like, whoa, what? And I never went back, actually, that was the very last time I went. I still wasn't okay with it, and I wasn't okay with it for years, but being like, oh being gay is fine, it is just like being a heroin addict, to me for some reason, that, they lost me completely. I was like, I am not a drug addict, I agree with you that this is a problem, but it isn't like, I think I had this idea that that it was a program for these actively gay people who had a lot of sex and were maybe addicted to it, but that is just not even for me.

After her initial disclosure, April "stayed depressed for awhile" as she struggled with this potential new identity. She came out to another friend, remembering,

So we freaked out together for awhile, and then we realized that the sky had not fallen on our heads, and maybe, maybe it wasn't going to. And then, I really, actively avoided dealing with the religion part of it for a very, very long time. I would sometimes have nightmares about it and then I would . . . yeah, push it down. Because I was like I can't cope with that.

April remembers intense fear that she was going to go to hell, and to counter these fears she eventually started dating a man. "So I got this boyfriend like, maybe this will fix me! It didn't. He was an asshole."

Jorge also remembers intense fear when he first felt that he himself might be gay. Jorge not only attended worship in his Baptist congregation, but also school, so the loss of his place in the congregation would also mean potentially not finishing school with his community.

I first started realizing my sexual attraction to boys in junior high. And during school we would also have Chapel. So we would have Chapel Wednesday, Thursday, Friday, so I heard sermons on Sunday all day, Monday, Tuesday we didn't have Chapel because we had gym, and then Wednesday, Thursday, Friday when a different teacher or speaker came in, it wasn't every day, but once a week I heard about it. And it was in junior high I realized my attraction for boys, and feeling that, oh my goodness if they ever find out, I am expelled. I wouldn't be able to come along, and then going through their high school, for the littlest things they were sometimes expelled because of immoral, or bring drugs to school was a big one, there was a boy that had to leave because he was going to get expelled for being gay, he was very feminine. I was never very feminine acting, actually if we were to look back everyone would call me the teacher's pet, or the most involved, because I got involved in chapel, I got involved in sports, I got involved in the candy sales, I got involved in everything. And I look back and this is after everything happened . . . and I look back and I realize I was doing everything to hide away my feelings. But it was through high school for sure, that I remember sitting in the chapel, hearing that and thinking, I am going to go to hell.

Despite these realizations, Jorge also recognized the risk of damnation he faced if he was found out. As other participants noted, the forbidden nature of any sexual activity outside of marriage, in many ways, protected him from any pressure to enter into a sexual relationship with someone of the opposite sex. If students were caught engaging in sexual behaviors outside of marriage, even just kissing, they were punished with demerits, or spankings. Jorge, as noted earlier, never even kissed his wife before they were married. In an attempt to fix himself, much like April entering into a relationship with a man, Jorge rushed into marriage to prove that he must really be heterosexual.

> That is the only thing I would take back, I would go back and not hurt [my wife], I would not get married, because I rushed into it thinking I was going to save myself and the same time hurt her, and to this day I feel remorse for that, and to this day I apologize to her, but I, it has made me the man I am.

Oliver, once he left home for college, immediately found a bible study group and started participating in Campus Crusade, a largely Baptist organization. The silence he experienced at his home church around questions of sexuality changed immediately.

> I was, so I joined, so going into college I was still trying to be the perfect little Christian Reformed person that you could be, I joined Campus Crusade, I joined a bible study freshman year. Campus Crusade was done, I think, by the Baptists, so a more stricter religion and there, going there, they wanted us to go to their Baptist church, and then I got the sermons, like you are going to hell for being

gay. At their church and also through Campus Crusade, they wanted you to sign stuff saying that you had never had gay tendencies or had sex with members of the same, and if you did, what are you doing to fix that? . . . I eventually left. I was like whoa, my church you didn't talk about it, but this is worse, this is in your face like you are going to hell.

Although Oliver was still not out to his parents, he began a relationship with his first boyfriend, though he kept that part of his life completely separate from the religious part of his life.

Because even the first, I had joined [a Christian Reformed] Church when I moved, when I finished law school. During the university and law school years I wasn't really a member of a church, I would go to my parent's' church with them when I would go home for breaks and stuff like that, and at that time it was still fine because I wasn't telling anyone at church or my parents about stuff, so that was one sphere. And back at school with my boyfriend and friends that was a different sphere. But then when I moved to [a large midwestern city] I joined . . . like a missionary church of the Christian Reformed Church. The difference between that and my parents' church there was still you don't talk about anything, that was still the same, the difference was the background of the people I think, I don't even know, I think they were okay with it, but they couldn't say they were okay because they might get in trouble with the denomination. Whereas back home they didn't talk about it and they weren't okay with it. We all knew that. But it still didn't feel right, because I was still hiding a part of myself from God or from church, and I don't feel part of the community because I can't be my whole self with the community.

Oliver also felt things might be okay if he didn't tell anyone about his sexuality, but once he met his now husband and they planned to get married he could no longer keep the spheres separate, and his non-accepting congregation could not continue under the false assumption that he was gay but celibate.

Now the Christian Reformed belief is, I think you can be gay and be a member of the church, but you have to be celibate. And it was weird because our friend's grandma who was a member at my parents' church, she was okay knowing that we were gay, but as soon as we got married—you are going to hell, I can't talk to you anymore. I mean, we weren't celibate still living together, but I guess in her mind you could have been or something like that. But once you were married, oh no, that was so horrible.

Lucas started attending a Pentecostal school and continued struggling with both the sexual abuse in his past as well as beginning realization that he might be gay.

Yeah, so it was like literally, we would have these, every Wednesday was a chapel service that was almost the entire day, and it was like people were casting out demons and speaking in tongues, it was like the full on shit show . . . So the theology side of things gets really interesting. I started to become, I think I started to develop, despite the weird God stuff, the way I would describe it now, despite all this chaos, I think, actual grace started to happen. I started to feel spiritual, I started to connect with something despite all the chaos that was going on, and all the ways that I was using the ideas of God to protect myself from psychological trauma, but despite all of that there was God's grace, and what that is, I started to feel like, just something, I don't know, sacred beyond all that, that was sort of at the center of myself. And I started feeling like I felt like even though I was fed here something was not right, and these people were crazy and their interpretation of the Bible didn't make sense, I started taking Latin, and I became quite the little bible thumper . . . And so I basically became a wannabe Catholic, I went from my obsession with scripture led me to these questions of interpretation of scriptural origin and all this stuff, so yeah, I started like carrying around a rosary to this Pentecostal high school and then I started getting really interested in deeper theological questions and philosophy and stuff like that.

Okay, I guess well, when I was about a senior in high school I started to, I admitted to myself that I was gay and told my girlfriend of four years, which is rough but she was somewhat supportive I guess. And so I think in the back of my mind what I was thinking, despite where I am now, what I think of the Roman Catholic interpretation of homosexuality is, at the time it was so much better than anything I had ever heard. At least Catholicism is like, you shouldn't abuse people, there should be equal rights, all present in Catholicism that wasn't in where I was from.

Lucas continued in the Catholic tradition, exploring what it might mean for him to be Catholic, while also trying to integrate his sexual identity. Being Catholic was a middle ground for him, it wasn't exactly tolerant of his sexuality, but at the same time there was more space for him to try to be both a Christian and a gay man. Finally, though, after studying Catholicism with plans to officially join the Catholic church, Lucas decided he could not live as a gay man and a Catholic.

So I didn't officially become Catholic, and that was because I felt like I couldn't ever agree with the interpretations around sexuality. So then I kind of was homeless, you know. I felt like I had spent my entire life in education chasing something and then in the end said no, so basically I started exploring my sexuality . . . I really struggled socially and unfortunately drugs and alcohol entered the picture then, and that took over very, very quickly. I went from trying my first drink to dealing drugs in like nine months. I don't know how I finished college in that fog, I did and then I moved and did this whole drug thing for like two years, and then went crazy, which is a wonderful blessing. I have always wanted to tell this story to somebody, you are probably the first person I feel this story is appropriate, so there is a lot of terrible stories from this time, the recovering addict always has to tell one. Here is my one. My one is one of the very last times that I used, I decided that I would get a very, very large amount of drugs, it was probably nearly a suicide attempt, and smoke like two grams of Meth and read the book of Revelation.

Lucas continued, like Oliver, April, and Beth, to believe that one could either live out their sexuality or be a practicing Christian. There simply was not space to be both. Lucas' drug and alcohol addiction continued to plague him,

> So my self-destruction was so tied up in my guilt and my confusion and this sort of encyclopedia of theologies and never picking one, not believing anything, self-destruction so I went crazy, which is the great gift, so then I had to ask for help, so I got help. And it took me probably five years to get my mind back.

Before Alex was able to process the idea that they might be gay, a number of people, including their own mother asked them on numerous occasions if they were a homosexual. They remember,

> But what it, I knew at some level, I just didn't really know. I hadn't articulated any of this, and hormones and puberty, and what the fuck is life, and switching schools and all of this stuff that like, there is a lot up in the air in all of that. And I didn't know a single gay person. I had never seen anyone that was openly gay, ever. Not at church, I mean . . . it is so sparse . . . So you know, what that was really, I didn't have the vocabulary, my only context for the word gay was this little stupid little song that one of my cousins and I used to sing, there wasn't any, I just had no concept of it. So I think it wasn't until the moment when I knew, I had no idea what was going on with me, I just knew I was really not in a good place but I had started testing things within myself. Like how I dressed, I started shaving my legs at that time, just things like that that I started, there was a lot of experimenting with myself and identity.

Alex continued to explore their own identity on their own, while also keeping their questions and struggles secret.

> It wasn't until I looked in the mirror, after watching Birdcage (laugh), I still don't know how I found that thing, I found a DVD copy of the Birdcage, I had to hide it. I remember taking books, and putting my DVDs in the middle of books, like fucking Holocaust, hiding . . . I think back to this and I am like, what the hell was I doing? But I remember I watched that and I just thought to myself, that feels like the most genuine thing I have seen in my life, what I just watched. And I looked in the mirror and I looked at myself and I said, I am gay. What motivated me to say that to myself at the time, I don't even know, I think

it was just a codification of all these years of just exploring and entering further into myself. But that is when I knew, but there were people who had asked me before and I said no, but at my core I knew, because I remember that feeling when they asked me because I was almost embarrassed and frightened and like defensive, and thought, no I am not, but ehhhhh there is something in there, something back there that is like, yes.

When Jasmine first started feeling that something might be different about her she recalls being terrified, especially given not just her religious background, but the general opinion about homosexuality within her black community.

It was around that time, this time was around middle school, about 12 or 13 and I was starting to understand that I didn't feel like normal like everyone else, so called normal, I wasn't interested in dating or anything like that, I didn't know what was going on, I couldn't talk to anyone because being exposed to all the judgment I was like how I can you go to a relative and say I think I like girls? And especially in the black church that is like the biggest no-no . . .

The feeling of being judged or rejected for her sexuality was too much for her to bear,

Yeah, I kind of knew something, but I didn't come to terms with it because I thought I was wrong and bad. But I didn't want to say anything if I was going to be judged. I was like, what's the point? So from like 25–35 stopped going to church, still interested in spirituality, but I wasn't faithful in it, I wasn't going to church or anything, or anything like that, still thought about God quite a bit, still coming to terms with my sexuality and wondering if that was something that God is going to judge me with, so wanting to be close to God and at the same time scared to. Because what if it is wrong, and what if He is judging me, and how could I deal with that, because I knew it was something that I couldn't change, it was just a part of me. So I stayed away for quite a bit of time.

Jasmine started therapy to work through her general dissatisfaction with life, her issues with self-harm and at some level, the continued questions she had about her own sexuality. Her therapist encouraged her to consider looking for a church, but she hesitated,

Because I didn't want to walk in there and feel judged, I don't want people asking me questions. But eventually I took her advice and I went to a Vineyard Church that a colleague of mine attended. And I participated for two or three months, people were very welcoming, it was a small congregation. I was still kind of self-destructive at the time, overeating, I was self-harming at the time. And I confessed that to the pastor because I just wanted to feel better and he was so shaming. "That's the devil! We need to pray for you." So he announced to the church that he was going to pray for me, he didn't say why, thank goodness for that, but he was like this sister here needs some help, the demons are in her. Blah, blah. So they were laying hands on me, this is in the Vineyard Church. So I was like, that didn't feel so good. And I like, what do I do with this?

It was embarrassing, and he did not have the training to deal with it and instead of saying here is another pastor who may be helpful or here is the number to a counseling center. Yeah, he clearly didn't understand. And I am like okay, this is not good. And unfortunately, the friend that I was attending church with, we had a falling out over something similar because she was like, you are sad all the time I don't know why you are depressed you are supposed to be Christian.

After attending the Vineyard church for a few months and the "laying on of hands" incident, Jasmine took another five-year break from church before she considered returning.

Though Sarah grew up in a "liberal" home, she admitted she did not know anyone that was gay,

I didn't even know gay was a thing until well into high school, and didn't really meet a really openly gay person until I was in college. So it wasn't even on my spectrum of awareness, and I really didn't want to talk about it. And I grew up in a pretty, I'd say inclusive home, my parents always wanted us to be open and welcoming to people, but it just wasn't something we talked about. It wasn't a thing in [the South]. It has the reputation, but it just wasn't in my world.

When Sarah heard messages about homosexuality in her non-denominational congregation while in college she simply decided she was not going to think about her sexuality at all, "yeah, I am always kind of hard and fast, black and white, so I was just like, nope, not an option, going to move on with my life. I was, 20, 21." After finishing college and feeling "burned out" by the views of the non-denominational church she had joined in the South, Sarah started a new life in a large city. Yet, within a week of moving, she found another non-denominational church and started attending worship. She recalls,

They have pretty weird views, but I liked the people there so I just kept hanging around. But when you move to [a large city], gay, LGBT community is very alive and well here. You see a lot of, I actually moved to [a historically known gay neighborhood], not knowing. (Laughs) There is a lot of gay people here! It is something you have to work through, so after about a year and half, I had met, when I moved here I only knew one other person from [the South], and she was here in law school, so I was just out with her and her law school friends, and one of those friends was openly gay. I had gay friends in college, they were all guys, so I was like, okay, that's cool. But I didn't know another lesbian, I knew of some, but they were outcast, but people didn't really associate with them, so I was like, nope, not my crowd. And I moved here, obviously very open, and that friend who was openly gay, one day just kind of called me out on it, just coached me out. (Laughs) But the church I was going to here was kind of similar in views of the LGBT community . . . They were just not going to talk about, I had heard people make comments about it that were a little bit homophobic, and so after that friend kind of coached me out of the closet . . . I realized I could not stay there if I was going to try to work out how I was feeling.

For Sarah, as well as other participants in this project, their initial realization about their sexuality felt incompatible with continuing to claim a Christian identity. They could either be queer, or they could be Christian, but they had no pattern for how one could integrate these two identities. For a number of these participants, they foreclosed any further development beyond identity confusion (asking who am I?) and identity comparison (recognizing themselves as different from others) as noted in Cass's model of LGBTQIA+ development. The cost of integrating their sexual identity was simply too high.

For all of these participants, the church provided them a desperately needed idealizable selfobject relationship, while at the same time, the church proclaimed a theology that kept that relationship from maturing. In order to develop a healthy internal structure, one must be surrounded by selfobjects that are presented in a realistic manner. As Jones argues, when religious institutions insist on their perfection and purity, adherents are kept in a "state of infantile dependence."[26] Just as God could not be complex, they could not develop a complex understanding of the self either, and could only mature in their self understanding through complete loss of this selfobject relationship. Development of their sexual identity as well as their selfobject relationship was foreclosed by the proclamation that queer people were outside of the love of God. The inevitable loss of this selfobject relationship with God and the church was further compounded by the potential loss of familial relationships, leading to a psychological foreclosure on the integration of a healthy sexual identity.

Due to the multiple pressures on development of this healthy sexual identity, one in which these participants could both "know and value more fully who they are," the coming out process for many of these participants is a primary site of the religious trauma they describe.[27] Several participants mentioned biblical literalism, the unchanging nature of God, and the inerrancy of God's word as central concepts to the theology of these congregations. As the participants began to question their own sexual identity and the sexual theology of their congregations, difficult questions arose. Brown argues, "For the [LGBTQIA+] person who, for whatever reason, is unable to reject the homophobic teachings of the context and instead internalizes those destructive messages, the coming out process leads to another sort of trauma, in which both perpetrator and target reside in the same skin."[28] For many of these participants the experience of this dual identity, and the incongruence resulting from it, was uniquely traumatizing. How could the God they were told loved everyone, determined the course of the universe, and held eternal life in His hands now believe that they were inherently evil? And, if they were inherently evil, how could they keep on living?

NOTES

1. Alex identifies as genderqueer and chooses to use the personal pronouns they/them. To respect Alex's self-understanding, I will use these pronouns when sharing their story. I have chosen to use plural verbs when using Alex's chosen pronoun.
2. Freud, S. *The Future of an Illusion*. New York: Classic House Books, 1927/2009, 17–26.
3. Kohut, H. and C. B. Strozier. *Self Psychology and the Humanities: Reflections on a New Psychoanalytic Approach*. New York: W.W. Norton, 1985, 261.
4. Kohut, *Self Psychology and the Humanities*, 264.
5. Kohut, *Self Psychology and the Humanities*, 74.
6. Kohut, H. and M. Elson. *The Kohut Seminars on Self Psychology and Psychotherapy with Adolescents and Young Adults* (1st ed.). New York: Norton, 1987, 5.
7. Jones, J. W. *Terror and Transformation: The Ambiguity of Religion in Psychoanalytic Perspective*. New York: Brunner-Routledge, 2002, 22.
8. Kohut, *The Kohut Seminars*, 124–125.
9. Kohut, *The Kohut Seminars*, 6.
10. Kohut, *Self Psychology and the Humanities*, 126.
11. Kohut, *Self Psychology and the Humanities*, 257.
12. Kohut, H., A. Goldberg and P. E. Stepansky. *How Does Analysis Cure?* Chicago: University of Chicago Press, 1984, 197.
13. Kohut, *The Kohut Seminars*, 78.
14. Kohut, *Self Psychology and the Humanities*, 10.
15. Kohut, *How Does Analysis Cure?*, 52.
16. Kohut, *How Does Analysis Cure?*, 44, 77.
17. Kohut, *How Does Analysis Cure?*, 44.
18. Freud, Sigmund, and James Strachey. *Civilization and its Discontents*. 1st American ed. New York: W.W. Norton, 1963, 11.
19. Kohut, *How Does Analysis Cure?*, 50.
20. Rizzuto, A.-M. *The Birth of the Living God: A Psychoanalytic Study*. Chicago: University of Chicago Press, 1979, 50.
21. Jones, *Terror and Transformation*, 65.
22. Reynolds, A. L. and W. F. Hanjorgiris. "Coming Out: Lesbian, Gay and Bisexual Identity Development." In R. M. Perez, K. A. DeBord, & K. J. Bieschke (Eds.),

Handbook of counseling and psychotherapy with lesbian, gay and bisexual clients (pp. 35–55). Washington, DC: American Psychological Association, 2000, 35.

23. Reynolds, "Coming Out," 36.
24. Reynolds, "Coming Out," 37.
25. Cass, Vivienne C., MPsych, MAPsS. "Homosexual Identity Formation," *Journal of Homosexuality,* 4:3, (1979) 219–235.
26. Jones, *Terror and Transformation,* 78.
27. Reynolds, "Coming Out," 35.
28. Brown, "Sexuality, Lies and Loss," 59.

Chapter Four

Estrangement: Leaving Church

Alex was open about their queer identity in their high school, but did not realize that the children of their Missouri Synod Lutheran pastor would hear that Alex was gay and tell their father the pastor. Alex's pastor, without talking to Alex personally, called Alex's mother and stepfather for a meeting and told them that their child was gay. Alex recalls,

> It was not pretty. It was really ugly. Yeah. That was the most, I would get panic attacks very frequently, ones to the point where I would fall to the ground and not be able to move it would hurt so bad this panic attack. And they would last for like, 10 minutes, and they were very painful, very painful. I still remember. And they would happen at random times, so it would be like, out at recess, or lunch break or whatever we called it at that time, and I would be over off doing whatever and then it would just like, oh, shit, I need to go. And I think my family were a lot of the cause of that. The church to me was like, okay that is not me, but my family was the one that really hurt, plus I am living with them, and they told me I was going to hell and God hated me and they didn't like me, "we love you but we don't like you" and all this stuff. They threatened to send me to a conversion therapy camp, and I left the house and said, I am not, no, I am not doing that, and if you think that I am doing that I am not going to be here with you all. I did go back, it was a very short thing, but nonetheless, it was incredibly difficult. So I have my mother, my stepfather and my half sister . . . she was also not supportive and actively combative with me on that. And my stepfather was, on a few occasions, physically abusive over the situation as well. So, yeah, it was a very difficult, very difficult time. I was thoroughly convinced for a very long time that I was going to hell and that there was nothing I could do about it. It was this weird sort of feeling of like being indoctrinated in a certain way for so many years and still feeling some connection to church and all of that, so I think it is really as a young person really hard to navigate all of that. And it certainly was for me.

Because of fear that Alex was going to hell and needed to be healed, Alex's parents insisted Alex meet with the pastor and attend "Christian counseling" in hopes that Alex would change. Alex says,

> I met with the priest several times; he gave me literature and books that were all about the leading research on homosexuality and the realities of whatever, so . . . It was, in a lot of ways, he was a very intellectual person, so he thought this is a condition, or a reality, so it does exist. Homosexuality does exist. It is just not a fruitful state of being. So most of the books he gave me, I actually read many of them because, first I was like, well, it can't hurt to at least read about this stuff, but then as I was reading I was like, no, this is just trying to, it is a sneaky way of trying to say the same damn thing as all of the rest of it. Eventually I told him, I was like, "Look, I am not going to pretend to be something else, this is what it is." Yeah, and that was not going well either because the one that the people that we were going to were "Christian counselors" and it was like, it made it worse in a lot of ways.

After unsuccessfully trying to convince Alex to abandon homosexuality, their pastor offered an ultimatum.

> So there was all that going on and then the priest said, you know, look, you and I have had these conversations, I cannot, if you are going to continue with this, I cannot knowingly give you the sacraments. So I, he said, what we need to do if you refuse to repent of this and to try to work with us here on our terms then we are going to excommunicate you. Then there was this tribunal in front of the elders of the church where they asked me, "are you a homosexual? Do you identify with that? Do you want recourse?" so in front of the six elders . . . Yes, two of my godparents, my stepfather's parents, his father was one of them as well, and then my two godparents that were there for my baptism, I was in front of them and I said "look, I am not going to change, this is not going to go away . . . " And I did it in the most badass way, I was really super into church so I consequently knew a lot about it, so I knew about this tribunal coming up, so I thought, it is obviously not going to go well, so I might as well enjoy myself as much in whatever way I possibly can. So I memorized Luther's speech as he is in front of, the "Here I Stand" speech in front of cardinals, there we go! (laughing) . . . I was convinced that the priest was going to give me a "well done" (makes approving look with face), but there was none of that. It was, not quite the right tone. So that is what I did, they were not exactly amused.

After the community recommended an excommunication, Alex received a bull, a formal decree from the Bishop, that Alex had been excommunicated from the Lutheran Church Missouri Synod. Alex still lived at home, however, and as a result did not have a clean break from the congregation. They remember,

My mother and my stepfather, they said, you need to go [to church], so I went for the first bit. But then I thought, I can't keep doing this, this is ridiculous and that is when I think things got the worst... I was just sitting, I wasn't an acolyte, he wouldn't let me be an acolyte, because he said that would be putting things, I don't remember how he phrased that, basically it would be like thumbing our nose at people. So no, I just sat in the pew next to my mother and it was the most awkward of times, because everybody knew, it is a parish this size (they make a gesture indicating a small size with hands) everyone knew.

Jorge was also "outed" to his pastor by a colleague from work. Already married to a woman, Jorge was working both at the church and in a hospital, while also, on occasion engaging in sexual relations with other men.

I was teaching, and of course, as a teacher I didn't make enough money, so I was taking out part time jobs, and I really thought, that no one would have thought I was gay, even though in my summers I would do weddings—floral, designing (laughing), so all the typical things that everyone thinks a gay man is! But I loved doing that, anyway, that took a kind of stop to it, because I started taking a part time job at a hospital, I worked part time in an ER, because I used to work there in high school and most of my college years at a hospital work as a medical records auditor. And it was an easy fit for me to go back to medical, so I went to an ER as their unit secretary taking notes, filling out charts, being the person to take notes for all the traumas that came in. So I started doing that and felt comfortable enough where by this time I was already second guessing who I was, and not happy with myself, going home to a loveless marriage from my side even though she was trying everything possible to make us work, but I was very depressed, down, even to a point suicidal, and then felt comfortable to a point that I thought, I could speak to somebody that I got to know there at the hospital as a friend not as a patient. So we went out for coffee kind of talked, and I brought up the fact that I was feeling and that I had acted upon it a couple times, and that I knew that was who I was and that I was trying to change who I am and having a problem of it. Little did I know he was a neighbor of somebody at the church.

This confidant told the pastor, which quickly led to the unravelling of Jorge's teaching career as well as membership in his Baptist Church.

Somehow it got to the pastor, by this time I was a junior high teacher. I taught math, music and science, fifth through seventh grade, and then on Sundays I was the choir director for the Spanish department, well involved I was the right-hand man to the pastor in the pulpit. I sat on the platform during services, so I was really looked upon as a leadership figure, and I remember it was right after my birthday, and school always ended the third week of May, and we had a walk-a-thon, the kids had to raise money to do this walk-a-thon, so we are doing this walk-a-thon, and came back from the school, and there was this message for me, the pastor wants to see you. So I think, great, I'll make an appointment, but they say, he wants to see you now.

I got a knot in my stomach, but to me, it was like, maybe he wants to talk about what is coming up in the future in the church, I know there is a lot of changes that are about to happen, we are about to move to a new building, we just moved to a new building, and I need to know what his vision is, so maybe he just wants to meet with the staff. So part of me was a little scared, because that is a little weird that the preacher would call me in and our school was in [another town than the pastor's office]. And that's a 30-minute drive, it is not around the corner. So she said he wants to see you right away, as soon as you get there see his secretary and they will buzz you in. So I drove . . . from the church and I waited in his little space . . . and I remember sitting there the old pastor . . . great man from the pulpit, this was his son-in-law that took over the church. He calls me in, I walk in, and he says I have gotten a letter with pictures of proof that you were kissing a man, is this true? Well, I know for a fact there was no pictures, so I, he's like, is this true or not? I requested to see the pictures. And I requested to see this proof. And he said I cannot show you the proof because it would incriminate someone as well, and that's when I said I do not have an answer for you then, it is neither a yes or a no, you will not get a concrete answer from me until I see your evidence that you have. And with that said, he asked that I go back to the school, clear out my room, and stop teaching, and I was fired. There was two weeks of school left.

Jorge returned to his school, but in some ways had already been preparing for the truth about his sexuality to come out. Though he was afraid to tell his wife, it was also the end of living with two conflicted identities. He recalls,

So they asked me to leave, I was fired. Got to the school, by the time I got back to the school the principal already knew of course, I had to go clear off my desk. The principal is a great guy, he, I wouldn't say understood, but everybody loved me as a teacher, and kind of helped me get my stuff together and put it in the car for me, and that's when I realized driving home I don't know what I am going to tell my wife. How am I going to tell her what has just happened? I completely believe in everything happens for a reason, the month prior to that in April there was a sermon at the church, Spanish department that the pastor was preaching, and he was like I need all my men up on the platform get up, and he used us often for examples, this was one of the sermons, of course homosexuality was preached from the sermon. I at this point thought no one knew about me, no one knew what my feelings are, and I was for sure, and to this day, I don't think he knew at this point. So he was like, okay, mix up yourselves, mix up yourselves, and he put us in line, and he was like mix up yourselves again, this is random. And he counted out one, two, three, four, step up, one, two, three, four, step up, and there was a total of I think twelve guys on the platform. And he's like, okay, the guys that stepped up, if society have it right, one in four men are gay, and I was one of the four, one of the four men that stepped up. So I was like, oh, my goodness, are you serious? Am I getting called out? It wasn't that I was getting called out, but that was the point to the message, and it just, in my heart, I, my stomach, I got upset, I could not wait for the service to be ending.

When Jorge returned home, he confessed to his wife both his sexual experiences with men during their marriage as well as the loss of his position in the church.

> As soon as that happened I told [my wife], and said okay, this is what is going on, and for the longest time she didn't believe it. She would say, I will pray it away, it is going to make everything better, our prayers will make it better. And I remember our principal from high school came into our house and asked [my wife] to step away and that he wanted to speak to me, and I remember oh, he's coming here to rebuke me, ridicule me, kind of things, and it was my home, so I am like you come in here to preach the gay away it is not going to happen, I need you to leave. And he is like, no I am here to support you, so okay, I will hear you out. So, [he says] I don't know if it is true or not, but if it is not I will stand next to you and I will back you up, and everybody that comes our way, and he cursed, he is like, fuck them.
>
> So, to me I was like, wow, one of the men I really looked up to, actually just cursed to me . . . but I told him, I haven't changed my mind, I am still going to the city, and I'm going to seek a divorce. And I remember him leaving and remember my wife coming back in crying, of course, and she was like, this is really going happen? And I am like, yeah, this is really going to happen. And so [that] was the year, a pivotal point for me. And so that's, and it really all came out to, and even when I moved back to the city I was so depressed, suicidal, I never end up, the bad part about that I never sought the help that I should have had, but I had my mother, which to me was all that I needed at that point. And, I remember getting text messages, I had to change my number, text messages from people at the church about me going to hell. They would send me a picture of a man's chest saying if this is what you like, you are going to hell. You are a devil's child, you, it was just getting ridiculed . . . All of those relationships were over.

With the loss of his community of faith as well as his employment, Jorge was left feeling completely broken. He moved out of his home, and into an apartment by himself. He recalls feeling

> Bitter. Pissed off. Angry at God, angry at the church, thinking, and always remembering the definition of a Christian to me, that is not how I was treated. *(What was your definition of a Christian?)* At that time it was stand in support, help each other out through whatever is going on in your life, but it was more of pointing the finger. And that is kind of what I grew up, and I remember kind of feeling, oh my goodness, I have always done that in my life as well, always pointed the finger.

> I remember being bitter, saying I am not going to talk about God, I don't want to do anything, and even to the point of where if I saw anybody from that church, if I saw them on a bus riding by part of me would be like "ugh, I wish they all died." Because I was so angry towards the church, I was so bitter towards the church.

Although April was open about her sexual identity on her college campus, and had shared with a small group at her Vineyard church, she waited for some time before she felt ready to tell her parents. She had already been sporadically attending a less explicitly non-accepting church when her parents came to visit. She remembers,

> After that, I ended up coming out to my parents, very bad. I probably wasn't quite ready, but they responded really, really poorly. It was a Saturday night and the next morning I was like, at least come to church with me, and they were like, any church that would have you there is not a real church . . . Yeah. And so that was bad for awhile. My parents started asking me if I had been molested. No. They started trying to ask me what they had done wrong. Nothing. They sent me some books they had gotten at the Lifeway Christian store, about like, ex-lesbians, and that was really just unpleasant.

When April finished school she entered the Peace Corps, where for two years she felt she could put religion on a "pause." She was open about her sexuality, but when she attended a "house church" in this new country she decided not to disclose to any of the other members. When she returned from her peace corps tour she decided to attend law school in a large midwestern city returning to her childhood home only very briefly. She says,

> My parents were pissed. When I went to [the peace corps] I left 2 weeks after college, and when I came back I spent three weeks at my parents' house before moving here . . . for law school. Which was on purpose. I was still really afraid that they were going to ship me to one of those conversion camps. They had threatened to and so when I was home in college my best friend had my itinerary and local police numbers and he knew to call the police if I didn't check in with him regularly . . . I really think if they could have afforded it they would have. Because those are expensive. I really think that they, people look at me like I'm crazy if I ever mention it, but I don't really talk about it, but they really do kidnap people. They drive up to your house in a van and they take you to the middle of nowhere bum fuck Alabama . . . And the whole you can't really do that unless your kid is under eighteen. That is flexible. They tried to unenroll me from college once, that didn't happen. I was really wary, so I tried to spend as little time as possible with them after that. My parents are pretty crazy.

With her rocky relationship with her parents and continued religious wounds that had not yet been attended to, April felt like her world was turned upside down. She began seeing a therapist to try and work through what was happening to her. She remembers,

> We ended up talking about how it was really unsettling because a lot of linchpins of my worldview had suddenly become unpinned. And figuring out how to build that stuff up, and I still have the same therapist, and now we are like, okay, we have some basic identity pins in the world, and now we are getting to existential philosophy and what happens when you die, and I don't really know, I haven't gotten to rebuild that part, because I had so much, let's not be super depressed all the time, let's not be suicidal, let's get back to functioning and we will worry about the whole heaven thing later.

April believes that both her depression and her suicidal ideation were tied to the theological worldview she desperately wanted to set aside, but which had an incredibly powerful hold over her. She says,

> It's interesting, I had to get an excuse letter when I joined the peace corps from the therapist, I refused any meds then, and now I wish to God I hadn't, my grades went from A's to C's. It is just really hard to be okay, and live and move and breathe in the world when you are like, I can't not be gay, and if I am gay and I am not adequately repentant about it I could get hit by a bus and go to hell in a moment. It is really hard to be like, "I should do my homework," you know? It just doesn't seem important. I think that is where it started and then worsened into clinical depression which was shitty, but once it started coming back, I was smarter this time, I saw the therapist, I took the meds, which helped tremendously. It is amazing how that works—antidepressants make you less depressed. But all of the depression, my therapists wrote the letter, it centered around family rejection around issues of identity. And that's what it is. Especially my parents, with having no siblings, and being so into this church family mesh structure, being rejected by that is hard. Because I am like, I have nothing. My friends, my family would be like, only your family truly loves you, your friends say they love you but they don't really. My parents are a little crazy in addition to the religious thing, but that made it really hard.

For April, the religious trauma is mixed up in both her family system and the religious institution in which she was a part. Growing up Southern Baptist with her father as the pastor meant that her life had a trajectory that she was setting aside by living as an out lesbian woman. When April eventually graduated from law school and planned to marry her girlfriend, the relationship with her parents had deteriorated so much that they were no longer speaking.

> I mean I think part of it is control and in their worldview daughters are always a little bit the property of their parents, even when they are married, and being unmarried I am pretty much their property, and they just can't deal with the fact that I am just really not. They fully expected that I would go to [college], come home and have a job for a few years if my husband really needed me to work, but something like an elementary school teacher, that's okay. Definitely not a career. And we would live like 15 miles away and bake cookies together and my mom would watch the grandkids. And I still don't think they have given up that, I mean I have a restraining order against them now. Because they threatened to crash my law school graduation and they sent a bunch of creepy text messages from them in [the city I live in]—they live in [the South], and so after that, we were getting married, I was like, they are not going to crash the wedding, and I don't want to have to worry about them crashing the wedding, this is bullshit we are getting a restraining order.

Oliver also experienced further rejection when he shared his plans to marry his boyfriend. While it was a false assumption that he was living a celibate life, the decision to marry his boyfriend made it impossible for his family and church community to deny his homosexual relationship.

> When I did say I was getting married at first both of my parents were fine with it, they were accepting. Then my dad told the pastor, I have no idea why, he told the pastor and he told some people on the consistory about me, that I was gay and I was going to get married and all that stuff. They told him to disown me. He listened to them, and he backpedaled on his acceptance of us, and he told me over the phone don't ever come home again I don't want to see you. The rest of the family was so upset that he was listening to the church and not his family, because my aunt was accepting, my mom was accepting, that they finally, my mom was almost ready to get a divorce from my dad, and then the aunts, his sisters, finally had to step in and say you do what is right, you tell [Oliver] you are welcome back home. (Starts tearing up) And you tell that pastor he can mess with his own life. And then my dad did that, he apologized and welcomed me back. My mom and my sister left the church and they go to a non-denominational church now. My dad still belongs to that church, he wouldn't leave it.
> That is actually the worst part of this whole thing, when he, first of all, I don't know what their business was, I wasn't a member of that church anymore, anyway. And then he told them and they said you have to disown [Oliver] he can't be a part of your family anymore because he is gay and he is getting married, and then that he actually listened to them.

Though his father did eventually concede to attending his wedding, Oliver still is not sure what his father believes about his homosexuality.

He might actually still believe it but he's just, I don't know, maybe he still thinks I am going to hell, but I am his son so he is going to be nice because the whole family said something like that, I don't know. Or he may disagree with that part of the church but he will never tell those people that anymore.

The potential break in his relationship with his family, and the encouragement by the church to cast Oliver out of the church and his own family, still feels traumatic to him.

> Definitely the incident with pastor and the consistory and my dad, I definitely think that was religious trauma because, especially in my own mind, if those people would not have said that or done that my dad would have accepted me the first time and we would have been fine. But because of that, and Dad actually listening to them had problems with my mom and the rest of the family and with me, and you know, it is hard not to blame the church, and say, because of them look at the roller coaster my family went through for a couple of years! Before they were able to get around it . . . What would have been so wrong, especially with the friend's grandma, she knew that [my husband] and I were gay and living together, but when we got married it was such a horrible thing. There was nothing that changed! It was the same relationship, we were doing the same things before that we did after we were married, we are still the same people. But for her that stuff was too much.

Oliver recognizes that if he had been able to live quietly, perhaps in a non-married relationship with his boyfriend, or as a celibate gay man, he would have been able to maintain his membership in the church. His choice to claim his identity as a gay man barred him from feeling like he could ever return to his childhood church.

> I think, for some of those people at my parents' church, I think before it wasn't acceptable, if you were gay you were excommunicated, but now I think you can be gay and celibate and they will accept you. But, they don't want you talking about it! It is not like you are going to introduce yourself, "hey I am gay and celibate!" It is keep your mouth shut, sit by yourself, live by yourself and we will tolerate you.

Lucas also experienced a decisive break from the non-accepting church when he determined that he could not enter full membership in the Catholic church while living out his identity as a gay man. As he reflects on his internalized theology and how it interacted with his spiritual life he says,

> The way it happened to me, is that my whole life it was, I was bathed in guilt, I was bathed in I am bad, guilty, no matter what I do, guilty, I can't, there is all these conflicting ideas, I can't pick one, I can't stick with it, and then, but there

is something so miraculous about going from where I went to where I was, in terms of recovery. All of my friends from then are dead.

Yet, without a spiritual anchor, Lucas "went crazy," turning to drugs and alcohol. Without a church to lean on as an ethical center, much like April, Lucas was left adrift, internally fragmented. He says,

> I went in my crazy mind, at least what made sense to me at the time, I went hyper intellectual, I went to I am going to be profoundly ethical, and invent my own ethics and all this kind of stuff. Yeah, I was doing drugs, but I didn't believe that to be bad, and I guess it took my, that's the problem with inventing your own ethics you only learn what is bad by your own process, you work it out in your own body, and so I did. I think that was news to me. If I left God, I wouldn't suddenly become evil, by anyone's measure really. Which is very different. And I really think in the long term that is what turned the tables on how I think about God.

When thinking back to his Pentecostal days, though, Lucas recognizes that part of his estrangement was the loss of the "chosen-ness" he experienced in his church community.

> My recovery is going to kick in here. I miss it, but it is not good for me. I miss feeling justified and holier than you, I miss these feelings of like, I mean to me, those, especially the sort of Pentecostal stuff, the sermons and the experience is so profoundly emotional it kind of breaks you down, and takes you on this emotional journey. But the end result of that is that it is us versus the world, and we gotta stick together, because they are out to get us. And in a weird way I kind of miss feeling that way, because it feels good to think we are the chosen ones, but at the same time the recovery in me knows that is ego, it is the opposite of spirituality, it is the opposite of pursuing anything that Jesus taught. I know that now, but I miss feeling that.

Lucas also claims religious trauma as part of his story, because his relationship with the church so mimicked the feelings he internalized about the sexual abuse in his past. To be gay was something that had to be hidden, ignored, or repressed.

> Well, because experientially it fits the same path as the sexual abuse trauma. It is that same fear based, hiding, complete lack of, I don't know, I don't know if this is good theology or whatever but when I hear the word grace I have sort of an involuntary word association of beauty or creation. And when I think of the sexuality that I was taught there is no beauty, there is no creation, there is nothing wonderful, there is nothing inspiring about it.

April, Oliver, Alex and Lucas recall a moment of estrangement, a decision which led to their excommunication or loss of their non-accepting church. Beth, Jasmine, and Sarah exhibit a different kind of estrangement, characterized by a slow drifting away from their church until they simply no longer participated. Though one might imagine that this would be less traumatic—they do not have stories of being cast out, losing jobs, or excommunication—these participants still talk about feeling fragmented after they no longer had a spiritual home in their lives. The language of hell and punishment, even if it was not formally declared to them, was still very real.

Sarah maintained some level of skepticism about the need for God's forgiveness in her life; she recognized that God was supposed to be loving, but she also needed to name her sin continually.

> It was, like loving, but also a level of shame. Not quite like Catholic shame, or guilt, but just kind of like, He is there, and you should talk, and you should forgive yourself and forgive your sins, and it always comes back to the sin stuff. You are basically never okay, but God can make you okay, so you have to constantly remind yourself of what you have done wrong and how God can forgive you for that. If you forgive yourself and all that stuff. I think it mixed a level of shame, looking back on it, that I couldn't acknowledge then. They were always having a big college retreat, or women's retreat, and you could write what happened, and then you'd burn the piece of paper, and that was a way to forgive yourself. And that was always a theme of retreats, forgiveness of doing things wrong, sin in your life. That game of you should always be asking for forgiveness, but also that element, He's a loving god.

Yet, Sarah was able to bracket her own struggles with sexuality, because although it was in her mind, she was refraining from being in a relationship,

> Because I wasn't acting on it. I was kind of playing the game of, I am not acting on it, so there is nothing wrong. And, sometimes I would be like, ahh, what do I need to be forgiven for? And I remember being kind of confused, at like the third or fourth retreat I had been on, like, I have nothing to write on this piece of paper. I think I always kind of had a healthy skepticism around me, but at the same time I was in it, recruiting other people to be in it, too. So looking back, there is a little bit of, ugh, I did that. But it is what it is, some people really needed that, and to build people up, and acknowledge that we aren't ever going to be okay, to be the focus, brings you down. They had a lot of bible focused small groups, making sure that faith was a part of all parts of your life . . . So it is hard to look back on it as the college kid who was really into it, because they never thought anything of it, they would just give me more leadership positions, I am a pretty all-American kid, I recognize that, other than this one part of my life that I have changed, and I got here, though, and I started to feel more guilt about it. That's when I started to really pray, I want to be normal. I don't want

to worry about this, I was in the worship band here for awhile, but then I was like, I don't like being on stage because I know there is something wrong. And so that is when I felt more guilt about it, and didn't want to be in a leadership position. So I took the more behind the scenes role of being in charge of their audio, because I have always been involved in that kind of stuff. But I was like, I don't want to be on stage, I don't want to be an example.

After joining another non-denominational church after college in her new city, Sarah finally realized she needed space to process her questions about her own sexuality. She recognizes that her supportive family is likely part of what gave her the ability to "get out" of her church before they cast her out. Though Sarah felt she had to work through and heal what was hurt by the churches of her past, she also recognizes that unlike many people in her life, she was able to avoid the depth of trauma many LGBTQIA+ people face in the South.

> So I was never really outcasted by a church, which was funny because, after I decided I was going to come out and told that church I was leaving, when I go to churches I don't just join, I really go in, I was there every Sunday setting their soundboard up, tearing it down, I was really integral, so I basically had to give them two weeks' notice. And the pastor said, I am just really shocked by this, is there anything we can do, and I told him and he was like, I don't talk about it a lot here, but you can be gay and Christian we just don't want you to act on it. So I could stay a part of the community, but I told him, I just don't think I can stay because there are some really homophobic comments said around me by people here, and I don't think I can stay and try to figure out myself and what that means, especially with the Christian faith.

Beth carried within herself the messages about homosexuality, messages that reinforced her belief that homosexuality was a result of the devil, a sin which puts you outside of God's love.

> Then I clearly heard, oh, and the colleges really, like when we would go to the state gathering of the Fellowship of Christian Athletes, they really hammered in that homosexuality, it was a sin against God, and some of you in this room, by next year, you are going to have fallen away if you aren't careful. And you are going to be in sin. . . . Yeah, you gotta watch it. The devil is everywhere, and the devil is coming after you. I just remember these things.

At the same time, despite these messages, Beth couldn't shake the internal realization that she was a lesbian,

> It was deeper than that. I couldn't get away. It wouldn't leave and why wouldn't it leave, it was like my core, and I knew this. Really, though, it was really

confusing though why God wouldn't take this away. Like, what was the purpose of this? . . . And maybe if I try harder, or be better, cause that is what you hear, you know, if you have faith, God will do anything. God can do anything. Yeah, very, very confusing. So I just immersed more and more in religion, went to seminary, I was a very holy, the only good thing about being that righteous and religious is that you didn't have to have sex with a boy. But I finally decided to give that a try.

In seminary, despite still ignoring her feelings about her sexuality, Beth had a dream that she shared with a professor.

> And I had this dream, and I wrote it down . . . So there was a wall, and I knew it was my faith, and someone had taken a sledgehammer and it was everywhere, everything I had ever known, but in the middle of this chaos was a bed, and I was invited, you know, to be there. And I wasn't ready to be comfortable there to lay in that bed, but I was okay in the midst of the rubble. And so I told him that dream, and he just smiled, because he was like, that's their job. He said, it will come back, brick by brick, and it will be yours. And it was very powerful.

While her faith felt like she had a "sledgehammer" taken to it, she finished seminary and moved to a large midwestern city. Even now, as she remembers her time in college and seminary she speaks with deep sadness and regret.

> Yeah, and I was like, how many missed opportunities have I had in this life? And that's sad. That makes me so sad sometimes. And other women, I met, and there was this connection, this energy, and I just pushed it aside, until I was 29, and I was exhausted, and I was out of seminary and here . . . I probably was more disengaged from church. I really walked out of seminary with a degree but no sense of God anymore. Those bricks hadn't built back up in any way shape or form . . . I felt very lonely, very lonely and very lost. And, it was hard.

When Beth considers what happened, even as she slowly drifted from the church, feeling lonely and lost, she feels comfortable calling this experience trauma.

> I think the trauma started so early, and I don't think, it really started early, it started from the minute I was taken to church at two or three, but I don't think I would have ever seen that. . . . In all of the theology, yeah. I mean, like, hell is real. Hell is scary, I was terrified of hell. . . . Yeah, and they have this whole thing, and they are really believing in the end times. And when I was little they were really believing in the end times. And they talk about it a lot. Being left behind and stuff . . . Yeah, and what was going to happen to you. All the suffering, and I just remember thinking how cruel God was, and there was nowhere to say that. I really do, just to say I don't understand at all, and you are telling

me it is the only way, and then when I realized I was gay, it was as clear as, I realized when I was driving to school, I was seventeen and driving to school and I was stopped at a traffic light and I was like, you are one of these people . . . It happens so young, and then maybe even before we know or have language for what we, that we are gay or lesbian and it just is double traumatizing. Because I will tell you, you hear that, from the time you can walk, and it is wrong.

Jasmine's background included attending churches of multiple denominations, where she heard sermons describing homosexuality as "sinful," and tantamount to murder. Despite her desire to know the God she felt lived in the church, she felt like she "couldn't connect to anything." Looking back, despite her attempts to repress her questions about her own sexuality, the messages still traumatized her.

It was the sexuality. Because it is an essential part of who I am. And it was such a big part of who I was even though I wasn't actively acting out of it at that young age. But it just sort of confirmed the fact that there is something about me that is bad, and it confirmed the feelings that I had when my dad left. And so every time I would hear things about homosexuality that was damning and judging it just confirmed what I felt at that age that there is something wrong with me, that I am bad, that I am not worthy. I am not worthy of love. Look what happened—he left, mother is depressed she can't really give the emotional needs that you have, the church is telling you that something bad is going to happen if you reveal it, you are feeling at that age you just feel hopeless and helpless. You know? So, yeah, definitely, the sexuality a lot of it.

Even when she attempted to find God in other places, staying away from the church for a number of years, and then returning to a Vineyard congregation, the lack of a spiritual center left her feeling lost.

Emotional wounds that took years to heal, and that is what I consider the trauma to me. And in their defense they thought that what they were doing was best, because it was something they believed and they lived their lives according to that same judgment and labeling, so I don't fault them for that. It was just, it didn't work for me. I can't live my life like that. So it was traumatic for me, one who needed genuine love and acceptance and I could not find that in the places where I went. So that was traumatic for me. It was harder for me, it took more of an effort for me to want to be here and to thrive. There were times I was suicidal. It got really bad at points. It took a lot more effort than it needed to be. But it made me stronger and more solid in my beliefs so I can't like totally down it, but it was rough, it really was for a really long time.

Selfobject relationships allow for the maturing of self when the disappointment or loss of those relationships is slow and measured. In all of these religious communities, the loss was immediate and extreme. Even in cases where the participants slowly drifted away, the loss of the church and relationship with God was immediately clear. You could not be LGBTQIA+ and loved by God. This conflict sets the stage for religious trauma—a community that inspires intense archaic idealized selfobject relationships and subsequently, without question, rejects the very people who believed in the God they proclaimed.

THINKING ABOUT RELIGIOUS TRAUMA

Jasmine, April, Lucas, Oliver, Alex, and Beth all claim their stories as religious trauma. Both Sarah and Jorge, though recognizing that what happened to them could be called traumatic, suggest that other people "had it worse." Yet, Sarah and Jorge are set apart from the rest of the participants because despite the loss of their spiritual community, they both had families who stood by them and supported them when they began to identify as queer. This support, though not sufficient to completely prevent the deep pain caused by the non-accepting church, provided a needed safe space for both Jorge and Sarah to continue to meet their idealized selfobject relational needs. Both Sarah and Jorge were open about the love and acceptance their parents offered them. This experience is supported by research on family acceptance as a protection against negative health outcomes, including depression, substance abuse, and suicidal ideation and suicide attempts.[1]

For the other participants in this project, religious trauma was a helpful category, and for many, something they had been trying to work through in spiritual direction or therapy. To think about their stories as religious trauma, a specific kind of trauma related to the loss and betrayal of religious system which, in a number of ways, defined and structured their lives, it is helpful to specifically address what about their stories made this loss traumatic rather than simply a period of suffering.

Religious trauma, as exemplified by these participants, requires six supporting conditions. These conditions, unlike a set of DSM diagnostic symptoms where diagnosis requires exhibiting only a few symptoms, were all present in the experiences of participants. Many participants in this study were aware that people remained in non-accepting congregations while both consciously and unconsciously refusing to integrate a queer identity. However, for these participants the presence of all these conditions led to the internal fragmentation of religious trauma. These conditions are:

1. Membership in a non-accepting religious community
2. An intense focus on the sinfulness of homosexuality

3. A belief in the reality of hell
4. A "decision" to integrate a queer identity
5. Recognition of one's place outside of God's love
6. Fragmentation as a result of loss and betrayal

Membership in a Non-Accepting Religious Community

All participants defined their previous religious community as non-accepting. However, defining non-accepting, especially given the changing nature of beliefs within the neo-evangelical community is difficult. For the purpose of this study, to solicit participants, non-accepting religious communities were defined as those who did not have statements of support for homosexuality either at a denominational or local level. Yet, the non-accepting communities of those involved in this study reflected a few important qualities beyond just a level of unwelcome for queer people.

These communities focused on biblical literalism as an important aspect of their religious life, and especially in relation to the biblical condemnation for homosexuality. Scripture was without error. This belief in the Word of God as an ultimate source of guidance led some communities to question climate change, evolution, and other "scientific" facts, while in others, the Word of God was the most important guide for ethical living. In all communities, participants noted that the Word of God was directly applicable to living your life.

The level of expected participation in these communities was incredibly high. Participants spent weekends and often at least one weeknight at church events. These were not communities where one was casually affiliated, for all participants in this study, the congregations in which they found themselves were central to their lives. Many of these participants took on leadership roles in a variety of capacities—leading bible studies, playing in a worship band, or providing needed services for the community. They felt as if they "belonged" and their presence was important.

Though many of the participants spoke about the pastor of their youth, the relationship with the pastor was not central to their experience of this non-accepting community. In some congregations, multiple staff people were needed to lead congregations of more than 10,000 people; in others, the pastor had such a senior role that they were removed from interacting specifically with participants in this study. The congregations in this study were quite varied in size, from small church to what might be considered a mega-church. In some congregations, even if the pastor played a large role in excommunicating them from the congregation, ultimately, their stories focused on the either the congregation or the denomination as the perpetrator of their trauma. In many of these congregations there was significant suspicion that Christians outside of their religious community might not be "real" Christians. At the same time, membership among the "saved" was a point of pride and connection with others.

Finally, these participants experienced God and the church as an important idealized selfobject. The church provided them with needed structure; it was a place of ultimate love and connection with the source of the universe. A personal relationship with Jesus was often expected. At the same time, these congregations did not allow for the maturation of this selfobject relationship; questions, doubts, or ideas outside of the accepted theology within the congregation were unacceptable. As Jones argues, "If a religious institution insists it is pure and without error; if expositors insist that a text is infallible; if a teacher or master insists that she or he is perfect; then the devotees will be kept in a state of developmental arrest, no matter how deeply they love the institution, or the text, or that teacher, or how powerful the emotions are that are evoked."[2] God specifically, and religion generally, had no space for imperfection, leading to the need to leave the group when their own identity was no longer acceptable. In several congregations women were also prohibited from being in leadership positions, further restricting their access to spaces where questions or doubts about the theology were possible. This structure led not just to the presence of an idealized selfobject relationship, but reinforced that this selfobject relationship remain archaic, setting participants up for internal fragmentation when that relationship was lost.

An Intense Focus on the Sinfulness of Homosexuality

All participants believed that homosexuality was a grave sin. In a number of their congregations homosexuality was regularly demonized; it was more than a disease one could catch. Homosexual people were threatening, and they wanted to trick the unsuspecting into the sin of their lifestyle. To do this, homosexual people attempted to "recruit" new members, especially targeting children. One homosexual could easily convince others, no matter how faithful, to participate in their sinful lifestyle. God was intensely interested in the sexual lives of Christians, and homosexuality was incompatible with living a Christian life.

In some congregations the sinfulness of homosexuality was communicated ritually through the excommunication of members who refused to repent of their homosexual behavior. Unlike other sins, homosexuals were not merely sinners, but a threat to their communities. The difference, however, between homosexual acts and homosexual thoughts was present in some of these communities. In some congregations, even having a homosexual fantasy was sinful, in others, you could continue in membership as long as you remained celibate; though homosexual thoughts were not encouraged, it was the homosexual act that was sinful.

In some congregations homosexuality was so anathema to being a member of these communities that the topic was rarely specifically addressed. At the same time, participants in congregations that favored silence were fully aware that homosexuality was sinful and in conflict with God's law.

Finally, the sinfulness around homosexuality meant that keeping homosexual thoughts and actions secret was of utmost importance. Fears that one might be a homosexual were meant to stay internal, and true belief in prayer could change these thoughts and actions. The use of conversion therapy or dedicated prayer groups to excise the sin of homosexuality was common.

A Belief in the Reality of Hell

For many who have internalized a less punitive theological structure, hell is often intellectualized, not a literal place where one can expect to spend eternity. But for participants in this study, hell was entirely real, and their visions of what happened to homosexuals were graphically violent. Lakes of eternal fire, unending excruciating pain, complete separation from everything they had ever known and from God was only the beginning of the pain they would suffer in the afterlife. April remembers, "you know when someone is 20 and they come to you and say that they are scared of going to hell, if you didn't grow up with that being an entrenched fear, people kind of chuckle—partially because they are uncomfortable partially because it sounds kind of silly," but for April, the reality of hell was not silly at all.

The belief that they were going to die and spend eternity in excruciating pain meant that many participants in this study recall periods of anxiety attacks, self-harm, suicidal ideation or suicide attempts. This correlates with studies which suggest that non-accepting religious communities lead to higher risk behaviors among LGB youth.[3]

Given that the traditional view of trauma highlights the threat or expectation of death as a primary indicator that an event may be traumatic, it is not surprising that the belief that one would die and spend eternity as a victim of unimaginable violence was considered traumatic for these participants. In many congregations the stories about hell and a theology which featured hell as a central vision of punishment started even in the earliest Sunday school education.

A Decision to Integrate a Queer Identity

In many non-accepting circles, homosexuality is often considered a "decision" which can be reversed through prayer or "conversion therapy." In this study, the possibility to foreclose on further development of a homosexual identity does not assume that one makes a "decision" to be homosexual, but rather that LGBTQIA+ people are active in the process of coming to know and value who they are and that activity, if the costs associated with it are too high, can be discontinued. Several participants recalled people in their communities and congregations who appeared "obviously queer," but chose to live an outwardly heterosexual life. In some congregations one could identify as a homosexual as long as no homosexual acts took place, a life which did not appeal to any of the participants in this study. Following initial periods of identity confusion, participants in this study often moved into a long period of varying levels of identity tolerance, a stage which highlights the difference between how LGBTQIA+ people see themselves and how others view them. At this stage, one tolerates their LGBTQIA+ identity but does not fully accept it.[4]

The risk of losing their relationship with God, with the church and, in many cases, with their families, left participants in this study with few good options when considering their queer identity. They could either accept that homosexuality was a sin, and actively repress their growing feelings and attractions, or they would likely lose a connection with the people and structures that were most important to them. Most participants simply said they "couldn't live any longer" without being honest about their sexuality, whatever the consequences. They could no longer ignore their queer identity.

Recognition of One's Place Outside of God's Love

For all participants in this study the cost of integrating a queer identity was the loss of their community and membership in the non-accepting church. For a number of participants this resulted in excommunication or formal dismissal; for others, they slowly drifted away from the community knowing that they were no longer welcome.

Just as many participants recall having no healthy examples of LGBTQIA+ people in their communities, none of these participants had seen an LGBTQIA+ person actively participating in a supportive religious community. Several participants were not even sure such a community existed.

Fragmentation as a Result of Loss and Betrayal

The belief that they were going to die, the loss of an idealized selfobject relationship, and the knowledge that their "choices" left them outside of God's love and damned to hell, resulted in religious trauma. This experience of internal fragmentation left participants struggling to pick up the pieces of their lives and go on. Rage, sadness, crippling anxiety, depression, suicidal thoughts, self-harm, drug and alcohol abuse, as well as suicide attempts all characterize the experience of participants after they left their religious communities. Many participants in this study spent years trying to understand what had happened to them and to rebuild the internal structures needed to function as healthy creative adults.

Trauma is different from suffering. Suffering is painful, but the world remains anchored. Trauma, as Root argues, destroys the basic organizing principles by which we know ourselves, our environment, and relationships.[5] Religious trauma, as these participants lived it, reshaped how they understood themselves in the world. Categories of good and evil were not as clear, spaces that were safe became dangerous, families were not stable, relationships could be discarded at will.

These participants could have left the church for good, refusing to return to a place that would remind them of their trauma. Yet, these eight participants eventually returned, and in their return tell stories of healing, of leaving behind the darkness that plagued them, and of working through their trauma. It is to those stories of return, and what they might tell us about how accepting religious communities might care for those who have been traumatized that we now turn.

NOTES

1. Ryan, C., S. T. Russell, D. Huebner, R. Diaz and J. Sanchez. "Family acceptance in adolescence and the health of LGBT young adults." *Journal Of Child & Adolescent Psychiatric Nursing* 23 (2010): 205–213.

2. Jones, *Terror and Transformation,* 65.

3. Hatzenbuehler, M. L., J. E. Pachankis and J. Wolff. "Religious climate and health risk behaviors in sexual minority youths: a population-based study." *American Journal of Public Health* 102 (2012): 657–663.

4. Cass, "Homosexual Identity Formation," 230.

5. Root, "Reconstructing the Impact of Trauma," 229.

Chapter Five

Psychological Analysis: Return

> Yeah, and I did leave after seminary for a long time, and I didn't go to church, and I missed it. God was always there, but it was like, we really, as I age, I understand the importance of community. We were made to be in community, to heal; we were wounded in our family, in our community, and we will be healed in a community.
>
> —*Beth*

Religious trauma results from an extreme break of the relationship one has with God and the community. Many participants felt lost with no church to call home. The doors of the institution which had occupied much of their lives were now closed to them; leaving them uncertain about how to navigate their new reality.

For Alex, the pain of their excommunication was so significant that they no longer felt they could call theirself a Christian. Alex says,

> I did a complete 180 from church and said, I am not going to ever be involved with that ever again. And flirted with many different faiths and things consequently throughout high school and into the first year of college before really returning back to any sort of church activities.

In order to deal with their concept of hell and the belief they were going to suffer there eternally, Alex says they simply decided they were no longer going to believe in hell at all. Having lost the church, their concept of God began to expand,

> It wasn't until my concepts of God really started broadening very very widely. So yeah, that time of exploration of faith and spirituality was a really beautiful one actually. Because of it I was able to make those things my own. Part of the beautiful thing about it was that I wasn't participating with any faith communities, which can be a good thing, if you are in [the midwest] where it is

very sparse, and very conservative, and the one little Jewish community [near my town] is lovely, but they are very conservative. So there is things like that. So I explored Judaism, and Buddhism and even Islam. Buddhism is where my thoughts and energies were into faith wise, for a while, and that still influences me to this day in some capacity. That concept of I am going to hell, that was there, that was there up until about that time that I stopped going to church, like I didn't think I was going to go to hell because I didn't believe in any of it really. So I was just going to divorce myself entirely and go to something else.

Eventually, Alex found theirself in a Catholic church, sobbing during an Ash Wednesday service. The rush of emotions, accompanied with what they understood as the "don't ask, don't tell" stance of the Catholic Church, drew them into the community. Eventually, they began discernment for the priesthood in the Catholic church. They say,

I think it was a lot of confusion of many years of confusion of just not knowing what the fuck is going on. And I think I was still feeling it then, I was just in the weight of that, of like, I hadn't really sat down and thought about all this stuff. It wasn't until now that I can look back and be like, oh, well, clearly I was upset with church because of this, so I was exploring other things because of whatever. But, it was just a really big experience, and I started becoming involved with the Catholic church to the point where the year after I was done with school, I started discernment with the Catholic Church . . . which was a very negative experience. What the fuck was I thinking? Now is what I think, but when I look back it makes total sense.

Alex wanted to find a church where they could be fully theirself while also discerning their capacity for church leadership. The Catholic Church felt like it might be that place for them, but the reaction to their sexuality felt similar to their experience in the Lutheran Church Missouri Synod. They recall,

In the moment I was thinking I identify with the liturgy, I identify with this church, this church feels like a homespace for me. Yes, they have teachings, a lot of teachings I don't agree with, but that didn't really, but yeah, that will probably change at some point someday, and that doesn't mean I have to believe it. And there is a lot of, in the Catholic Church today, I believe personally there is a big, for clergy, a separation in their minds between the realities of teaching, and dogma and doctrine and the realities of practice. So that's all, I was having conversations with priests, and I have priests in my family, I have Catholic priests on my father's side, and I grew up with priests and nuns and it didn't feel weird to me. And then we go through the entire year process of the first year of discernment. So this is, they never asked me, and this is the part where, a year in, and you have you do a psych eval, you do all these things and that was actually a really positive experience, and then you have this in front of a panel "are you a homosexual?" And I am like god damn it, is this thing on? (makes hitting microphone gesture) Three times, third time's a charm, so I said yes, and they said wrong answer. Even if you are, you have to say no. And I am like, you are telling me to lie? They literally told me that. They are like, it is fine if you are, you just have to say no.

Alex, having already been through an excommunication experience, simply could not accept the idea of living a half truth, acting on their sexuality while lying about it in a significant part of their life. Alex eventually began work with a non-profit organization resettling refugees and came into contact with a number of people connected with the Catholic Worker, a social justice minded community started by Dorothy Day. Alex moved to a large midwestern city and began working and living in a Catholic Worker community, starting discernment for the priesthood again, but this time with the Franciscans. The process with the Franciscans felt entirely different to Alex.

> They ask you a hell of a lot of questions, and they are not afraid of the answers, or they don't necessarily care what the answers are just that you are asking these questions. The most in depth and comprehensive education I have ever had on sexuality was with them and probably ever will . . . Like, yeah, you are going to masturbate, but most Catholic priests would not be able to say, like no no no, but they are like, no you are going to do that, that is just, and everybody knows it and half of them are gay and they know that, it is not just that they are gay, but they know that. There is a sense of by naming it you are showing support, it is like I know this to be true with you and I still love you as a Friar Brother.

Alex felt as if their mind was expanding within this community, and when the time came for them to take the next step in discernment, they felt like they could be more open and honest about who they were. They say,

> That was big, and for me to feel like honest in how I am telling this story and not like I have to code language like omit things because they won't accept me, I am like, okay, I am just going to do this, I am like living this life for a while, I am feeling pretty comfortable in it, that is not going to change for me. So it is like, y'all need to accept me, and this is what you are going to accept . . . I come to the panel, they accept me, I kept that piece of paper, too. And I keep nothing, the only reason I ever say I kept something is because it actually means something. I toss everything. And I kept that because it meant so much to me and it still is.

Yet again, though, something did not feel right to Alex, and they ultimately decided they couldn't continue. They recall,

> And a month later I told them, I so appreciate all this, but I am not going to be able to be celibate, I just know me, I feel like it is a good fit in so many ways,

but I am just not the kind of person, I started doing a lot of thinking about that, and I am like, that is when I had that conversation with myself because they are so frank, and had asked the good questions that I was like, you know, that doesn't seem like, I was really struggling with that. Because I started thinking in my head more and more and I have got all these urges, and I don't think it to be a bad thing, and they are not going to go away . . . Yeah, especially for a pastoral relationships and just the basis of your entire vocation being founded on some sort of lie. Because I also was starting to see what that looked like for certain people, for certain priests, it takes . . . And it is not that they were, by any means, bad priests or bad humans it just, I saw it takes a toll. And it limits what you can do in this world. So I looked at that and I said, that doesn't feel right. So then, back to square one. Again.

Jorge felt such bitterness and anger at this church after being fired that he felt he could not call himself a Baptist anymore, but he still identified as a Christian. Once proud to call himself a Baptist, the experience in the church made him realize that his relationship with God had to be outside of the church. He was unwilling to give up on God even though he had been rejected by the church.

Jorge, separated from the church, also felt the power of the messages he had always heard about what was going to happen to him, that his life would no longer have meaning. He says,

As soon as you become a gay man, you are going to have AIDS. When I finally accepted the fact that I was a gay man through my marriage I was like, well, I am going to have AIDS, I am going to die one day of this . . . But it is, being naive to it all, I thought I am going to die of AIDS. I am going to die of loneliness and never find another Christian man out there that believes the same thing I believe and is gay. So it was a lot of things adding on, that I thought, oh my goodness, I am going to have a horrible life.

But Jorge missed the church, and even though he was filled with "bitterness and anger," he also felt like something was missing.

I always missed it. I wanted to go back to a church and I remember going to, I started dating a guy, and he actually was part of [a church] . . . however, I didn't go with him, because I was scared of what was being taught. I never realized that [this church] was a church that accepted gays, I was like, no, no, I am going to be ridiculed, I don't want to be looked down, I hate that feeling, I don't want to sit in the back and feel like every eye is on me. So I really didn't go, and then I kind of, secretly would listen to sermons from [the] Baptist Church because they are online . . . but when they were on homosexuality or anything about drinking I would just turn it off.

Jorge admits that for a while, he just "flatlined"; he didn't want to attend church and didn't believe that there was a church that could accept him.

Jasmine, after a short experience in the Vineyard church, stayed away from church for five years. She admits that she still felt a "spiritual" side to herself, but did not do much other than, "talking to God sometimes, reading books, talking to friends sometimes, but I would never discuss sexuality, we would talk about everything else. That was it, that was as close as I got."

Lucas, after "losing his mind" to drugs and alcohol, eventually clawed his way back, now with the knowledge that,

> All of my friends from then are dead, and I was chosen, and that is when I know, no matter what a theology, no matter what an interpretation anyone has to say about me, I know I was chosen, and I know that is divine. And it is so powerful to me. And so then I started seeking out whatever fed my soul, like anything. I always say I learned to meditate by going tanning (both laughing). Anything that would feed my soul. I started doing yoga, I started seeking out anything. Someone gave me this book called, it is the Sermon on the Mount but I can't remember the guy's name, but it is a Unity guy, anyway, and I really connected with it, and I looked up his spiritual background and I started following this sort of Unity path.

For Lucas, though following the Unity path was healing for him in many ways, it was still missing an integral piece of his spirituality. He says,

> [Unity] is like a, it is like, kind of like Oprah, kind of like the power of now stuff. But they identify it from a Christian perspective, but other people wouldn't call them Christians, they are almost like Unitarians somewhat but a little more woo-woo, whereas Unitarian is kind of reserved. So I did that for a long time and it goes so hand in hand with twelve step that I am involved in and therapy that it really worked for me for a long time . . . Part of it is music, part of it is the spiritual stuff which is that I feel like I missed Catholicism, like ritual, I missed that process, and I felt like I loved Unity but I couldn't deny, it is the philosopher in me, the academic philosopher, that I couldn't deny that no matter, even if what Unity says I believe, the reason I believe it is because when I was young I heard these stories about Jesus and I loved what this guy had to say, and the things that he said led me to the kind of interpretation that landed me at Unity. And so I was like, I think it was relationship that started that. So I missed talking about Jesus, frankly.

Beth, after finishing seminary left with "no sense of God anymore," and realized, "I had this degree and I needed to do something with it," so she began a position with a social justice organization in a large midwestern city. She recalls that she felt, "it's kind of like I was a leaf on a stream. And I was being taken, so I was like, okay, let's go with this . . . and see what the hell . . ."

Beth was introduced to a spiritual director by a friend, a relationship she remembers as,

> Yeah, spiritual direction slash therapy, and I think, she was the first person, the first Christian to embrace me, to hug me, knowing everything about me. Yeah, it was very powerful, very freeing . . . yeah, and I have said this to other people and they have looked at me cross eyed, but I will say this to you, I think it the closest, her love for me, her acceptance of me, is the closest I will find of Jesus on this Earth . . . She wasn't just seeing me, it turns out how many Catholics, and other folks of different faiths were also wounded, and not just from being gay, but abused, all these issues. So this one day she says, you know I am starting this bible study group, and it turned out it was these four or five other women, and we met every month for like 10 years as a group.

For a long time, Beth was "soaking up" the messages she received in this bible study with other wounded people.

> Yeah, so we had bible study, and man, she made the scriptures real again for me. Like the bible, I could look at it again. And yeah, I just took so many notes . . . Yeah, I no longer had to hide. I could be an open vessel again, it sounded so new, like I could hear it again, the Exodus, the way she told the Exodus, we spent months on that story, but it was us. That journey was your journey, coming to be found again by God, what was your journey like, what was your desert? And the prodigal, that was beautiful, the way she described that and I still have all these notes. I typed them all up, I have them in a book, and I gave them to everyone else in the group. Because to me it was just the most freeing thing, and I know not everyone felt that, one of them laughed, because [she] would just start talking and I would write and write, and she was like, you have already filled up seven pages. And I would just laugh, I can't help it, I want to remember everything. It was like, love, love, acceptance.

April also found her way to another "liberal but not super liberal" church when she was invited to attend a soup supper with a friend. She says,

> Second half of my junior year, a friend invited me to like a soup supper bible study thing at the local Lutheran church . . . And the pastor there was actually really really sweet. And I liked it, it was nice. And very low pressure. Like theoretically it was supposed to be a bible study but generally we talked about a mildly religious topic maybe, and the church had a homeless shelter in the basement and that's where we ate and hung out, and we'd be like, Jesus said we should feed homeless people, so let's go feed some homeless people. And that is pretty much what it was, and I feel like that is what helped me to re-acclimate to the concept of religion and faith. Because everything else, whether it was the church I grew up in or the Vineyard, they were both very intense experiences, while the Lutheran experience was a lot more chill . . . Both of the other

churches I went to were very much black and white, us and them, saved and not saved, if you come here we are going to swarm you because we have to get your plugged in as soon as possible, and this church is like, hey, you want some soup? That's cool, or not. Hey, do you want to come to church? That's cool too, or not . . . I thought they were really weird, like you people are not very serious. But then they did a lot more walking faith than talking faith. And I was like this feels a lot less hypocritical than before, and that's why I kept going.

She continued to attend the Lutheran church, drawn in by the social justice work they were doing in the community, although she never felt like she was ready to become "officially" Lutheran. She wasn't hearing messages about homosexuality in the church, and so she felt like she could "press pause" on thinking about her own sexuality and what that meant for her faith.

I started going with my friend because I like soup. I kept going because I didn't realize until I started going to worship that I missed the structure, the community, the singing especially. The quiet reflective time. Because even though I didn't get tons of that during my childhood, and I didn't like going to worship, it was such a chunk of my, a well-defined chunk, of my life that not doing it felt weird, and doing it felt nice and it was nice that it wasn't super abrasive. And I kept going because I felt like they had some good things to say. The church was liberal but it wasn't that liberal. And they'd be like lots of people have things to say about gay marriage and abortion and stuff, but that's probably important, but we have much more pressing issues. They did a lot of local action, like they had a homeless shelter, and that was great because then I didn't have to deal with the large existential concepts. And I could do the church thing and plug into things, like yes, we should do something about all the kids that are getting asthma from public housing.

April even met with the pastor, bringing her questions about whether it was possible to be a Christian and lesbian. Though she did not find all the answers she was looking for, the church felt like a place she could stay and continue to explore her identity.

I actually had a couple sit downs with [the pastor]. And he gave me a couple books by gay Christians that were like, hey, the bible is confusing, because Lutherans are so big on the whole grace thing, which was a new concept for me, really. And I mean, the Lutheran take on it, even before they were really okay with gay people was like, well, probably not ideal, but God loves you anyway. Which is a hell of a lot better than what I had been getting. So I felt better, I felt better about all of that.

Oliver also joined a somewhat less conservative church, though he admits he kept the two parts of his life separated, thinking of his church as one realm of his life, while his homosexuality occupied another realm.

> Because even the first, I had joined [a church] here . . . when I moved, when I finished law school. During the university and law school years I wasn't really a member of a church, I would go to my parent's church with them when I would go home for breaks and stuff like that, and at that time it was still fine because I wasn't telling anyone at church or my parents about stuff, so that was one sphere. And back at school with my boyfriend and friends that was a different sphere. But then when I moved . . . I joined [a church] which was like a missionary church of the Christian Reformed Church. The difference between [that church] and my parents church there was still you don't talk about anything, that was still the same, the difference was the background of the people . . . I think, I don't even know, I think they were okay with it, but they couldn't say they were okay because they might get it trouble with the denomination. Whereas back home they didn't talk about it and they weren't okay with it. We all knew that. But it still didn't feel right, because I was still hiding a part of myself from God or from church, and I don't feel part of the community because I can't be my whole self with the community.

Oliver refers to that time in his life as the "dangerous years," because he recognized that, like many of his friends, he could have given up on God entirely. Yet, he felt like there was always something pulling him back to the church. He recalls,

> Maybe just because, I would think my upbringing. Because it was such a strong, such an important part of me for so long, just because of the bad experience with one church it wasn't something I was going to throw out the window, just right there. I am like okay, something is wrong with this, I don't want to be a part of this, but I have got to figure out how these things, could go together. God can't be this awful person that is just judging people and sending people to hell and stuff like that.

Sarah also felt like she had to figure out how her faith and her sexuality could possibly be compatible. After joining a non-denominational church in her new city and taking on leadership roles on Sunday mornings, she would pretend that she was going out of town in order to visit other churches that she thought might be more accepting. She eventually emailed the pastor and told him that she could not continue to worship there and explore her sexuality. She heard members of her church discussing how the neighborhood needed to be "saved" because of all the gay people, despite the church's theological belief that celibate homosexual people were acceptable in the eyes of God. She said, "You hear those comments, and it was like, I am not going to be able to be here. And if you can't invite your friends and you never want your family to come, that is not where you should be, and I knew that already."

All participants in this study, at varying levels, continued to live out their spirituality, despite the loss of their church community. For many, estrangement from the church meant a new openness to the larger world; when all was lost, their relationship to God and the church had to be built up anew. Feelings of anger and bitterness, as well as fear of further trauma kept several participants away from the church for quite some time. Others practiced their spirituality on their own, not sure if they would ever return to a church community, while some participants found a middle ground by returning to a less explicitly non-accepting, though still not accepting community.

This time, referred to as "dangerous years," by Oliver, felt like a period of being unmoored from the ethical, ritual and community systems participants in this study had come to know. Cultural anthropologist, Clifford Geertz, describes religion as that which "tunes human actions to an envisaged cosmic order and projects images of that cosmic order onto the plane of human experience."[1] One might argue that the "danger" expressed by participants in this study was not just the loss of a present and cosmic order, but a loss of the cultural-religious world that had been a primary source of meaning making in their lives. For the non-religious, the depth of this loss can seem overexaggerated, yet, if we understand the lost religious community as the primary cultural system of meaning-making the "danger" becomes more apparent. Geertz goes on to argue that the symbols and symbols systems that are so integral to how we understand ourselves; they might be called central to our "creaturely viability."[2] Without symbols and symbol systems, we are left in a state of chaos. Through ritual in a religious community, humans form and maintain social bonds that establish human community, unconsciously appropriate common values and categories of knowledge and experience, resolve conflict, and transform or renew community life.[3] The loss of a ritual community, one that had so deeply shaped the way that participants understood community, values, and life upended their sense of how they functioned in the social and religious world.

What was lost to participants in this study was not just a community, but a system of making sense of life, through religious belief and religious ritual. They were, whether they drifted away or were cast out, no longer welcome in the ritual community. In his work on rites of passage, anthropologist Arnold Van Gennep suggested that all rites of passage involve a three-phase form: separation, transition, and incorporation.[4] Participants in this study often described a "middle time," or liminal stage, when they were no longer a part of a non-accepting church community and had not yet found an accepting church. Between their non-accepting and accepting congregation, participants in this study were "neither here nor there; they were betwixt and between." This liminal time, in ritual studies, is often likened "to death, to being in the womb, to invisibility, to darkness . . . to the wilderness."[5] The religious allusions in this language about liminality are obvious; this middle time was, for many participants, a pilgrimage through the spiritual wilderness, often considered, in scripture, as a place of great danger. Liminal time, occurring after a separation before reincorporation into a new community, leaves liminal beings powerless, without identity, "they have no status, property, insignia . . . " In many rituals of passage, this liminal time is a "moment in and out of time," when hierarchies of status are flattened.[6] For participants in this study liminal time was a struggle to be seen—were they a beloved child of God anymore? Was there space for them in the kin-dom of God? The loss of their religious community, the separation described by Turner and Van Gennep, left them without a sense of themselves in the Christian world, yet the liminal space also allowed them the opportunity to explore this wilderness, despite the "danger." What did it mean to live and move and exist outside of the Christian community? Would they, as many had been warned in their non-accepting church, die alone and afraid? Was the world really as dangerous as they had been told?

Eventually all participants in this study became reincorporated in a new community, but the liminal time they experienced would deeply shape how they imagined the Christian life ought to be lived. Yet, the risks of return were very real. Was there a place where they could be both openly LGBTQIA+ and Christian? Was healing even possible? Why the time to return felt right, and how they summoned the strength to darken the door of a church again required a kind of courage that still puzzles many of the participants themselves.

RELIGIOUS RETURN

Alex's return, in many ways, began when they first entered a Catholic Church for an Ash Wednesday service. After being excommunicated from the Lutheran Church Missouri Synod, practicing Buddhism, and finding theirself unsatisfied and still searching, they did what "made no sense" and went to church. They continued to follow this path, somewhat disillusioned with the Catholic Church, still unable to find a way to live as a queer person and a Christian while being open about both of those identities.

As a musician, Alex took a position directing music in an Episcopal Church. Almost immediately, something felt different. Alex says,

> That was an interesting time because it started those thoughts like, I am connected to something larger through this massive international billion people

faith of Catholicism is starting to crumble because I am like oh, I can actually be as open as I want and basically say anything I want and it won't be heretical in the Episcopal church. And that was, it felt so liberal to me, it was almost like beneath me, like you heathens! Almost, not quite, but there was almost that. And it was uncomfortable at first. It is not that I disagreed with anybody, it was just that I wasn't used to that in a faith place. I was between a rock and a hard place before that! (Laughing)

This freedom, to explore what they believed and say it all out loud, felt entirely different to Alex, who had, in their experiences in the Catholic Church, been living somewhat between identities. It wasn't until their own Rector celebrated his marriage to his partner in the church that Alex realized something completely different was happening here.

So that was interesting, and I started thinking, this seems like a much better fit. Because I had never really been in a Episcopal Church, I had been to Evensong services I was getting paid to sing at, but I was never going to worship at an Episcopal church. I just thought it was where white people go. It consequently is, but I always thought it was just Catholics who don't care. And there is some of that, but there is also a healthy sense of other things. I started thinking about that and we had a gay priest who got married to his husband by the Bishop, and that was my third month there, and that to me, I will never forget that. To think back a decade of what was going on in my life, and I was getting excommunicated, and I was just like, and here I am watching the priest that I work with, my rector, my confessor, my friend, get married to his husband by the Bishop, and that was big, and I was like, you know, there is something going on here that I really am.

This ritual acceptance, especially with the blessing of Bishop, was deeply healing for Alex. Alex recalls,

And that Bishop's hand is on this. He is saying the word gay. The kind of, like any good homilist you have this phrase you repeat, tricks of the trade, but he had that, he said that, "it is about time," that we are doing this, it is about that I am here, that was his refrain, and I am like, yes! Sobbing in the back, literally, I mean, everyone was sobbing, it was just beautiful. It was a big deal for me, and working with a priest that was in that relationship and working with him and being friends with him and his husband, and there were other gay, [this church] is a historically gay church, and that was, just seeing couples hold hands, in church, or a cute little peck on the cheek like you would give to anybody.

Alex recognizes that in a progression of moments—from entering the church while telling himself, "Fuck no I will never be an Episcopalian," to seeing their priest married, to realizing that this church was a space where he could be fully queer and fully Christian—the Episcopal Church became his "spiritual home." Alex says,

> I just really remember thinking that, like, wow, this is like it is my polity, my, it all resonates with me . . . when it was founded they were like, you actually have to be, you have to allow for a lot of broadness because there was a lot to encapsulate at the time because otherwise they would have had a coup, so that is part of the beauty today is that it still exists, each person bringing their own experience, in fact, the three legged stool, I don't know if you have heard about that, tradition, scripture and reason. And so tradition is kind of like church, tradition with a lowercase t, but the reason part is like, what do you bring to the table, and I love that part a lot.

Jorge admits that his healing began when he heard that the pastor who had thrown him out of his church and fired him from his position in the school was arrested for having sexual relations with a minor. Jorge says,

> Because I was so angry towards the church, I was so bitter towards the church, and my mother gave me probably the best advice that I could take at that time, "just remember everything that is done in darkness is going to come into the light," and growing up I always heard that saying and it never really clicked, and it didn't really register. And when a couple years later the same person that fired me is now in jail for having sex with a minor. So that's when, ah, that came to light, and karma is a bitch, kind of mentality, and that's what actually helped me process to heal . . . And I know it is a bad thing for me to start healing on someone else's whatever, but it made me realize everybody is human, and you know, compassion is I know how he is feeling right now because I felt that. Like no one else cares, no one else is on his side, even though of course he did something horribly wrong, but no one is on his side, where mine I was just being who I was, and even to them was something bad and to me it wasn't, no one was on my side . . .

When Jorge started dating his current boyfriend, it felt important to him that his new partner understand his religious background. Jorge felt the pull to return to church when he started dating Orlando, who is Catholic. Jorge says,

> It is hard to find a gay man that is religious. It really is. And I am pretty sure, all for the right reasons, they have the same background that I did, they were ridiculed or preached from a sermon that they were going to hell, or from the pulpit. And [Orlando] was Catholic, or is Catholic still, and I remember him inviting me, and I was like, "ugh, I don't want to go, I am not Catholic." And finally, I thought, you know what I am going to go, and went. And it wasn't something that I enjoyed completely, because I still felt that I was ridiculed, but

we were at church and he held my hand and I was like, no one is looking at me, no one is looking at me.

The Catholic Church did not resonate with Jorge, and though he sporadically attended with Orlando, he found his church home when he was invited to visit an accepting Methodist church.

> One of [Orlando's] friends invited us to [church], and he had gone before to [that church], and that's when I was invited, and I was like, okay, you know what, I will go. But scared, because it is a new church I am not sure if they are going to ridicule me, fought it for awhile, and then the first Sunday that I went I bawled my eyes out because it was that powerful.

When the time came for Jorge to visit this new church at the urging of a mutual friend, Jorge felt like he wasn't ready. Yet, he believes that God was pushing him to go to that first service. He recalls,

> I, the funny thing is, and I think God works in amazing miracle ways, I look back at some of those things like, wow, God, you really put thought into this. We were invited way before . . . and I kept putting it off because I was so scared, and that morning of that going to church at that point, I had a bad break up two years, it has been three years, and I moved back with mom for six months that turned into two and half years, cause Mom is like, no, no, I don't want you to move out. And I would go on the weekends to [Orlando's] house and stay there, and I remember getting up in the morning on Sunday morning and we had kind of a little argument and feeling like, I don't want to go, I don't want to go. And we talked it through and we had to go in our separate ways in different cars, after church I would stay in the city and he would go back home to the burbs. And in the car up there I am like, okay, I am going to give this a chance, it isn't going to change how I feel, I know it isn't going to have an effect, I am a Baptist, at that point I am still thinking I am a Baptist and there is nobody that is going to come close to that service, like what I am used to, and I remember turning on [the radio] and the song coming up "God is Love," and bawling my eyes out while I am driving all the way to the city. And I parked nervous, [Orlando] met me at my car and he was like "are you ready?" and I was like, no but I need to do this before I change my mind . . .

There was something different about this church for Jorge, and he felt the change within himself almost immediately. He says,

> So the first thing, one of the student pastors got up, and I was thinking oh, she's a lesbian, I called it right off . . . yeah, I just knew, I called it. And so I was thinking, I am feeling more comfortable now, but she got up and the opening message, or not message really, but greeting, was like, we don't care if you are

gay or bi, we don't care if you are black or white, she went through this whole list, and said, we just want you here. And that's when the tears started.

I have never felt at home. [Orlando] realized it and he started squeezing my hand, and I am like, okay, this is just maybe coincidence, and the next thing that happened, the music director choir person sang a song from a hymn that I knew that kind of brought all these memories back, and I started bawling . . . And then [the pastor] got up and preached, or gave a message about how love is love and how we are accepting of who we are but the doors are always open and we are a church that believes in what we believe and we won't send you away, and God works a miracle in different ways. And I sat there shocked, and there was, after church there are always treats in the back for after when people drink coffee and stuff and [Orlando] was like, do you want something? And I was like, I have to get to the car right away. I couldn't even make it to the car where I started bawling. He's like, are you okay? And I am like, I am not okay, I am not okay, I am overwhelmed with emotions right now. And we sat there and we both cried, and I felt for the first time welcomed into religion again. Where I felt this is home again, almost, I am back home.

This return, the feeling of coming back home, transformed many things for Jorge, including the way he understood his relationship with Orlando. His liminal experience gave him new eyes to see himself as both a member of the Christian community and a gay man. He says,

We go to mass on Saturdays for [Orlando], and then Sunday mornings we go to my church. So we, he's a Catholic still, believing in Catholic church and I am a Christian going to Methodist church, but he will go with me. He likes it as much as I do, and I would say it brings us a lot closer. For sure. Because we believe on the same things, and having church back in our life is a changer . . . because it was so, such a great feeling again, of knowing that I belonged to a church, knowing that I belonged to a congregation, where I am sought for if I am not there. And that I can sit next to [Orlando] and hold his hand or reach around and give him a kiss if I have to, do communion with my partner next to me the whole time. And that to me is a huge thing.

After meeting with the pastor for a one-on-one conversation, a common practice at his new Methodist church, the pastor encouraged Jorge to offer testimony to the entire congregation about what had happened to him and how God was working in his life.

It is funny because we were supposed to meet one on one and I couldn't make it because of work, and then he reached out and he's like, hey we are moving locations and I would love for you to give your testimony. And I was like, I am not ready for that at all. He's like, how about we talk about it over coffee and let me know what you are scared of. So we met over coffee and I told him where my reasons were, and why I didn't want to do it, and he was like, I think you should, if [this church] has been that much of a change for you, and a healing for you I think you need to. I am remember sitting there at coffee almost trembling telling my story because this was the first time I had actually told anybody other than [Orlando], because I was very upfront with [Orlando] in the beginning, what is he going to think of me, he's a pastor. And when [the pastor] right in the middle of the coffee shop we prayed it was like, oh, wow, I'm okay with this, I am okay that my pastor knows I am gay, and he is okay with me being gay and yet a Christian. And I remember going to the service giving my testimony and . . . it was such a burden lifted off my kind of shoulders kind of feeling when I gave my testimony. And going back to my chair and knowing that I feel loved, I feel accepted, I feel like I am not going to be ridiculed for who I am, what I do, who I decide to love. This is what Christianity is, and that feeling of it is just not a religion anymore, it is a Christian community.

Jasmine was also looking for a community when she finally felt ready to see if there really was a church that would be accepting of her identity. Her life felt better, she was back in school and on a path toward a career, she was seeing a therapist, but still felt like she was "missing a connection" with her spirituality. Jasmine didn't feel ready for a full church, but when she heard about a bible study meeting over her lunch hour, she decided she could give it a try. She recalls,

I was not willing to go to a church, I was like I want to do something different, I'll start with a bible study. You can't go wrong with a bible study, that is what I am thinking (laughs). And I needed some, I was starting to read the bible again, and I had a lot of questions. So I was like, I will look into a bible study. So at the time I was a member of meetup.com, and so I was looking on that website, and I saw and the meetup said "doing church differently" that was their motto. So it piqued my interest, obviously. Doing church differently, hmmmm . . . And how different? . . . So I went to the first bible study [the pastor] had, he was the first person I met, and it was a small group of us, maybe 6–8 professionals, it was held during lunch time so people could go from work. And that is where I met the current members today. So I have known them since that first bible study. And he taught me a lot! I really liked his personality; he didn't judge me. He was so open, he revealed that he was gay, and I had never heard of such a thing as a gay pastor.

Meeting a gay pastor and other queer people at this bible study surprised Jasmine, but she still was not ready to be completely open about her own identity. She continued to attend the bible study, slowly coming to trust the community of people gathered and the way they understood God. When meeting the pastor, who was openly gay, for the first time she recalls,

> I was shocked! I was like, is he confessing something to me? Is this wrong? Can this be? So I had a lot of questions. I did not tell him that I was, too. I just had a lot of questions. I kept a secret. He explained to me a different way of looking at God, I told him about my past and stuff and why I felt judged, and I remember he was like, but God is love. He never really said, no this is wrong, you are wrong for thinking this, or my way is the right way. He just introduced a new way, and what he thought it was. And one thing I liked about that was that he never claimed to have the answers. And I have never been to a church that was that humble. And that is something that really attracted me to the church, for example, the mission the values system, they were humble, every church I ever went to had the answer. The fact he said, God is love, God doesn't make mistakes. And I knew God created me, really that today still that makes me really emotional, because that's right, He doesn't make mistakes so if He created me, then what could be wrong about this? It was a lot to digest.

When Jasmine finally revealed to the community that she was a lesbian, they welcomed her with open arms. She admits, though, that she was still unsure if she could really trust what was being taught in her new church. She says,

> No, I questioned it, I questioned it. Because most of my life has told me the opposite. So I questioned it, like oh my god, we are all going to hell. I like this church, but we are all going to hell! (Laughs) If I accept this, what does this really mean? But I could not deny the fact that I felt loved, and I kept going back to the feeling as opposed to the words. And I kept thinking, I feel loved, I feel safe with them. I felt like I could tell them almost anything and still be accepted. So how could that be wrong ultimately? And the only way I have come to that conclusion, counseling played a huge huge part in that, in helping me to explore those questions, and just the fact that I was allowed to have questions, that [this church] talks about—it is okay to question, it is okay to doubt. Even though you think you know it all, it is okay to question. I have never been totally accepted by family, even before I came out, I have never been totally accepted so this was huge. And I could not, I refused to give that up, I needed that to survive. And it helped heal me out of the depression and it played a huge part.

April was also somewhat skeptical about the new things she was hearing when she visited an accepting Lutheran church. She remembers her first visit,

> I think I actually cried in my very first service, because I had gone with my friend who coincidentally had been my close friend I went with in [college] and lived here—craziness. Complete coincidence. And we went together, and you know [the pastor] does a thing like, no matter who you are, no matter the color of your skin, no matter who you love and marry, you are welcome? I totally lost it. Like, I had heard it was an okay thing, but then I looked around me, and some churches are like, we love gay people but then they don't really have any, and you are like, I feel like a specimen. I mean, it was just a thing . . .

Yeah, [LGBTQIA+ couples] clearly together and it is just, it was really, it really impacted me emotionally. And I was like, oh, no, this is a good place for me.

However, even attending services did not erase the messages that she had internalized about hell, her sexuality and the way God felt about her. She recalls,

> Well, it is still kind of a battle. It was really tough because they just aren't like even the same religion. You really can't look at Lutheranism the way [this church] does it, and the Southern Baptists the way I grew up doing it, and say they are even the same religion. They are just not. And there is really no way that you can squish them together. And I realized I was sort of converting. And I had a lot of meetings with [the pastor], and he gave me a lot of books to read because I like to read books, and I don't remember any specific moments, but I started realizing maybe there is this hell thing, and maybe I am really screwed, but I started realizing that this God is love message not only does it feel better, and it makes a lot more sense and I feel like it is better for the world, so let's go with this. That isn't to say that I was magically fine, or that I didn't have any issues.

The internal change was slow for April; she was not sure if she could fully integrate this new way of understanding God. She says,

> I wouldn't say I didn't like it, but it did make me uncomfortable . . . And so [the pastor] was like, did you have a diagram that you used to explain salvation, and I was like yeah, and I drew a cliff here and a cliff here, and the gulf was sin and hell, and the cross was the bridge, but you have to choose to walk it, and if you stay here the cross doesn't do you any good. And [the pastor] was like, well, to Lutherans that is kind of like heresy. And I am like, oh, we aren't pulling any punches here. I was a little offended, and then we started to talk about grace and he was like, well, heaven is here on earth and maybe hell is, too, and no one can definitively say what happens when you die and so that is not where we choose to live our faith. This is not a prologue, this is life.

Soon after beginning to attend worship in this new religious community, April started dating Leslie, the woman she would eventually marry. Coming to church together was a totally new experience for April. She says,

> It was sort of funny, because I started dating [Leslie] maybe a month after I started going to [this church] and she did not, she went to Catholic church with a friend in high school but her parents are not religious at all, and so she was like, I should go to church. And I was like, oh, I go to this really cool church you should come sometime, and so our fourth or fifth date was going to church. It sort of went from there, because people thought we were together together because we went to church together even though we sort of weren't, and when

we moved in [Leslie] was like, "hey Pastor, guess what, we moved in together!" And I was like ugh, shhhhh, (makes silencing motion with hands), and [the Pastor] was like "that is amazing! I am going to get you a plant!" So stuff would just pop up, and I would think—"can we say that?" I guess we can say that. And I was so in love with her and having that reinforced at church, I feel like it kind of healed a lot of things I felt about it . . .

Once Lucas realized that what was missing from his spiritual practice was his desire to "talk about Jesus," he began to slowly visit congregations every few Sundays. When he wandered into an Evangelical Lutheran Church in his neighborhood, he knew almost immediately this was the place for him. He says,

So I walked in here and like literally from the moment it started I was like, this is perfect. Like perfect. I am pretty involved in some social activism things, and from the pulpit I heard someone say white privilege and I was like, (looks around confused) they are aliens, and I haven't heard anything like this, but they are like me! What is going on? Yeah, so it was literally like, these are my people . . . I would say it was identity, I completely so identified, I felt comfortable being gay and I saw some other gay guys, and I saw families and kids and that's a big thing for me, is like, so many like "gay" churches are literally gay. And that's not my thing, I don't want to go for a political lesson, I have my own political involvements. Yeah, just deeply, deeply connected here, from literally the first moment I was here.

Lucas was especially drawn to the openness of the congregation, he saw both gay and straight couples, and felt that this was the place where he could fully be himself. Yet, even as Lucas was drawn to the community, it also made him uncomfortable. He says,

I would say socially I felt that at first, but that was me projecting, I am relaxing into that I belong here, too. But that is me, I have my own social anxieties that come through. And that is part of why I know I need to be here is because, the gay guy with the issues around straight men, there are straight men here! And that is healthy for me, to be my authentic self, to be a musician and all these things is exactly where I need to be.

Being a Lutheran brings together Lucas' experience in the Catholic church while also honoring his sexual identity as a part of God's beautiful creation. For Lucas, worshipping with a variety of people makes him feel connected to God and to the community around him. He says,

And I would hope that the church would be with people of all colors and types, and that is what I see, and that is what I wanted. That is what is here. It is so amazing to me that this has been here a long time, because it is all new to me! (laughs) It is like, wow, people discovered this path a long time ago. And how I missed that Lutheranism is a constant reformation of the church Catholic. That is so brilliant, and I love it, I am so connected to it, so connected to it.

Sarah also found healing in returning to a community that was not solely a "gay church," but honored her identity while not forcing her to make it the centerpiece of her experience in church.

So I met with two pastors of the church, because I decided if I was going to join another church I really wanted to make sure I understood what they believed in. So I met with both of them, and [one pastor] was definitely like maybe one day you will find more stock in being a part of the LGBT community, and I was like, maybe, probably not. (Laughs) I'm still not, it is still not one of my focuses.

Sarah felt it was important to join a church where there were a variety of people from a variety of backgrounds, even while acknowledging that she specifically needed to find a church that was accepting of her sexuality.

I am very talkative in one-on-one situations, but not so much in large groups. So at first I would just sit back and watch. Once I met with [the pastor] and started to get to know other people in the community I was like, this is going to be a really good spot for me, really good growth. So I joined a small group and it was great, getting to know people there, and they legitimately when I told them [I was a lesbian] were like, okay, and filed it away as another piece of information about me, because at that time I had come out to my family and my close friends and I was kind of coming out to the public, it felt like, especially when I got into my small group and I found those people, this is a good spot, this is a good church. As I have talked, I really get involved, and start doing a lot, and I wanted other people to feel that in a small group. For me it has been a really open and accepting community. I hope it is that for other people as well, I try to make sure in my role now, I am kind of the operations person for the [the church], I just make sure the services are running and all that. We try to make sure that the services are not just friendly but also open and welcoming, and that people are having that experience when they come.

Oliver was invited to an accepting church by a gay friend he had known from his hometown. The first time he visited, the message about acceptance was quite explicit. He recalls,

And you go there, and they say, like right out, that everyone is welcome here whether you are gay or straight, democrat or republican, believer or doubter or whatever, and it was just kind of like, whoa, I have never ever heard a church say something like that before. To be honest, at first I was a little shocked, and nervous. Did they just say gay in church? And also, did they say, gay and then did they also say it was okay? . . . and I was like, wow, I think I am finally home.

Oliver was dating the man who would eventually become his husband and had never felt like he could be open about their relationship in any of the churches he had visited. The pastor invited Oliver and his boyfriend out for coffee, and though Oliver was nervous, he also felt free to be completely honest about his sexuality. He remembers,

> I think, I mean, we did tell him that when we first met with him. I think it was weird, but it was also like, you knew that it was okay. Because I had never said that to a pastor before, ever in my life. Whether it was the Baptist ones at school, the church where I grew up, or the transition church, I didn't even think about it. None of those I ever said that to a pastor . . . Yeah, I think he said things like, you know, God loves you.

Slowly, as Oliver made friends at this new congregation and found himself taking on other leadership roles, he felt as if the "demons" that haunted him were exorcised. He says,

> I am not sure if there was some, I could say that this one sermon or this one act I feel like I was healed or repaired but I do think that now I am I can't put a specific thing, I think it is more of being accepted and realizing that this is, real is not the right word, but genuine faith in the Christian community that you can be gay and part of it . . . I think what needed to be healed more was just my view of the church, not necessarily with God . . . This might seem stupid to you, but that the church is on your side.

For Oliver, realizing that the "church was on his side," that a community loved and accepted him and honored his relationship and identity, was the beginning of healing what had been broken inside him.

In Beth's case, much like when she "accepted Christ" in the non-accepting church, after a process of spiritual direction and therapy she woke up one day and felt like she was ready to return to church. She remembers,

> Yeah, I think I was trying to reconnect again. Because during all that, I did want God, you know when I was 17 I did want God, and I did want that love. But somehow because of my sexuality, because of the messages about judgment, hell, grace was kind of thrown out there, we sing Amazing Grace, but I don't know if I ever really understood it, because I really tried hard to be okay, I wanted to be okay. And it wasn't being gay. But at this point in my life, it was like too much, and I was doing the spiritual direction at that time, which was a big process of healing, and it was during that that I think I started looking

again. I just woke up one Sunday and said, I'm going to church, and I did and I never stopped.

For Beth attending church was also very much tied to the changes that were happening for LGBTQIA+ people in the political world. Though her congregation was open about their acceptance of LGBTQIA+ people as Christians, many denominations still had clear policies excluding people. She remembers,

> I was, I had a large group of lesbian friends as this point that I am with, gay men here, this hunger and thirst for inclusion, and we were going to get that. You belong, you are loved, you are welcome here, and some of this talking about our journey . . . Because not just here at [this church], but down the road there is another Lutheran Church and there is a Methodist Church, and everyone was just, the pastors and staff was just speaking out for the inclusion of the GLBT population, not so much T yet, but it was finally getting introduced, so it was a movement here. And in the gay pride parade, clergy, everyone was just marching, and speaking out. And AIDS was still killing people, antiretrovirals were just coming out, but so many people had died, and churches were just coming out [here] and had met that challenge and stepped up, and that kind of fueled it as well. It was a movement . . . Yeah, it was like, I'm in a movement. We are not going away, we are not going back in the closet . . .

At Beth's church, the pastor was openly gay himself, though he had not spoken about his own identity from the pulpit. Beth was serving as an assistant minister on the Sunday when he came out to the congregation and the invited media.

> And there was one sermon . . . when he came out to everybody. And I was the assisting minister, and I was sitting up there, and I just was bawling. I couldn't stop weeping, I wept. I wept to the point where . . . all these women in the congregation noticed it, because I couldn't stop, and everyone made a beeline for me at the peace. And afterward [the pastor] came back and we were both like, "Ahhhhh." But I couldn't stop, I mean, I wept. I just wept. It was just like, something just left when he shared this, yeah, it was so powerful. And I think that was the start of it. It had already started, but boy that sermon, man it spoke to me. And everyone. Because he, basically he, a few people had known that he was a gay minister, but he put it out there, and there were members of the press, so I don't know if people knew that this was happening, and this was, but he was taking a big chance with the [Evangelical Church in America] . . .

Watching her pastor come out to the congregation was a deeply healing moment for Beth, a time when she felt like she finally belonged in a congregation as a woman and a lesbian.

I would say it was before then but I can't pinpoint it, because I felt God's presence here so strongly, and that I was being led here, like I belonged here. That was a beautiful, a very freeing moment, and I could not stop crying. I mean, it just, this release, I had to set communion . . . and I remember saying, "I'll be right back." Because I had to leave because I had to try and get some composure. I had already been hugging people, they made a beeline for me. But I just couldn't stop it . . . I just couldn't stop it, so I had to go behind the little, to the left, I don't know if [the pastor] knew what the hell was going on, but I just had to leave to get it together . . . I think it was all of it. It was just gone, like no more, no more hiding, no more, I was alright, I was finally, I think I understand I was alright and I was okay just the way I am.

BEARING WITNESS: ACCOMPANYING RETURN

Visiting an accepting religious community was an initial act which led participants in this study down a path toward recovery. They sought a community in which they could be open about their identity, but their healing was not just found in attending worship, it required specific actions by the church and pastoral caregivers to counter the reality of isolation as a result of trauma. The emotional magnitude of trauma makes it difficult for victims of trauma to trust relationships and the world around them. Witnesses to trauma often desire to minimize the reality of trauma by blaming the victim, refusing to acknowledge the trauma itself or shifting the focus of the story of trauma to the story of healing rather than the wounding itself. It is imperative that the accepting church recognize the power of trauma for many LGBTQIA+ people, while also acknowledging their own historical proclamation of theology which has, in many cases, also supported that religious trauma. For many participants in this study, the accepting denomination in which they now participate only recognized the full participation of LGBTQIA+ people within the last decade. Though certainly, through the history of the church, congregations, pastors, and Christian people have fought for the full recognition of LGBTQIA+ people, in order to provide care in response to religious trauma, even accepting congregations must reckon with their own history.

Reckoning with this history requires that congregations and pastoral caregivers deal with the uncomfortable truth that many LGBTQIA+ people have stories about religious trauma that began in our own denominations. In order to provide a space for healing, we must seek to speak truth about our own history, while also recognizing that religious trauma is a result of the interpretation of biblical texts that both accepting and non-accepting church communities hold sacred. Congregations and denominations on both sides may suggest that they are the only "real" Christians, and those who either welcome or condemn LGBTQIA+ people are interpreting tradition and scripture correctly. But, as many participants in this study expressed, the person who has experienced religious trauma likely has both positive and difficult memories and experiences in non-accepting and accepting religious communities. Throughout this study, participants, even when describing the extreme hatred for themselves they internalized in non-accepting congregations, would also remember people, rituals, and songs they loved and still missed. The relationship with the congregations that harmed them, in a majority of cases, remains an ambivalent one. Demonizing another denomination while erasing the history of the accepting church does not adequately address trauma or lead to healing. As James Jones argues, "if the relationship with the beloved, religious, or interpersonal object allows its shortcomings to be acknowledged, its failures recognized, and its limitations supportively worked through . . . then there is the possibility for genuine transformation towards maturity."[7] It is the acknowledgment of the imperfection of the church, like a child slowly recognizing the imperfection of the parent, that allows for the maturing of the selfobject relationship and which provides the opportunity for continued religious growth and recovery from religious trauma.

When considering the question of healing from religious trauma, it is imperative that pastoral caregivers see themselves as active participants in creating an environment where healing can occur. It is important here to differentiate between healing and cure. Healing, especially as it relates to trauma, is not a magical return to a state before the trauma, but rather a restoration to relationship with self and the community of the self-object world. Cure suggests that trauma can be erased, but healing is much more complicated. Healing is possible even when cure is not, because healing means carrying the wounds of the trauma into a new way of being in the world. For communities that want to promote healing, simply having the "right" theology, inclusive of LGBTQIA+ people and their concerns, is necessary but not sufficient when caring for those who have experienced religious trauma. Focusing solely on narratives of healing to the exclusion of the stories of trauma does not lead to recovery from the experience of religious trauma.

Bearing witness, a common theme in trauma literature and in scripture, is a helpful lens through which to see the work of pastoral care among those with a history of religious trauma. Bearing witness requires not just hearing the stories of trauma shared by LGBTQIA+ people who return to our church communities, but actively participating in the healing work required of the larger church community. The work of bearing witness reflects in words and actions the statement, "I see you, I believe you, it is not your fault, and you are not alone."[8] Acknowledging the trauma experienced by many LGBTQIA+ people is a first step toward witnessing, but must also be accompanied by the confession of the anti-LGBTQIA+ history of the accepting church. As theologian Shelly Rambo argues, this kind of bearing witness might be described as "thick witness," a more "textured and multilayered" vision of what it means to witness suffering and trauma.[9] Rather than simply understanding witness as the means by which we "observe, stand by or look on," Rambo argues that witness in the context of trauma requires us to stand in the middle space between life and death, a liminal space, where what is witnessed is an unknown that cannot be contained.[10] In the context of this study and the experience of religious trauma, this "thick witness" likely entails seeing the experience of religious trauma and the return to accepting communities as a process fraught with twists and turns, uncertainty and fear of further harm. Participants loved the God they came to know in their non-accepting churches so much so that they still dare to hope that God had not given up on them. The idea of thick witness also pushes pastoral caregivers to recognize not just the depth of trauma, but the ambivalent feelings many religiously traumatized people still hold toward the congregations that harmed them.

For pastoral caregivers, this means refraining from demonizing non-accepting theology as unchristian. Bearing witness also suggests that pastoral caregivers, active in accompanying survivors of religious trauma in the work of healing, remain aware that agency is always centered in the survivor of trauma.[11] Religious trauma rips away the relationship one has had with God, and the return to that relationship cannot be forced; it is restored by allowing LGBTQIA+ people to move at their own pace into a new and safe congregation. For some participants in this study, this meant immediately volunteering for positions in the church, for others, it meant starting slowly and taking time to build up relationships of trust. Bearing witness to trauma means letting LGBTQIA+ people find their own pace in our congregations, and knowing that allowing them to write their own story in this new community is integral to healing.

Given that the historical view of trauma within psychological circles has been centered around direct trauma, recovery from insidious or indirect trauma is rarely discussed. However, drawing on the studies of direct trauma, several key themes emerge which are applicable to working with LGBTQIA+ people who have experienced religious trauma.

TRAUMA AND RECOVERY

Judith Herman, in her classic text *Trauma and Recovery*, argues that there are three stages in recovery from trauma—establishment of safety in the first stage, remembrance and mourning in the second stage, and reconnection with ordinary life in the third stage.[12] In many ways, this three-stage recovery echoes the three stages described by Turner and Van Gennep—separation, liminality and reincorporation. Though the tasks associated with each of these stages are likely different in congregational settings as opposed to therapeutic relationships, these three stages can provide a framework for understanding how to work with survivors of religious trauma.

Establishing Safety

In establishing safety, Herman argues that naming the trauma is central to creating the kind of relational alliance that can lead to healing.[13] For pastoral caregivers, this means acknowledging the severity of the trauma inflicted on LGBTQIA+ people in non-accepting religious contexts, while also believing the narrative and naming the experience as trauma. For many participants in this study, the naming of what happened to them as religious trauma was helpful and was greeted with sighs of relief. Yet, for people like Jorge and Sarah, the use of the phrase religious trauma did not feel like it fit for them; both suggested that "other people had it much worse," and that what happened to them made them who they are today. Naming the experience of LGBTQIA+ people as trauma is a gift to some, while it remains a poor fit for others. For pastoral caregivers, the offering of religious trauma as a frame for the narrative of some LGBTQIA+ people is not meant as a blanket statement about all religious experience, but as a way to bear witness. Offering this label is only one way of saying, "I see you, I believe you, it is not your fault, and you are not alone."[14]

Establishing safety also extends to the creation of a safe environment for the reestablishment of a relationship with God and with the church. For almost all participants in this study, the first time they returned to church was a moment filled with deep anxiety and fear. They were often moved to tears when even considering the possibility of returning to church, and shared fear that they would be ridiculed, ignored, hurt, or retraumatized. For many accepting churches, statements of welcome on web pages or the back of the bulletin are helpful signs that the church is a safe place but are not sufficient for establishment of safety for LGBTQIA+ people. For all the participants in this study, their accepting congregations explicitly named their welcome in a statement during worship, every Sunday. As Oliver said, "they say, like right out, that everyone is welcome here whether you are gay or straight, democrat or republican, believer or doubter or whatever, and it was just kind of like, whoa, I have never ever heard a church say something like that before." April said, "[the pastor] does a thing like, no matter who you are, no matter the color of your skin, no matter who you love and marry, you are welcome? I totally lost it." These explicit messages about welcome, naming LGBTQIA+

people as both welcome and loved in the congregation is integral to establishing the congregation as a safe space.

Creating a safe space, however, cannot simply be on the surface. Many participants also highlighted the importance of "doing the work" required to face the internal assumptions and prejudice people may have toward LGBTQIA+ people. "Doing the work" for participants in this study meant going beyond the tokenism and surface level welcome found in some congregations. For Alex, this means going beyond just "flag waving." Alex says,

> And I think it has to be also sort of in the culture of that church, otherwise it sort of just flag waving. And I feel like the Episcopal church has done a lot of flag waving with things like gay and lesbian rights and at the end of the day it is like, well, what did you do to really enter into relationship with us? Because it is one thing to say we stand with you, you are welcome here, but then when you welcome people in you have to be open to change. It is not this sort of, you have a tree and you are bending down one branch, what the church is doing with black people and other groups, oppressed minorities, it is like you can do church we will bend you down this little branch but it is on our terms, and we are the ones bending it. And it is still the same tree, and it is going to be the same tree, this is just your little branch. So I really wonder about that, it has to be in the culture where it is real relationship where you are open to change. Otherwise it is just flag waving.

Alex recognizes that doing the work of establishing a safe space is hard, and it doesn't work in all congregations, but it takes more than just welcoming LGBTQIA+ people, but requires a conversion of heart. Alex says,

> There is like the flag waving, let's say with trans rights, it seems rather poignant, you have the banner waving by the church, let's say the Episcopal Church saying we welcome you, let's even say my church . . . we welcome you, we love you, you are one of us, you are completely unquestionably welcome in all capacities, step one. Step two, oh, okay, let's de-gender bathrooms . . . that might be step two, still not conversion of heart stuff, but real steps that are making that person's reality better. And then there is the third step and that is the hardest one and I really don't know a lot of places that do that, and that is like the real conversation. There are not a lot of places that have the capacity for that, they just don't. They aren't healthy enough, and not just, and not just that they aren't healthy enough that is a really specific place to be in, where you are able to not divide a church over a conversation like that, because you are in a relationship with each other, and you have deep enough roots with each other that you can have these kind of talks that are going to be unsettling and disorienting.

Beth recalls when her current congregation considered changing the time of worship on Sundays, and how it felt to her like there was a "revolt" at the idea of change. Knowing how difficult it is to make even practical changes in congregations, she believes you must do the internal work among leaders to truly make an accepting church a safe space. She says,

> Some really basic things, like letting it be known that you are open and affirming, and if possible, have a gay, lesbian, bi-person on staff, very helpful and talk about inclusion of all people in sermons, just saying it, touching on it, as we have done a lot of work on racial, you have to name it, be able to name it and be okay in that, and the council has to be on board, it has to be because if the council is not on board and the leadership, whoever that is, then the pastors are really flailing in the wind. There has to be buy-in, so maybe, if a church is going to consider being open and affirming, welcoming, they are going to have to do some searching, and maybe it starts with the leadership, but you have to get the buy-in and if that means having church retreats, workshops, getting people, because I guarantee you getting people in the church, people who hold those beliefs at different, maybe even unconsciously, like marriage is between a man and woman and that is a biological . . . does that make sense? So it is a lot that you are asking. . . . But today in 2016 it has got to start, if they really want to do it, it is more than putting out a sign, and they have to do some internal, they have to do some work. The council and then the congregation. And healing.

Many participants recognized that internally they were attuned to the safety of a space in a new way, and congregations that had "done the work" felt emotionally safe to them. Jasmine says,

> The energy, I can't describe it any other way than the energy. I just knew. You know how sometimes you just know in your spirit whether something is right for you? It was a knowingness that I really can't explain.

She felt that "knowingness" in her new congregation. The mission and values of the congregation are the foundation on which the safety is built, but for Jasmine she is also aware of when the space feels "toxic" and won't be able to value her sexuality and her race.

> Total acceptance, inclusiveness, their mission pretty much lined up with what I believe church should be and what God says church should be which is acceptance, nonjudgment. When I walk in there having a sense that I am welcomed, I am loved, regardless, there is no judgment. I know no church is perfect, but walking in there and not feeling like it is a toxic environment. I can pick that up right away, that there is some unhappiness whether it is with leadership or the congregants, so just having a sense that it is okay . . . There should be when I say acceptance, I mean not just at face-value, total acceptance where I can talk about me, the whole part of me, that I don't have to hide anything, because I have done

that, and it is not fun. It doesn't make you feel good about yourself. So there has to be total acceptance of who I am as a woman, as a black woman, as a lesbian.

For congregations seeking to provide this kind of safe environment, participants in this study were quick to recognize that simply tolerating LGBTQIA+ people was not sufficient to creating a safe space. Just as pastoral caregivers must examine their own internalized views of sexuality, the congregation must also openly confront their views on LGBTQIA+ people. Herman argues that working through this first stage is much like running a marathon; it is a "test of endurance, requiring long preparation and repetitive practice."[15] This means continually reminding the congregation and the LGBTQIA+ people present that they are beloved by God, and that their sexuality is a welcome gift to the larger congregation. It involves work on the part of the congregation, not simply an open door. Conversations, establishment of trusting relationships, study and reflection are all a part of creating a safe space.

When this stage has been completed and safety has been established is rarely a specific moment in time. Many participants in this study couldn't name one particular ritual or moment when they felt that they belonged in their accepting congregations, but rather saw the establishment of safety as a progression, with stops and starts along the way. For victims of trauma, safety is always tenuous, though the longer they remain in relationship with trustworthy people and institutions, the more they are able to value themselves and trust their relationships.[16] For congregations and pastoral caregivers, this means that accompanying the traumatized through the process of returning to a congregation is never done. Maintaining a safe congregation requires continued attention to the theological, pastoral and ritual dimensions of safety.

Remembrance and Ritual Inclusion

In Herman's framework, after safety has been established, the traumatized moves into the stage of remembrance. This stage first requires telling the story of trauma, "in depth and in detail."[17] Ghislaine Boulanger, in her work on adult onset trauma, argues that it is not just the telling of the story, but the moving from a "lifeless" to a "living" narrative.[18] For many victims of direct trauma, dissociation was a primary coping strategy, allowing them to separate themselves from what was happening to them. In creating a living narrative, or in telling the story of their trauma in depth and detail, the victim is able to engage a witness in the telling, a therapist or pastoral caregiver who will bear witness while also demonstrating that they will not be destroyed by the horror of the story. This bearing witness provides the needed strength that can allow the traumatized to eventually "witness their own experience," reintegrating what has been dissociated.[19]

For LGBTQIA+ people who have been religiously traumatized, the concept of stories is present on several levels. The telling of their personal narrative, with the hopes that the congregation or pastoral caregiver will bear witness to what has happened is integral to recovery from the trauma. The realization that their own story can be a part of the larger story of God's people is a unique aspect of religious communities. This realization, in openly sharing their own story while also connecting to the story of God's people demonstrates they are not separated by their sexuality, but a part of the Christian history proclaimed in scripture and tradition in the congregation in which they are a part. This is a powerful kind of storytelling which is unique to religious communities; the story of the people of God is not frozen in time, but rather retold as both a past story and a present reality.

Serene Jones, writing on trauma and grace, suggests that there is a powerful opportunity to consider the place of theological imagination in the telling of stories of trauma. In her own work with a survivor of trauma, Jones suggests that the biblical stories, rituals, and traditions of the church order the imagination in such a way that it can be said to be "shaped by grace."[20] This shaping by grace happens as stories are told and reenacted about "people who were agents in their own lives, with God-given grace to act, moving through concrete embodied history in time, coherently connected to their own pasts and the stories of others who came before them, related intimately to other people and to the good creation that sustains them, and looking forward in hope to a flourishing future. In cases of direct trauma, Jones suggests that often survivors are left without "a world, without speech, stories, memory, community, future, or a sense of self; theology's task is to renarrate to us what we have yet to imagine."[21]

In the case of religious trauma, this imagination and renarration is lived out through the acceptance by a new community and rebuilding of a relationship with God and the church. As noted earlier, religious trauma shatters the worldview that God and the community of God is trustworthy, just and good. Theological imagination is a building block of this renarration. Through the experience of ritual in a safe community, theological imagination is restored, helping to rebuild the relationship religious traumatized people have with God and the church. For many of the participants in this study, that renarration was a result of participating in the rituals of the church while also being open about their identity as an LGBTQIA+ person.

Ritual theorist Tom Driver argues that humans long for ritual. Driver claims that ritual is "the close relative" or even the "progenitor" of art and the source of "speech, of religion, of culture and of ethics"; rituals "invent" us as a people shaping how we understand ourselves and the world.[22] Ritual, as a source of speech, religion, art and ethics is intertwined with culture, and to be human is to develop within a particular culture; no one is "universally human."[23] For many participants in this study, the loss of a ritual space, where they were baptized, or received communion, or met the divine, was one of the most significant parts of their loss. When they were estranged from the church, they were, in a very specific way, estranged from their access to a ritual community, with the blame for that loss placed firmly on themselves. They were not allowed to access ritual because they were sinful, and, in some cases, told that God hated them and was disgusted by their participation in these rituals. This ritual loss is a story that must be renarrated in their new congregation, when they can again participate in the rituals of the church while also being fully themselves, open about their sexuality.

By participating in the rituals of the church, as openly LGBTQIA+ people, participants in this study renarrated their past while reimagining their place among God's people. As Driver states, "we cannot well appreciate the power of ritual unless we see its usefulness to those in need, especially those who, having little social power and, being the victims of injustice, have a need for the social structure to be transformed."[24] The best kind of ritual, according to Driver, is transformative, confronting power with power, throwing off the chains of oppression and moving toward freedom and liberation.[25] For those outside of the church, there may be an assumption that worship is simply the ritual deadness of a leader speaking words in a monotone, but for those who have been denied access to ritual, and yearned for inclusion, the presence of their bodies in the worship space, the ability to access the tangible elements of ritual (wine, bread, ash, oil, water), is a powerful act. The rituals in this new community echoed rituals they already knew but functioned in a new way. To take part in the rituals of the church is to "confront power with power," to boldly claim access to the sacred while recognizing that their estrangement was an act of injustice.

Most participants in this study could name particular ritual moments when they either felt they belonged or could express their faith freely without fear. For Jasmine, the ritual of anointing feels like the "perfect way" for her to express her faith in a tangible way. She says,

> Yeah, because usually with most churches, with the churches I visited I would last a month here or there, but when it was like a solid year, and I was happy getting up and going to church—I have never been happy going to church—(laughs) just looking forward to that one day of the week where I can feel accepted and I am giving back to other people and I feel like my spirit is fed, when it was a solid year of that I felt like I belonged. It is so funny, I was still learning about Christianity and I was like, can I get re-baptized? They were like, it doesn't work that way. But I do like the fact, the Vineyard church baptized me by the way, I do like the fact that they have the, what they call, I forgot what they called it, they take oil and ash . . . They make the sign of the cross on your

forehead. So we have that occasionally, the church has it when we are doing a baptism . . . and you can still get baptized in the church, but for those of us that have already been it is a way of us to sort of show that we are rededicating our lives. So I always try to make church when I know that is going on . . . It is telling the whole world, well people in the church, how you feel about Christ. It is saying it in a ritual, sometimes we as humans don't have the right words to express but it is so deep and it is so personal that it is like the perfect way to express that love. Like, he died on the cross, and that is like the perfect way, instead of just saying something. It is the perfect way.

In Jorge's case, the ritual of testimony was a significant part of feeling as if he could be honest about himself in the presence of God and his community. In sharing his testimony, something that "lifted the burden off his shoulders" and made him feel "loved and accepted" for who he is, Jorge took part in a ritual of his community that engaged this imagination shaped by grace. He saw himself, his sexuality, and his community in a new way. He says,

It is funny because when I gave my testimony I didn't even write it down, I wanted to go out there and speak whatever came to heart. And I remember closing right before I did this testimony, I went to see the movie *Sisters*, and one of the things was, you know, home is not where the frame or structure is, but home is where the heart is, and I remember closing the testimony and I am like, home is not where the structure the frame or building is, home is where the heart is and that [this church] has started rebuilding my structure, and I am now calling my heart a church home. Didn't even plan on saying that, and I sat there, and I kind of analyzed, I over psychoanalyze everything, and I am like, oh my goodness that just came out of my mouth, and almost like, I am living that, I am rebuilding my church, quote unquote of what I think a church should be, even though church to me could be in any room, any time, in my car, in the woods wherever I want to be. But a congregation a structure is such a good feeling of me coming home.

April had internalized the message that LGBTQIA+ people were bound for lives of unhappiness and pain. Seeing LGBTQIA+ families participating in worship transformed her view of what her life might look like in the future. She says,

When you see a same sex couple and their baby is getting, not Christened, baptized, or blessing of a same sex union. I mean, [two women] had their renewal of vows or whatever a couple years ago now, and it is just so, it is not even like a newsflash when we do that now, it just is, and I feel like that is very, I don't know if I would say healing for all of them, but like soothing and comforting that I am normal and this is a thing we do and it is fine. And also getting married in that church and having a liturgy and a Eucharist and a homily and all of that, that was one of the hardest things for me when I came out, I didn't think I would ever be happy, I didn't think I would ever find anybody, I thought I would be alone forever and I would be super depressed, and once it got a little better I was like, even if I do find somebody, I will never be able to go to church, I will never be able to get married, I will never be able to have kids, I'll never have an extended family, like anything like that. So helping to peel away some of those layers is really good.

When April and her partner decided to get married, they planned the service in their accepting church. They knew they wanted a religious wedding and, as a lesbian couple, they were able to find a way to express the newness and the sameness of their experience in the liturgy. It felt new to marry as a lesbian couple, but it also felt the same as weddings that had happened before. They particularly highlighted songs and readings about justice, again, as Driver argues, confronting the power of estrangement and trauma with the power of religious ritual. April remembers,

> Well, it was awesome, because [the pastor] loves this sort of thing, and because it is a queer wedding, you can kind of do whatever you want. A lot of the traditions you can't even do, so you can do whatever—we did a full liturgy we had [the church] put explanatory notes, not just about what things were but why it was important to us, like the passing of the peace and it means this to me and [my wife]. We sang all the social justice hymns like "Let Streams of Living Justice Flow" so we put it together as a very us service, most of our friends and family are not church people, so we made it super clear to everybody we talked to people, it was in the service plan, [the pastor] said something about it—you don't have to stand up, sit down, sing, you can do whatever you want and no one is going to mind. People totally adapted to their comfort level and it was wonderful. It was really, really great.

Sarah also had a marriage ceremony in the church. The ability to call her service something that was "real Christian," considering the knowledge that others may identify it as un-Christian was significant for her.

> Yeah, [our pastor] did our service. And everyone, we had a lot of, [my wife] is also from the South as well, and everyone was like, that pastor, he is really great, because he is also just really charismatic. Really good with his words, but also with being charismatic he's also really caring and wants to understand people so it is an okay balance. Yeah, so we had a religious ceremony, and it was great. None of our families had anything to say about it not being a real Christian or anything. I think at this point they have all gotten used to it.

After Oliver had attended an accepting church for some time, he invited his mother and sister to attend. Oliver's mother had already accepted his sexuality but was concerned that Oliver might be attending a church that wasn't "biblically based," and instead focused more on personal stories and feelings rather than scripture. Oliver was excited by the ability to show her how his church conformed in many significant ways to the kind of religion he was brought up with. He says,

> To me it felt really good, almost like an accomplishment or something like that. It was like, I have found a church and I was able to share that with the family and they also enjoyed it it wasn't like they just went and were like "oh, well, this seems sort of crazy" . . . My mom, because she has heard of some liberal churches that aren't very biblically based, so she said she was happy to hear that it had like a normal sermon, and they read the scripture and everything like that but just being more progressive on just other issues. I think that in her mind she wasn't so sure about.

Oliver was proud to introduce his mother and sister to his church, and to show them the importance of his community. Though his new community is different in many ways, including in their welcome of Oliver and his husband, the community also provides a needed place of belonging and support that, had they not found it, would have "worried" his mother and sister. Oliver says,

> They had known a couple of the friends because we introduced them at our housewarming party last May and some people from church had come to that party, so they met a few of the people who they recognized. But then they met a lot more of them, too. And mom was like, "wow, [Oliver], you have a lot of friends here and everybody seems to know you." And she was also part happy being a mom who was like they have a church here now that they are actively involved with and I don't have to worry about that part of their life anymore now . . . Whereas I never really had that before so I think she was happy to see that.

Alex, when they witnessed the marriage of their priest to another man, presided over by the Bishop, felt something within theirself healed. The service was a counter to the messages they had internalized that "gays are bad, this is disgusting," even seeing two men kiss to seal their marriage vows before God was a healing ritual moment. The service of marriage, seeing love between two men blessed, was a ritual that countered the belief that LGBTQIA+ love was disgusting and bad.

Beth felt like the ritual community was giving her "spiritual food"; she was hungry and took in all the lessons, and the readings, and prayers like it was nourishment for her soul.

> I remember when the real healing was happening, the really profound ways of healing just good, good stuff, the healing, like everything [the pastor] said, I was one of those people, it really was like food. This whole new way of presenting scripture. Telling a story. It was like I have notebooks full of things I got from sermons, and I type notes, and I just go back and flip through and read and read. And it was really like that . . . Yeah, and it was like food, it was like nourishment. It was like, you couldn't have moved me, it was just such a wonderful retelling, and it was getting in there, it wasn't. I remember once I was assisting him, I was just listening, just so, like everything, and it was time to flip the page and he was like, are you okay? Because I was just like, wow, you know how he is like, create, you are the water, and it was just this telling of God and I just couldn't move, because I was like, yeah.

Many participants shared their story of trauma in "depth and detail" with other LGBTQIA+ people in the congregation and with their pastor. Some had participated in testimony during worship. Yet, their theological imagination was shaped in the most significant ways by participating in the rituals of the church as an out LGBTQIA+ person. These were not people who were "ritually bored"; rather they were ritually starved, hungry to be fed by the community.[26] The rituals of the church helped to reshape their worlds, allowing them to reimagine themselves as recipients of grace, beloved children of God.

This reimagining is born out of the power of rituals, according to anthropologist and ritual theorist Roy Rappaport, to transmit both self-referential and canonical messages. When participants in this study engaged in ritual, they not only transmitted information about themselves to others, but they also transmitted "such information to themselves."[27] This kind of self-referential message is central to the way that ritual communicates. By participating in worship, in the sacraments, or other aspects of liturgical life, these participants not only communicated to the gathered community that they were Christians, but that message was also reinforced to themselves. Surrounded by other Christians, participating in rituals alongside them, ritual functioned like a mirror reflecting to them their status as accepted and beloved members of the community. All liturgy is a public liturgy according to Rappaport, and in so being, the very presence of these participants, open about their sexuality, suggests that they have a place in the larger community of God. These rituals also transmitted canonical messages, the kind of messages that transcend the here and now and point to the universal. Canonical and self-referential messages are interwoven in liturgy. Rituals do not just transmit messages about our current state of being, but they also transcend the present, representing the enduring and eternal.[28] By participation in the rituals of the church, participants in this study did not just receive messages about who they were, but how they were also bound up in the grace of God over time, part of a church beyond the present. The theological imagination, belief that they might be recipients of grace and love, was reshaped by the self-referential and canonical aspects of these rituals.

How might pastoral caregivers create ritual spaces where this kind of theological imagination is inspired? According to Driver, ritual must not just proclaim the freedom and liberation found in the Christian story, but it must embody that freedom and liberation.[29] For participants in this study, ritual was meaningful not just because it told a liberating story of God's people, but because by participating in these rituals, open about themselves, their sexuality and their relationships, their participation was an act of liberation and freedom which had been denied for far too long. As Beth said, "God was always there, but it was like, we really, as I age, I understand the importance of community. We were made to be in community, to heal; we were wounded in our family, in our community, and we will be healed in a community."

Reconnection and the Double Coming Out

In Herman's framework, the final stage of trauma recovery involves reconnecting with the world as a newly integrated person. After the trauma has been remembered, the work of reconnecting buffers one against future trauma. Herman says, "Traumatic events destroy the sustaining bonds between the individual and the community. Those who have survived learn that their sense of self, of worth, of humanity depends upon a feeling of connection with others. The solidarity of the group provides the strongest protection against terror and despair, and the strongest antidote to traumatic experience."[30]

For participants in this study, the process of reconnection is not a final stage, but present throughout their return to accepting religious communities. As they establish safety, remember their trauma and ritually reimagine, they are also forging new connections in their congregations. In this way, congregations are unique environments that can provide a powerful experience of healing. Further, this process of reconnection means taking the newly integrated self and living authentically in new spaces as both a victim and survivor of trauma.

In this study, the process of reconnection is most apparent in the new task of living as a religious person in the LGBTQIA+ community. Participants in this study were intensely familiar with what may be called the double coming out process—the secondary coming out as religious in community that often remains skeptical of organized religion. For all participants in this study, the initial coming out story involved intense trauma; their coming out led to the severing of a relationship with God and with the church. After returning to a new accepting congregation, however, participants described a second coming out process, when instead of coming out as LGBTQIA+ in the church community, they instead came out as *religious in the LGBTQIA+ community*.

This secondary coming out process is a rich opportunity for the church and pastoral caregivers to accompany a LGBTQIA+ person who has experienced religious trauma to "re-imagine" their story in a new way while remaining connected to both their religious community as well as the LGBTQIA+ community.

April is aware that coming out as religious in the queer community is a difficult process for many queer people. She says,

> In a lot of queer spaces it is not one of the first things you want to talk about. Whereas with straight people church is usually a pretty safe topic, like, ah, did you go to Catholic church and school? Because most white people have some sort of church involvement, it is a safe topic. With queer people you definitely don't want to bring that up until you know somebody pretty well . . . Because they might be like me and at a different stage. They might think church is terrible and have had really bad experiences. They may be in a place and assuming that anybody that does go to church is going to try and ram church down their throat. Because there are a lot of churches that do do a lot of hurtful things, still. And I think there are a lot of people who are still really hurt by that and don't want to have anything to do with it, and there is a balance between, sort of helping them with that and also respecting their need for distance.

When April does feel ready to talk about being religious, she recognizes that for many LGBTQIA+ people, her religious life may appear as if she is setting herself up for trauma. When she talks about her church she often says,

> I guess for me it takes the form of (speaking really quickly) "I go to church, but my church is really cool, we support a homeless shelter, we do lots of fun things" . . . I definitely, the very first time I mention it I sort of lead with all the stuff I like about [this church] before I am like, and it is a church. Because people really don't understand, especially people who know my background, why would you do that to yourself again? And I am like, no, no, it is different. I think a lot of people in [cities] have a pretty easy time understanding it because I think they do have a pretty good idea that there is a lot of different kinds of churches, but other people, maybe people that don't live in cities, or don't have access to progressive churches, I don't know, they kind of see you as a traitor. Usually once I tell them that my minister is gay they are like, okay. I guess that is proof they are bonafide. It is definitely something that as I have been more involved at [this church] I have made a point of telling people more, because I was like, hey, this is a part of myself that I shouldn't need to hide because I happen to be religious, and people need to know there can be religious people who aren't trying to make them religious, too.

April recognizes that having LGBTQIA+ people in leadership in her congregation is one way that she legitimizes her narrative about being religious.

At the same time, having a church that is willing to wade into some of the LGBTQIA+ events and issues in her community also helps her to talk about how she has managed her identity as a lesbian and a Christian. April says,

> The fact that both of our main ministers are gay, that helps a lot. I think also the fact that we march in the Pride Parade, because I feel like, the Pride Parade is a lot of very in your face, very penis-y, naked man, out there stuff, and the fact that churches are willing to go cheek to jowl with men in bikinis, I think that says a lot to people. Especially the people who are really hurt by the "it's fine if you are gay but we don't want you around our children," that's another really hurtful thing that I think a lot of people get even if they are not religious, because you know, we are all child molesters and we are going to prep them or whatever.

She also recognizes that the theology of her new congregation speaks to other issues of gender and identity within the LGBTQIA+ community. April sees a strong connection between theology and the presence of her community at more "fringe" LGBTQIA+ events.

> I think that especially with a lot of transgender issues, there is a cartoon going around about how Jesus was a virgin birth so he doesn't have a y chromosome, but he is a dude, so like, whoa . . . It is really great, people's minds are just blown by that. But if you want to talk about a person that has a non-standard gender identity, I think God is a pretty good example. I think there might be a lot of room to be supportive, and to be like, this is not only compatible with our theology, it props up our theology, you know, that kind of stuff.

April shares about Dyke March, an event that runs counter to Gay Pride to highlight the most marginalized people in the LGBTQIA+ community. She believes that having a religious community present at the kind of events that speak to the continued injustice in her community and her religious identity would help her to be more open about her religious community.

> So they started [The Dyke March] and recently it has become co-opted by immigrant and trans people. It is sort of a beautiful, it is a march, it is kind of led by whoever is the most marginalized person in the queer population. So last year it was undocumented people and trans women of color because they were the ones getting screwed the most by the system, and so it is a march that is sort of counter to Pride. And I am not sure how welcome a church would be there for those reasons of like, you are the establishment and we are not, but I think that is where a church could be like, we are not the establishment and here is why. I think that could be awesome . . . Yeah, because I think it is really easy for a church coming out of a conservative history to be like, we have a [gay], white, cisgender, married man pastor and that is so progressive. And it is, but that is

not nearly enough, it does not speak to the majority of queer people, better than nothing, but it is definitely not anywhere near where it could be.

Like April, Alex understands that coming out as religious in the queer community raises a lot of questions for people. Alex suggests that when coming out with this identity many queer people respond with,

> These people hate you. Are you self loathing? Are you fill in the blank. And, yeah, so I can imagine it might be more of that, questioning why or how all of this. And, it is, my understanding of the gospel is very radical, and it is hard to explain it to even other Christians what I believe in Christianity, much less to someone who grew up in a place not understanding any concept of Christianity. So that is really, that is really, that is a really tough thing.

In Alex's case, the theology and tradition of the Episcopal Church give them the space to talk about what it means to blend their Christian and queer identities. The ability to trust the sense of belonging they have in the Episcopal Church allows them to come out again in a new way.

> I think, so I think that the polity of the Episcopal church makes it possible for me to say the things, and do the things, and feel the things that I feel and consequently communicate that. Because there isn't a lot of dogma and theology that is codified as "this is the Episcopal Church" that there is room for that but it is not bound by any of that. Or it is not built on any of those as a foundation. So that gives me personal platitude to do this. If that makes sense . . . I feel confident saying I am member of this church, I don't have to make concessions about what I believe and don't believe, and things like that. Or feel like I am going to be rejected as I am coming out all of this stuff. So I guess that is something it is helpful with.

Beth notices less animosity in her circle of LGBTQIA+ friends and more confusion about her religious identity. When coming out as religious to friends Beth thinks they see her as "I am kind of revered. Like an oddity in a way. There is some curiosity around it, questions." Since Beth finished seminary, she acts as a safe religious person for her group of lesbian friends. She says,

> Yeah, it is a lot easier with gay men, where there is much more religious, and it seems to be more accepted culturally. With women, I think there is a lot of misogyny and oppression and there is so much anger. But it is more about patriarchy and misogyny, it is big. They don't want to deal with it. But I don't know one person, and I have been in this group for twenty something years and I love this group of women and they love me, and I do their marriages, I marry them, and I pray for their babies, we get a baby in the group, I'm the one, "my father died, can I get a prayer?"

For many lesbian women in Beth's community, the question about how to raise their children leads them to her as a spiritual resource. She recognizes her responsibility to speak for a God that is very different from the one she grew up with. Beth says,

> Yeah, I am in this group, yeah, and they do, and the children, and I know the next step with the children will be, they are asking about God, what do we do? What can you do? Can you take them to church? And I bet they are going to, because they are getting there now, five and six, and they are going to start asking . . . I feel fine about it, I honestly wouldn't, I don't know what to do with a six-year-old and God, I would have to read, or like . . . what do I do? [Pastor]! Do I just bring her to Sunday School? Because my life was so structured, yep, you go to Sunday School, you go to choir, you do this, boom, boom, boom. And you just sit there, you went to adult church, that is where I got terrified about God, there was no children's, I was like, oh, shit, this guy is mean. Mean, I just remember that, like God damn, so mean.

Beth sees church as a complement to the work she had to do in therapy and spiritual direction.

> When I was coming here, when I just knew it was time to reconnect, that it was time, coming here, the spirit of God is truly here, [the pastor] is very loving, and that comes across. And you know [the pastor] is out so being a part of it, being a part of the community was healing. But the work you have to do, you just have to do that on your own. Through spiritual direction, therapy and spiritual direction, I don't think spiritual direction can do the, I mean, it can be an aid in the healing, but I think it takes therapy. But it is good, because I know that is done for now . . . Oh, it takes a lot of work, it takes your own work, it takes silence, oh, yeah, it takes going inward . . . and the community here is great, and then like I said, making friends with gay men, and hearing their stories, we do share our stories, we go out to dinner and breakfast and lunch and I feel so fortunate, I love my male friends, and their stories, and hearing their pain as a gay men. And the culture puts a lot on that, too, good lord.

Beth believes that by developing her own identity as a Christian and a lesbian she is the safe space that friends need when they feel ready to confront questions about God and their sexuality. She says,

> I mean, I think it is there for everyone. Either it is therapy, asking where can I go to church, I have been thinking about this, what do you think God thinks? (*Interviewer: So you will probably become, in some ways, a safe space to say, what do I do?*) Because I think I am that to them now. I really do.

Lucas, despite doing significant internal work in his own recovery from drug and alcohol addiction, did not realize until later that he still needed to work through his openness about his religious identity in the queer community. He recalls,

> I, there was a GLBT spirituality retreat that was at Unity headquarters in Kansas City, and I flew down there and I went to this retreat. They had a twelve step meeting and I am very public about being in recovery, so they asked me to run this twelve step meeting, fine, great, and I realized that I am public about my recovery which is supposed to be anonymous and private, historically, and I am, not only was I quiet about my religious or spiritual beliefs, but I would say I was ashamed of it. And that, being at that place, doing that meeting is what made me realize that. And I was like, wait, and then I realized that one of the big conflicts I had with [my previous] partner was around spiritual things, it wasn't literally church, but it was around spiritual things. And, so I realized that I needed to have a spiritual component to relationships, it needed to be central. And I needed to work on that in myself, those issues.

When Lucas met his current partner he decided to immediately open up about his religious beliefs.

> So when I met him, I brought that belief with me, that needed to be central to me. So I was like, good sign, good flag! Proceed. So I did. And so, he's very, he is a lot older than me . . . he is a cradle Catholic, and, but gay, and so has a mixed relationship with Catholicism . . . And we talk about those ideas constantly. And so I, it is one of the things I love about our relationship, and even though he will argue with me about theology and I call him a heretic, it is great, I think it was what I always wanted.

Yet Lucas also recognizes that he is still learning about how to continue to come out as religious in queer spaces. When asked about whether he was always open about his religious identity Lucas says,

> Okay, to be honest, I would say no. But what I would say is that I don't *not* talk about it. When it comes up I am honest about it. Like, I am in this Leather men of recovery, this like kink-identified recovery social club and I insist on telling them on Sunday I am busy, I am open about that. That to me has been, sort of, I feel like I am still in, I have training wheels to some degree on it. It is wonderful to feel like I know that I am growing, that is where I want to be, to know that I am growing, to know that I still maturing in this, and that I am at the right place to learn how to do this.

Jorge also sees the difficulty with coming out as religious in the LGBTQIA+ community. He believes that the church has an important job in helping people to learn to be open about their religious beliefs but must value patience and compassion when working with people who have been traumatized by the church. He says,

> Yeah, absolutely. I really think as a church they have to understand that one, we are coming out again for something, it already took us hard enough to come out as a gay person, we are different, we are already different and it is hard for us to have stepped out and done that, so it is hard for us to build up that courage, trying to build up that courage of oh my gosh, I am trying to come out as religious in the gay community now . . . And it is a very small minority within the gay community, so it is now another minority that they are coming out to and it, and they could be looked down upon, so it is nothing, I wouldn't say, it is more of compassion. As a church already has, have compassion towards them and realize if they are not ready, they are not ready. When they are ready they will know when it is ready, when it is time, they will come to the right person and they may do it on their own.

In Jorge's own experience, it took him time before he felt ready to share publicly that he was attending church.

> But now I post (on social media) I am at [church], oh my goodness, another great sermon by [the pastor], or [the pastor] got up and gave us a great message about this and this, and I tag [Orlando] and I and I am tagging, and now I don't care. But I remember the first time I was going to post, and I was like, do I really want to do this?

Jorge recognizes that being a member of a church has given him the strength to openly talk about his religion in the LGBTQIA+ community,

> It has pushed me on being open again to accepting religion and accepting a congregation, and calling [this church] home. I guess it has helped me post on Facebook that I went there, or that I was tagged by [the pastor], I did my testimony and [the pastor] wrote about it on Facebook. So I don't know if it, of course I wouldn't have done it without [this church], it has been a part of me all my life, religion.

Yet Jorge is aware that he is different; that coming out as religious in the LGBTQIA+ community is something that runs counter to most of his friends. He feels, however, that by being open he is slowly changing the anti-church attitude that many of his friends hold. He says,

> I most, and I say this very lightly, most gay men communities and most lesbians are very atheist, and again it is all how they were raised, bitterness toward religion, bitterness toward the church, bitterness toward families that let them go

because of "what the bible says" . . . So it was just, there is so much hate toward a church idea in the gay community that it is not, it is not something pretty, and I wish it would be different, I really would . . . I think of my friend that sits next to me that does the partying that does the drugs that does the everything and he is a great friend, but I personally cannot see him going to church one Sunday with me and saying, oh, I go to church. I would take multiple times before he even started opening up and saying, this is something I like, this is something I enjoy, let me start going with you more often, and him realizing that not all his gay friends are going to be that way. Anti-church, because he isn't going to know if anyone is going to accept him or not, once again, coming out. So I would say that a church could be compassionate, understanding and just give it time. Give it time.

Sarah feels like she is not really in "the queer community," although she is married to a woman. When she first met her wife, she told her that she was attending a "book club" when she was really at a bible study. After a month of dating she finally felt ready to be honest about her religious beliefs. She says,

I was kind of like, I don't know how she is going to respond to this, and she was like, okay, that's cool. And then like when I met all of her family her grandparents loved that, that she had met someone that goes to church, because in their mind that is so great, especially one of her grandmas before she passed away was like, that is so wonderful, and you get her to go, that is so great.

Though Sarah doesn't see herself as part of "the queer community," she has found herself opening up about her identity at work, especially after her company took on a non-accepting religious college as a client. Since her company claims to be inclusive, the decision to work with an anti-LGBTQIA+ school was shocking to Sarah. She says,

It was a bold move and I think I have shocked all the straight white men that lead my team that I took a stance because I have always lived a really private life, because I am from the South and it is better, silence is a privilege, and I am unfortunately very passable in what someone wants to believe, so I think that's probably why they thought, oh, she won't care. But they have crossed a line in my opinion, and they weren't expecting it, I ended up turning to . . . my pastor, to talk about it, too, and he was like, this is something really courageous that you are doing, yeah, it is bolder than what I would normally do, because I don't want my life to be a political statement, it is just my life, now I am having to make it more of a statement because I think what they are doing is actually really wrong. But on the outside I don't think they thought about it in terms of what it really means.

In Sarah's case, the courage to come out in her work environment and to stand up for LGBTQIA+ students is at least partially related to her membership in an accepting church. She says,

> Even with what has been going on at work, [my church] has played a big part in why I feel encouraged and bold enough to do it because they, there is a whole person there that is not just gay, we all get to define ourselves how we want to define ourselves, and I think they have given me that courage to be accepting of myself first off, especially when I came out, so I had already come out and I could be in a spot where they are already accepted me and I could grow and be who I wanted to be and so [this church] has been really instrumental. I have been there for like 3 years now, and they have been a really strong support that I am really grateful for, but I haven't really taken advantage of all the different things they offer to work for LGBT people, but I know that it is there, so I think that helps a lot, and I think when people come into it that is really important when they are having struggles with that, or because they were fired for being gay from a religious institution, and now they are here, they can see that it does, that it can be different, that there are people living out Christian lives, faithful lives.

Oliver also sees himself as "different" than most gay men in his community. Like Sarah, he does not believe he is as "in" the gay community as others. He says,

> Yeah, I think I do realize it is not the norm, but I don't think that bothers me, but where other people might have more of a problem with that is where they might be more into the gay bar or club scene and those kind of areas and [my husband] and I aren't so much, and that, like we have gay friends and stuff like that, but it is not like we are in big gay community groups. Where I think they might get more push back.

Oliver is open about his religious life, posting on social media and inviting people to go to church with him. When a gay couple recently visited, he made sure they knew that on Sunday mornings he and his husband went to church.

> So they came to visit us and because they were a gay couple they wanted to come to [the culturally gay area of town] to see that and I said, sure, let's go, but we are going to go at 10:00 and come back at midnight because we are going to church the next morning! And I think they kind of did a double take but they were like, okay! (laughing) . . . And I think sometimes they look at you funny, but most people trust me and they don't think I would be someone that lies, and that I am pretty honest and open, so okay, if that is what [Oliver] says that has got to be what it is, so let's go and see what it is like.

Oliver credits his openness about religion to his experience in his accepting church, a community that has given him immense courage to share honestly about his religious beliefs.

> And it is funny that you ask me that, because I have also gotten the question and told some people, [Oliver] you are quite brave saying things or doing things. And I am like, I am not brave! I am a nervous wreck, I don't know why you think that . . . I think just that I say that, or something like that. [I am] unapologetic about being gay and going to church and that the things can go together and work together . . . I think [this church] kind of give you the tools and the strength and the background knowledge to be able to be like that. Oh, I could never be like that on my own . . . Even with [my previous church] I don't remember inviting people to go. When we moved to our new space I was emailing all my friends like, "we moved to a new space! You have to come check it out, it is a great church!" I think it helped to make me come out of my shell, come alive more.

Jasmine recognizes that people are often "taken aback" by her identity as a Christian and a lesbian woman. She notices this most often in online interactions with women she could potentially date. She says,

> So I haven't really, I mean, I have had a few instances that people were a little taken aback, like, you are lesbian and you are Christian? How do you do those two right now? These are primarily people that have left the church for whatever reason and were online dates that I have had the most questions about. I have a few lesbian friends who aren't involved in church at all, and they haven't really asked me about it. They have been burned by church so we don't really talk about it. But the most questions I get are from people online that I am talking to, because they don't understand how you can be both at the same time.

Jasmine draws on the mission statement of her accepting congregation to talk about how she manages these two identities. She says,

> Because they say that, they say well, how can you go to church and are you at peace with God and things like that. And I am like, yeah, because the God I believe in, and I always preface it with the God I believe in, the God I believe in is inclusive and loves me the way I am, God does not make mistakes, I am not a mistake, obviously I am okay. It is just humans that have the judgments. So I think that I do fall back on their motto of being inclusive, of being accepting and non judging as to how I could be a Christ follower and a lesbian at the same time.

The experience of God Jasmine had in her church helped her to see God in a different way, as a God that does not make mistakes. Though she is open to talking about her religion, she also doesn't feel as if it should be "shoved down the throats" of people that have been burned by the church. She says,

> Because my ideas about God didn't change unless I had an experience with God that allowed me to see a different way, you know what I mean? Because you can't see. You can't see him, so it has to be an experience. And I think if the person, I don't know, that, I don't know how to explain it. I am not sure. I would hope that the church could encourage or train, I don't know, train isn't the right word, but just offer a different perspective but that is really tricky. Because on one hand they want you to evangelize and bring people closer, and that is the one thing about the Christian church that I don't really agree with, and that is a big thing. (Laughs) Sounds funny saying it out loud. Like what do you mean, you don't believe in talking about Jesus; I don't believe in forcing it on anyone that didn't ask. If there is an opening, I will take it, maybe that is the way it could be approached, if there is an opening, a question, a random conversation, then sort of introduce God as being inclusive, and all loving and forgiving, and perfect in his creation, and how we are the ones who have all these ideas because we are trying to make sense of it, but God already knows what it is and accepts. Maybe there is an opening to that conversation, then it could be done, and maybe it would be more welcomed in that circumstance.

All participants in this study recognized their uniqueness in the LGBTQIA+ community; being religious and queer set them apart from others. At times, this experience can be difficult, causing discomfort in their relationships. Several participants recognized the importance of testing conversations with other LGBTQIA+ people to see if it was safe to talk about religion. However, all participants were at varying stages of trying to live as an openly religious person in the LGBTQIA+ community and valued being fully open about their sexuality and their religion in all areas of their lives. As Herman notes, a final task in resolution of trauma is reconstructing a "coherent system of meaning and belief that encompasses the story of the trauma."[31] The accepting church has both the opportunity and the honor of accompanying people who have experienced this kind of religious trauma in constructing a coherent system in light of the trauma they experienced.

Herman notes that often, for those who have worked through the experience of trauma, they "face life with few illusions but often with gratitude."[32] Though the church must resist moving too quickly or pushing survivors of trauma into gratitude before they have intentionally engaged their trauma narrative; for participants in this study their story did not end with their membership in the accepting church, but continued beyond. They reflected on their experience of religious trauma while also acknowledging the ways the trauma had helped them to grow.

POST-TRAUMATIC GROWTH

No theorist would suggest that trauma is "good" or that trauma is inherently positive. Yet, many participants in this study, looking back on their experience, noted that they would not be the people they are today without it. They expressed some surprise that they have ended up where they are today, living happy and fulfilling lives with rich friendships and relationships. Making meaning of their trauma, naming what good has come from the trauma and how they understand themselves differently on this side of the trauma echo findings in the study of post-traumatic growth.

Post-traumatic growth is the study of the "positive" outcomes after major events of suffering or trauma. Survivors of trauma, despite the numerous negative feelings following the trauma, often report experiences of personal growth.[33] Theorists in this field are quick to note that this area of study focuses on growth that often occurs alongside intense grief and suffering, and in no way minimizes the significance of the suffering. Not all those who experience trauma will experience growth; the study of post-traumatic growth merely recognizes that in times of intense suffering, some positive psychological consequences are reported.[34] In their study of post-traumatic growth, Lawrence Calhoun and Richard Tedeschi argue that many survivors of trauma name three particular categories of growth—perception of the self (including strength and new possibilities), relationships with others, and changes in philosophy of life (including appreciation and spiritual change).[35] Participants in this study reflect growth in all these areas. Their post-traumatic growth in areas of self-perception, relationships and philosophy of life highlight significant personal strengths.

Oliver sees himself as stronger because of his traumatic experience. His perception of self and his spiritual life have changed for the better because of what happened to him. He says,

> I feel like my faith is a lot stronger now, and I really feel part of a community. And I also feel like I have made it through the maze or the difficult journey like how do you navigate all of that? I came out the other side and I came out okay. Even my mom said that, about both me and my sister, she said you never know what happens with your kids in that time but she is like I am glad you guys both, my sister was a bit wild in her younger years so that is why she says that about her, but she is like with me being gay I could have rejected the church completely or had bad experiences with it or whatever, and we both kind of made it through.

It is not just his faith that is stronger; he notes that he is a "better person" because of his trauma, even if he would rather have grown up in a different way.

> I think so, I am better as a whole person, maybe I am not perfect and I still have things to work out but I am better in general as a whole person because of that, and I think that was a big part of it. And also my professional life is going very well and I am happily married and those parts are also set up nice in a row, too. . . . Sure, it would have been so much better to grow up in a progressive Methodist church because you could save yourself all of that drama. I mean, I realize with talking with friends who had a much worse experience than I did, and there are people who had a much easier than what I did. Of course you would pick the easier route if you could, but I think there is something about going through the struggles and trying to figure things out yourself that makes it all, either more important or meaningful than, because when you grow up in it it is easy to say this is what we have always thought and just go through the motions, when you have to figure it out yourself it becomes a lot more meaningful and impact for you, because you actively have to do something.

Oliver feels some responsibility to his community as a person who has come out on the other side. His experiences have changed the way he connects with others who have been hurt by the church. He says,

> And I can identify with more people that way, because I have had to go through something myself. Because I think it was easy for the people who grew up in a progressive church, it can be very easy for them, so sometimes they might not understand all the difficulties that someone else had to go through, and I can relate more, and I think that helps some of my friends because I can say, yeah, you know I went through some of that, too, and this is where I am now. So if I can get there you can get there, too.

Beth knows that what she has discovered about God and herself is a gift she can give others. She is stronger and able to trust the relationship she has with God and the church. She says,

> I feel like I am a whole person, I don't feel fractured. Again, you know, to get to the other side you have to go through, and it sucks, but it is beautiful at the same time. And it just changes you, and I think I just know now, there is nothing that is going to separate me from the love of God. And I stand in that, and I can say that, and I can offer that to other people. And maybe that is what it was all, that is the witness . . . Yeah, and I can give it. And I will. I will not withhold that from anybody. I don't understand everything, but I know that.

Like Oliver and Beth, April knows that the way she sees others is deeply impacted by her religious experience. Her ability to understand the struggles of others is rooted in her own traumatic experience. She says,

> I think I have learned that I am really resourceful, not like McGyver style, but mentally resourceful, and being able to hold a lot of things in my head or in my heart that are painful or difficult or contradict each other, and being able to hold all of that and then sort through it, even though there is a lot of stuff. I also think that I have learned that I am very empathic; I think a lot of that was caused, or a lot of the empathy I have for other people in any kind of suffering anywhere, I not only care, but I am motivated to do things, that is literally my job that I picked because I think I, it is sort of the classic I have been there, and I really get it, I really get it, and I want to make sure that other people don't have to stay in the situation that I was able to get out of. You know? And I really feel for them because I know.

April's empathy and ability to "hold a lot of things" in her heart also impacts the way she functions in the LGBTQIA+ community. She sees the influence of her past on those relationships as well as the way she interprets theology.

> So one thing I have frequently noticed is that I am probably the most open-minded queer person among the queer folks I know who generally pride themselves on being open-minded, and I think it comes from being in that place of having your entire world collapse and having to start over. Because like a lot of gay men and some gay women are racist, transphobic, misogynistic, and I used to be, but all of that was part and parcel, it all collapsed at the same time. So I really had the chance to start from scratch, so I guess being gay is okay, what do I think about trans people? Cool. You know? Whereas I never had to, I think if you never have had to do that radical breaking down it is a lot harder for you to overcome your earlier biases, and societal prejudices and what have you. I think that really carries over into church because I think a lot of people like to say "we worship our way and you worship yours," I actually think that we are both worshipping the same God. Like I actively think about that. I don't have a super developed theology in my head but I guess there is some sort of God figure and we are sitting up like, yeah, and people over here are doing their thing and they are like, yeah, and it looks completely different but it is all sort of sending positive energy to God, which sounds a little ridiculous, but you get the idea.

Though April experienced the complete fracturing of the world she had built up in the non-accepting church, she also recognizes that the rebuilding left her with the ability to see others in their struggles in a new way. She says,

> I think that it really is a firmer foundation, open-mindedness and really being egalitarian. Because when you start at the bottom and you see yourself as the

worst person on the planet and everybody is above you, like your previous levels and layers all look the same because they are all up. So when you get to restructure those layers it is a lot easier to put them down. Because I think a lot of people they were like, well, I am not super poor, and I am not black, and my parents have a college degree, and I am straight, oh, shit, I am not. And they just went back to like here, and then they are still kind of racist and they are still kind of classist, and they are still kind of xenophobic. Right? I think that is the benefit of all of this for me, and thank God there is a benefit, because otherwise it would just suck.

Jorge can see how his experience has changed the way he understands his spirituality and relationship with God. The loss of his church community forced him to build a new and deeper relationship with the God he now knows intimately. He says,

Yes, absolutely. [Orlando] and I spoke about it, he was like, I don't understand, I have a great relationship with God but you have an intimate relationship with God, I want to get there. And I was like, I can't tell you how to get there, I can't explain it, I can't say this is what you have to do, and do a,b,c and you will get d, and I look at my family all four of their kids went to church, none of them now, none of my brothers or sister go to church, none of them follow, I would say in their life, Christ, or any aspect of the life of Christ. So I would say from my family I kept it, not because I was pushed to keep it, because I could have let it go as soon as [it] happened. But it was something that I wanted and that was part of me. So I for sure would say I have a different relationship.

Jasmine draws on her experience in a variety of churches to strengthen her decision to join the accepting church. Her understanding of church and her relationship with God is stronger because she had to decide for herself what she was willing to believe. She says,

That I have a unique journey, in that I experienced him in all those different churches in different ways, but even with all of that it doesn't fully explain who he or she is to me and it never changed our relationship. So I just think of the churches as like buildings, it is not churches, it is so much more complicated than that. I guess what I am trying to say is I am glad I was exposed to a lot of different things and a lot of different ideas despite the emotional harm it did, I am glad I had that experience because I had an opportunity to see how each denomination viewed God and I had the choice whether to accept that or not. And so far [my current church] comes closest to what I truly believe in myself about how God is, it comes closest. It doesn't have all the answers, no church will, but it comes closest.

Jasmine can see the way that each of those experiences, despite how difficult it was for her, also changed her in unique ways. Despite her experience of religious trauma she also looks back on her time in the non-accepting church as not entirely bad. She says,

> Not to say that all those places were wrong, either, it is just from my perspective in what I was able or not able to get out of it, I guess I am saying I am trying not to put judgment on all those churches. I am just saying there was some good in all of those, too. Like even the Catholic church how you are praying for different things, it helped with the sense of ritual that I liked, that I miss, that I don't get from [my current church]. Each one had their good and bad parts so I am grateful for that, too.

Jasmine can also see how her experiences have changed the way she functions in relationships with other people, and in recognizing her own needs. She says,

> I am persistent. I am open. I am very sensitive. And not just in the respect of being emotional, but even being in a room with another person, I can sense their energy, if the energy is really strong whether it is good or bad, I have a good sense of people in that way. Yeah, that I am persistent, that I am very aware of when there is something missing and when it needs to be taken care of in order for me to feel whole, and feel safe and feel okay. Now that is something I have always had since I was a kid, and that is why I knew when it was time to go back to church, because I felt a void, and no matter what I did it wouldn't be filled. And it needed that, it needed the Jesus piece. The Jesus piece that was accepting, that is what it needed.

Sarah views God differently on the other side of her struggle with her sexuality and faith. Despite praying to be "normal," she knows that her life is good and fulfilling because her prayers were not answered. She says,

> I think for me it was, like, you may pray for a very long time that you want something to happen and it actually turns out for the best that it didn't. So whenever there is something that I really want to happen, and that has taught me to be like, whatever you want to happen I will take peace in that. So maybe kind of taking my want to control things out of it, that is maybe the biggest lesson, that is a lesson you struggle with your whole life. But for me, it is like, I am glad He didn't change it, or turn me straight or anything, because now I have a really great relationship with my partner and it is a relationship that gives me a lot of encouragement and support and that is really important in my life to give me the courage to stand up for things that I know are right and wrong. So I am glad that didn't and if He had given me what I asked for I wouldn't be here, so I have to take some peace in that, so I think that has been the biggest lesson about

what I am asking for and what is going to be next and having to really trust it. But again, that's something I will be learning my whole life, so that's the biggest lesson I would say.

Alex feels like their experience has opened them to the mystical. They encountered their own vulnerability in living through this experience. Their theology is deeper and more engaged because of the trauma. They say,

> Yeah, because if it would have just been that I was gay, and then fit nicely into that box and continued on, I don't think I would be in this spot today, I don't think I would. I wasn't. I think life would have sort of continued, and it would have been fine, not that it would have been bad, but just, I don't think I would have gotten to this point, really, like, bones kind of vulnerability. I don't think that would have happened. And also that, I am in love with thinking about God, and I don't know a lot of people who actually are. (both laugh) You know what I mean? Even Christians who love church that for whatever reason God is this like, I think people still just have this baggage and because I have had baggage that was so visible, or so right in front of me and in my ears I am now able to say, hm, well, yes, it is actually very easy to say that if God is a white, hetero, male, bearded reigning from a throne on high it is pretty easy for him to say these things in this way from these people, but if God is not that what is God? If God is not this, if God is not the Lutheran Church Missouri Synod for me, if God is not whatever, of that one priest or whatever, then who is God, what is God? And that to me is just beautiful. I love thinking about that. And it is an entirely mystical process, it can't come from, I believe it can't come from reading and this is coming from someone who reads non-stop, I don't think it comes from reading, I don't think it comes from theology, I think it comes from just experience and sort of clocking those experiences.

Alex sees their concepts of God broadened by the rejection they experienced in the Missouri Synod Lutheran church. Their concept of God is now so broad that they see all of humanity as in the image of God.

> So I am going along, things are going okay, things are going well, I have a concept of God, I have a concept of church. Something in my life happens, people are telling me that I am not okay, I am not good, that changes things, so there is that. So God then is super super super super one thing for that time period, and it is a process really, of making God that one thing by colonizing the imagination and then opens up when I say no more of this Lutheran Church. And then it is so open that I am like, oh my god, I am looking at different faiths, different faith experiences. And then it is sort of finding, for some reason at that time, it was really narrowing again, that idea, and then certainly into the Catholic Church it was definitely a narrowing. And then since I think it was probably the Catholic Worker when shit got real, it was like, oh, wait, not this, not the closing off of, let's err on the side of broadening the concept of God. If we are made in the

image of God, which I have never liked that part of scripture, because I think it is always like flippantly passed through and it is like, do you understand? That doesn't mean that God looks human it means that God is as vast as humanity! Just as a starting point, never mind all the rest of creation, but just as humanity. And I think about every single person's story, and that is part of God. So that process to me is one of broadening, so the phases of my life where I am either broadening or restricting possibility of what God might be to the point now where it is like, wow, it is pretty broad in a real and theological sound way. So it is more of that, and more and more and more of that, and just living into those questions.

Alex had to learn to live with the doubt about how much they could know about God, and the world, and even theirself. The ability to tolerate the unknown and to trust their own experience changed for them as they worked through the trauma.

And I think that approach is less fruitful than living into your questions, and living into your fear, and living into your doubt. Not fear, your doubt, living into your doubt. Because I think I became very rigid about myself, and how I presented to the world, and, just all of this stuff. And it is like, that was one approach, and maybe that was the approach I needed for that time at such a young person, my God such a young person, maybe that is what I needed, I had plenty of other questions running through my hormonal mind that I don't know if I could have done anything else, and that is what I needed for that time. But now I am looking back and thinking, hmmmm, okay, that was one way, and that got me to a certain point, and now I have realized this other way that can be used.

Post-traumatic growth is a result of the trauma experienced by participants in this study but is a gift that comes at an incredibly high cost. Through their struggle, participants in this study had to reckon with their theological beliefs, understandings of self and others, and on the other side of the trauma see themselves differently. Many participants in this study felt immense responsibility to people who are still struggling with religious trauma, and several people felt that their participation in this study was one way they could "give back" in order to try and help others. Though they have grown, participants yearned for a world where LGBTQIA+ people were accepted and loved in all religious communities.

IMPLICATIONS FOR PASTORAL CAREGIVERS

It is natural for those who observe trauma in others to imagine that with the right help, with the most appropriate treatment, with the most thoughtful care, that trauma can be healed. The purpose of pastoral care among folks who have experienced religious trauma is not to "cure" them of what has happened, but rather to accompany them in their journey toward healing, whatever that journey looks like. For many LGBTQIA+ people who have been traumatized by the church, the pain is too deep to ever return. Even among participants in this project, many named friends who would never cross the threshold of a church, and that were finding healing outside of the church. This project is meant to support pastoral caregivers in care for those who have experienced trauma, but this does not mean that the progressive or accepting church is the best or only path toward healing. Though there is no specific study on the impact of religious trauma on the return of LGBTQIA+ people to religious communities, the Pew Research 2014 Religious Landscape Study found that in the United States, 41% of gay, lesbian and bisexual people are religiously unaffiliated, while only 22% of straight people identify as religiously unaffiliated.[36] Another Pew Research Study suggests that most LGBTQIA+ people believe that Catholic and Evangelical Churches are unfriendly to LGBTQIA+ people, and only 1 in 10 believe that mainline Protestant Churches are friendly to LGBTQIA+ people. Approximately 3 in 10 LGBTQIA+ people can name an experience of being uncomfortable in a place of worship.[37] For participants in this study, however, the return to the church was the beginning of a process of healing that has helped them to further expand their own belief in their inner strength and deepened their trust in relationships with others.

Participants in this study offered a few key practices that are important for pastoral caregivers to implement in attempting to accompany the religiously traumatized as they seek a new relationship with the church.

- In all accepting congregations, pastors and other leaders shared explicit messages of welcome every Sunday. These messages named LGBTQIA+ people as specifically welcome and beloved by God. Helpful practices for pastoral caregivers include messages of welcome on the church website and in bulletins as well as explicit messages of welcome for LGBTQIA+ people during all worship services.
- These accepting congregations were committed to "doing the work" required to support those who had been religiously traumatized. This "work" included facing internal assumptions about LGTBQ people as well as internalized beliefs about sexuality and demonstrating a willingness to move toward a "conversion of heart." Dialogue, listening, and

continuing to acknowledge the unique experiences of LGBTQIA+ people in the congregation made these congregations feel safe to those who had been religiously traumatized. Helpful practices for congregations include opportunities for listening to the experiences of the religiously traumatized and for the open dialogue about LGBTQIA+ concerns in the congregation.
- These congregations recognized the importance of ritual as a site for theological reimagination. For many participants in this study, the sharing of testimony was a powerful experience of healing in an accepting congregation. For others, seeing LGBTQIA+ people in worship leadership was a powerful message, while participating and celebrating life events in worship helped them to trust that they were truly a part of God's community. Helpful practices for pastoral caregivers may include offering opportunities for testimony from the religiously traumatized. Additionally, recognizing the importance of ritual participation for those who have been cut off from a ritual community can help pastoral caregivers accompany the religiously traumatized as they return to an accepting community.
- The congregations showed awareness of the unique experience of coming out as religious in the LGBTQIA+ community. Participation in queer events like Pride Parades and the Dyke March are important steps that congregation can take to accompany people who are now facing a "second" coming out as religious in the LGBTQIA+ community. Practices that demonstrate patience, compassion, and a willingness to support the religiously traumatized as they live out their identity as a religious person are extremely helpful.

Though some may suggest that the gains in rights for LGBTQIA+ people in the last decade have expanded beyond what many imagined possible, participants in this study were aware that the experience of religious trauma is not over. Many participants could name people who were still struggling with their trauma, and recognized that trauma was still occurring in religious setting all over the United States. As a result, the accepting church must recognize and respond to the presence of traumatized people in our midst. Liberation and freedom are at the heart of our scriptures, but liberation and freedom require work on our part. To use our theology as a source of liberation and freedom for the oppressed, we must establish safe communities, allow for ritual participation and narrative reimagination, and accompany LGBTQIA+ people in integrating their religious identity. The call of our gospel requires us to proclaim the radical life giving love of God, and so this work is not just a requirement of our faith, but an opportunity to proclaim the power of God's love in places where that love has been denied for far too long.

NOTES

1. Geertz, C. *The interpretation of cultures: Selected essays*. New York: Basic Books, 1973, 90.
2. Geertz, *The Interpretation of Cultures*, 99.
3. Bell, C. M. *Ritual: Perspectives and Dimensions*. New York: Oxford University Press, 1997, 59.
4. Van Gennep, A. *The rites of passage*. Chicago: University of Chicago Press, 1960, 10.
5. Turner, V. W. *The Ritual Process: Structure and Anti-structure*. Chicago: Aldine Pub. Co., 1969/2008, 95.
6. Turner, V. W. *The Ritual Process: Structure and Anti-structure*. Chicago: Aldine Pub. Co., 1969/2008, 95–96.
7. Jones, *Terror and Transformation*, 65.
8. "Tips for Talking with Survivors of Sexual Assault." *RAINN*, www.rainn.org/articles/how-respond-survivor.
9. Rambo, S. *Spirit and trauma: a theology of remaining* (1st ed.). Louisville, Ky.: Westminster John Knox Press, 2010, 22.
10. Rambo, *Spirit and Trauma*, 36.
11. Herman, *Trauma and Recovery*, 133.
12. Herman, *Trauma and Recovery*, 157.
13. Herman, *Trauma and Recovery*, 158.
14. "Tips for Talking with Survivors of Sexual Assault." *RAINN*, www.rainn.org/articles/how-respond-survivor.
15. Herman, *Trauma and Recovery*, 174.
16. Herman, *Trauma and Recovery*, 174.
17. Herman, *Trauma and Recovery*, 175.
18. Boulanger, G. *Wounded by reality: understanding and treating adult onset trauma* (Vol. 6). New York: Psychology Press, 2007, 134.
19. Boulanger, *Wounded By Reality*, 137.
20. Jones, *Trauma and Grace*, 21.
21. Jones, *Trauma and Grace*, 21.
22. Driver, Tom. *Liberating Rites: Understanding the Transformative Power of Ritual*. Charleston, S.C: BookSurge, 2007, 31.
23. Driver, *Liberating Rites*, 24.
24. Driver, *Liberating Rites*, 166.
25. Driver, *Liberating Rites*, 190.
26. Driver, *Liberating Rites*, 7.
27. Rappaport, R. A. *Ritual and religion in the making of humanity*. Cambridge, U.K.; New York: Cambridge University Press, 1999, 104.
28. Rappaport, *Ritual and Religion*, 53.
29. Driver, *Liberating Rites*, 200.
30. Herman, *Trauma and Recovery*, 214.
31. Herman, *Trauma and Recovery*, 213.
32. Herman, *Trauma and Recovery*, 213.

33. Calhoun, L. G., R. G. Tedeschi, A. Cann and E. A. Hanks. "Positive outcomes following bereavement: Paths to posttraumatic growth." *Psychologica Belgica* 50 (2010): 125–143.

34. Calhoun, "Positive outcomes following bereavement," 127.

35. Calhoun, L. G. and R. G. Tedeschi. *Posttraumatic Growth in Clinical Practice*. New York, NY: Routledge, 2013, 5.

36. Wormald, B. "Chapter 4: The shifting religious identity of demographic groups," 12 May 2015. Accessed 21 Feb. 2017. http://www.pewforum.org/2015/05/12/chapter-4-the-shifting-religious-identity-of-demographic-groups/#religious-composition-by-sexual-orientation.

37. Pew Social Trends. "A survey of LGBT Americans." June 13, 2013. Retrieved February 21, 2017, from http://www.pewsocialtrends.org/2013/06/13/a-survey-of-lgbt-americans/#religion

Conclusion

In the month following the election of Donald Trump to the office of the President of the United States of America, the Southern Poverty Law Center saw a surge in anti-LGBTQIA+ hate crimes as well as a growing fear that these crimes would become more violent and frequent.[1] The election of President Donald Trump as well as his running mate Vice President Mike Pence, who has both instituted anti-LGBTQIA+ policies in his own state as well as argued that civil rights bills for LGBTQIA+ people are part of a "radical social agenda," increased the fear that LGBTQIA+ people may find themselves victims of violent assault, discrimination or loss of civil rights.[2] The fear of violence or the loss of civil rights is an intense stressor, highlighting the precariousness of their position within the social and political world. Even with the election of more liberal and openly LGTBQIA+ persons to positions of power doesn't guarantee that the next election cycle might not bring with it another round of politicians who seek to dismantle the rights of LGBTQIA+ persons.

As Maria P.P. Root, a feminist theorist, argues, in cases of insidious trauma "dimensions of security are not very secure," and the tenuousness of the recent gains in civil rights for LGBTQIA+ people reflects the reality that as political leaders change, the world cannot be trusted to remain organized in predictable ways.[3] The rise in hate crimes also intensifies the fear that the physical bodies of LGBTQIA+ people are not safe, a reality that suggests both the potential for direct trauma as well as the continued threat to life and safety that keeps LGBTQIA+ people second guessing the safety of the world around them.

Though this threat to physical safety took on a new level of intensity in the Trump administration, Vice President Pence also embodies the non-accepting religious agenda described by many participants in this study. Vice President Pence has described himself as a "Christian, a conservative, and a Republican in that order," and argued before Congress that when marriage is broadened to include same-sex marriage, we ought to remember that "societal collapse was always brought following the advent of the deterioration of marriage and family."[4] Vice President Pence, while Governor of Indiana, signed the Religious Freedom Restoration Act, a bill which, given that LGBTQIA+ people were not considered a protected class in Indiana, allowed businesses and individuals to claim First Amendment protection for their religious views when refusing service or employment to LGBTQIA+ people. This bill, though reminiscent of a federal law of the same name, was significantly different, in that it was supported by a number of conservative Christian groups including Advance America, a "pro-family and pro-church" organization, who proclaimed the bill as a victory for Christians, stating,

> Christian bakers, florists and photographers should not be punished for refusing to participate in a homosexual marriage!
>
> A Christian business should not be punished for refusing to allow a man to use the women's restroom!
>
> A church should not be punished because they refuse to let the church be used for a homosexual wedding![5]

In an interview Pence asked, in relation to the bill, "is tolerance a two-way street, or not?" suggesting that Christians themselves needed a state law in order to protect themselves from having their religious beliefs "substantially burdened" by the overreach of the government.[6] This reversal is central to the conservative Christian political movement; it locates the power in the hands of LGBTQIA+ people. In this view Christians are the victims of persecution, not marginalized LGBTQIA+ people.

How does all of this matter to the eight participants in this study? If religious trauma is a helpful category for us to understand their experience, we must recognize the ways that religious trauma, as a kind of insidious trauma, manifests itself in the shattering of the belief that the world is a just, safe, and ordered place.[7] This belief is not just shattered by conservative Christian individuals, but by the sum of the conservative Christian movement, leading to not just trauma perpetrated by an individual, but a pervasive state of religious trauma where even the world outside of the church is not safe. These bills, written specifically for the benefit of conservative Christian groups, are not simply about being LGBTQIA+; they are a reaction to the "danger" LGBTQIA+ people supposedly pose to Christian communities. LGBTQIA+ people are a threat to those communities, not a part of them. The stories of these participants are not of a trauma perpetrated by an individual, but of a trauma that is a result of the theology, political action and even threats of the entire conservative Christian movement. The elevation of a conservative

Christian Vice President who has a record of dismantling the protections for LGBTQIA+ people, suggests that LGBTQIA+ people continue to be a "category" of debate in our highest levels of government. As Laura Brown argues, "Until we know we are queer, in sexuality or gender or both, the world works in predictable ways for those of us who grow up with the good-enough experience"; it is this coming out process, to self, to family and to religious community that becomes a site for the shattering of the carefully built worldview that one is loved, cared for and good.[8] When even the Vice President of the United States believes that LGBTQIA+ people are internally misaligned with the ideals of the country, and could potentially be the site of "societal collapse," the world in which LGBTQIA+ people exist is one of continued insidious trauma.

As a result, the question of justice considering trauma was at the forefront of the stories of participants. Trauma is a valid response to injustice. Trauma represents something deeply wrong, and recovery requires the traumatized to reckon with the new reality of an unjust world. For participants in this study, what would justice look like? Could the wrong that has been done ever be made right?

For many participants in this study, their membership in a congregation that loved and valued them as co-participants in the kin-dom of God was the best kind of justice they could imagine. At the same time, many of them yearned for the congregations that traumatized them to understand what they had done, and the emotional pain it caused. Oliver says justice would be if the congregation,

> Like changed their doctrine because I think that right now the official word is that you can be gay but you have to be celibate, like if they came back to say, we are sorry, we realize that was wrong after careful study and consideration or something like that . . . I don't think it would solve all the problems but I think it would feel nice for that.

Oliver has moved past hoping that the non-accepting congregation will ever change, but worries that the church still has power over the young LGBTQIA+ people who have yet to realize their sexual identity is different from those around them.

> I think that I have worked it out, and now I don't care, and maybe that is a cruel or a cold, like, I have come through it and I realize I don't believe that is the right way, I am at a church that I feel is doing it right, not that I wouldn't want to see the other ones apologize for the hurt that they have done. I'll never get that, but even from my dad's old church, to say that we are sorry we never should have told your father that, it is wrong for us to break up a family or to tell parents to disinherit their children, because that is a horrible thing. It is one thing for a

whole church to say the doctrine is this, it is another thing for a pastor to say, I don't want you to ever see your children again because of that . . . Yeah, because at least then they would admit that they had done something wrong. Because right now they all think that is the right thing, and that is what you have to do, and that means that some younger child now, if they come up in that church they are going to do the same thing to that child.

Oliver sees his own story and his return to an accepting church as part of this narrative of justice. If Oliver had the chance to talk to young people in his non-accepting church, he knows what he would say,

This isn't the way it has to be. Get out! Get out while you can! (laughing) . . . And that's what I do now, like people say I want to leave my church, and I say, okay, then come to ours, don't give up on God or the church . . . or I can say, you know what, look at me, I made it through and you can do the same. Don't give up hope. Because I didn't have anybody like that. I had to figure it out all on my own. I think it is easier if you have a mentor or a friend, or someone that can kind of walk you through a little bit . . . Or even to just share, here is another viewpoint on it! Read this and see what you think. Don't just believe what they are saying.

Beth knows that there is justice in living her life and showing others that she is both a Christian and a lesbian. There is justice in her knowledge that she can be both of those things, even if changing the theology of a non-accepting church seems overwhelming. She says,

So I think, other than being a witness and living my life, and speaking, and people seeing that, because I know when they are around me they see God, there is just no doubt in my mind, this, my spirit, my energy, and I believe that people know, they are okay, because I am okay. Does that make sense? And they see all of that, and I don't know, I don't know how you tackle a system that is so ingrained. Let justice roll down. It is not like the civil rights movement, which was, I don't know how you take down 500 years of theology, and rooted in so much fear, like about segregation, women, unfortunately, it has kept order and structure. And I honestly believe right now why Donald Trump is doing so well, is because last year the Supreme Court said gay marriage is now the law of the land, booya. And now, here goes these uppity gay people, these trans people, it is a backlash. These people are feeling threatened at every level, at everything that they believe and hold sacred, it is being taken away from them.

Beth recognizes that the power of fear leads many non-accepting folks to think any LGBTQIA+ person is speaking for the "devil." The fear that thinking differently might lead to alienation from God is strong. Beth knows, though, that she embodies something that leads to questions, and questions might lead to a change of heart.

> I might be the only thing they see, and like, you know, I know I make people question. I know. Does that make sense? It is beyond me right now. It is big. I don't know if someone has an idea, I am in, let's do it, if we just, do we just go down and ask if we can speak, if they just let us in, are they going to let us in?

Alex wishes that there was some way they would be able to tell their story in the congregation that hurt them, and that the congregation would really listen. Alex fantasized about the possibility that if they knew what it was like to be gay, they would understand.

> I think I just really, there was a time that I thought, especially when I was younger, that oh, well, if everybody knew what it was like to be gay that would teach them, but you can't force an experience on somebody, you can only speak from your own experience, so I think that is ultimately really what I think would probably be best. Let's say with the church that I grew up in, the Lutheran Church, I think for justice for that, it is the same thing, I just think it would be, I don't think there is anything that I could tell them other than my experience and what I felt during that time, and actually I would add into that the phrase that you used, they put me in hell, the idea the concept of, they put me in hell that day when they told me that I would go to hell and just let them kind of sit with that and realize that is not the most loving way of approaching even if you believe that homosexuality is wrong that is not the most loving way of dealing with that situation. I don't know in those situations if there is anything else that could be done beyond that that is going to be effective or honest or not sort of forced, and with something so deeply personal I think it has to just be deeply personal . . . Just them sitting there, no questions, just me talking for an hour and half to them, this is what I felt, this is what I feel now even from that time. And just sort of let them live with that for a minute.

Alex's presence as a leader in the Episcopal Church feels like some type of justice for them. For Alex, the right use of power is justice, and Alex sees how justice goes far beyond just their experience.

> Oh, yeah. Definitely. Just the idea that there might be a genderqueer priest in this diocese, that to me, that in and of itself just seems like some type, not full justice but a part of the whole thing . . . I think, tokenism, and flag waving is detrimental to justice because it is like checking off a box and then their lives are continuing on those people in those little boxes that are checked off, but you are kind of helping to solidify those boxes a bit and that is not helpful. Even if it is including more boxes in the puzzle, but that is still not quite, in the pursuit of justice is the pursuit of justice, it doesn't matter what cause it is, to me, it always

has to be the same, it is the right use of power. And that it is, when you go home, or let's say you go out to the grocery store, you have all these choices, and what choice are you going to make? That is what justice to me looks like. And that comes only from conversion of heart, and that only comes from relationship and from experiences.

April, like many other participants, does not really believe that what happened to her can ever be "made right." She, like Alex alludes to, can sense that some people accept LGBTQIA+ people while not examining their own motives for doing so. She says,

> I don't think that this sort of thing can ever be made right. I think all you can really do if you are the perpetrator of this kind of thing is only to do better going forward. You cannot make up for it, so don't even try. You apologize for it, but you do right going forward, because it is the right thing to do not because you are going to make up for it. With my parents in particular I think there is about a 0% chance that there will ever be any sort of reconciliation there. And with other people, they have this sort of, I am going to do right by whatever kind of community it is because my son is whatever is this. Like, if that, like Nancy Reagan and stem cells, against it, against it, against it, now your husband gets Alzheimer's, now it is a great idea. Oh, I am really sorry I had those ideas, but you only care because it affected someone you knew, and that doesn't make it okay that you . . . you know? It is selfish still. Or like the Republican I think it is a House of Representatives person who did an ad with her son who is trans, being like, we loved him before, we love him now, stop being hateful that isn't helpful. She doesn't give a shit about trans people, maybe she does, it is very unlikely to me that she does, I know plenty of people like this, they don't care about birth control until their sixteen-year-old daughter has a baby.

For April, her life is the embodiment of justice; she recognizes that she can't keep looking backward but can use her own experience to help others.

> But I don't think the answer is looking backward but figuring out where you are and the best way to move forward. And sometimes that involves looking at the wounds and the handicaps you have suffered in the past and trying to move on from those particularly, but trying to get revenge or justice or pay back from the past is not a good way to live . . . I think, what is that saying? The best revenge is a life well lived? I am a big fan of that, and not so much like the revenge part, I guess what I am saying is that if you are always looking backward and trying to get recompense and you know, amends, for things that have happened, you are not really living your life, you are rehashing the past, and I definitely think that me being able to take what I have been through and help other people with it, that is absolutely the right thing to do if you want to call it justice or paying it forward or increasing the level of happiness in the world, whatever it is.

Jorge, like others, can remember a time in his life when he wanted those who hurt him to feel the depth of emotional pain they caused him. Now, living as a Christian gay man, and having the ability to help others feels like justice for Jorge.

> If you would have asked me that [back then] I would wanted pain, emotional pain to everybody that caused it to me. Asking me that now, I would say justice for me is still being on the other side looking at them is saying I am still a Christian gay man now you may have affected me a little bit, my dad always told me that you kill them with kindness. And now I am on this side . . . a gay man and you follow Christ, you have God in your life. Only because I don't do everything for a church, I still have my secular job, I still go to school, I still follow Christ, I still have a place for him in my heart, it doesn't mean I am not a Christian man, back then I would have told you karma is a bitch. And even to this day I would think that about my pastor that is in jail, karma is a bitch. You know, you have looked down on me, it goes back to "He without sin throw the first stone." I would say that, but now in the, there is a kid, I was his teacher actually at [the church school] and he is having a hard time with his family and he has reached out to me a couple times already. And he has been going through some hard times with his family . . .

Helping this former student through his struggles as a Christian and a gay man has been healing for Jorge. He says,

> Yes, and he is feminine, and so he is having a hard time of accepting who he is and he likes to dress up in drag and enjoying it, and he asks me is that wrong? And I am like, no that is not wrong, you can be in drag and still be a Christian man, you could be whoever you are and you still could be a God believing God fearing person. It doesn't matter what you have on. I am like, we were born naked, so simple as that. And he is having a hard time, his family disowned him, his family moved away and let him go, and he is trying to fight for himself so he goes to church up there, and he found a church that is progressive and he is going to that church. So I regularly talk to him and he is like, how do I deal with that? He will reach out to me like I am having a hard time, there is no right man out there for me, and I am like, just give it time. He is like, you found [Orlando], but I am like, yeah, and how long did it take me to find [Orlando]? And as much as I want to believe [Orlando] is the man for me, he may not be what God has planned for me two years from now, I don't know that. However, just open your eyes and allow God's work in where you are. And he still has a hard time, and he lives out there in [a rural area] so he deals with a lot of people when he runs to Walmart, and he is like, oh, here comes so and so and they make fun of him. And he has a hard time with that. And I guess my thing is, I wish when I was there, that there was a community that I could run to and not be suicidal.

Jorge can see himself in this student reaching out to him but realizes that there aren't a lot of accepting church communities available outside of the city.

> I know where . . . this guy that is reaching out to me now, is coming from. Thankfully he is not like, "I am getting married!," but . . . he remembers coming out to his parents and my ex-wife, he came up to her and said, oh hi . . . and he is like, how are you doing, and [his] parents walked up and said we heard what your husband did to you, and he is going to hell. And [this student] is like, I remember hearing that and thinking, dad, how could you? I just came out to you not too long ago. So it is just that.

Jasmine sees justice as an awakening to who God really is, which could lead to real change within the church. She, like others in this study, does not see a place for punishment, but wishes others could know God the way that she does. She says,

> The only justice I would like to see, it wouldn't be a punishment of any sort with my experiences and the people who brought that on, it would be more like an awakening, that would be perfect. Just for them to realize that is not how God really is, and, yeah, punishment would do nothing, and awakening, because with awareness with the truth and everything, that is when change takes place, real change, and people feel more inclined to act different and to say different things and to not judge and to welcome people and to love people for who they are if they have that awareness of what God really is. So justice, to answer your question, just an awakening.

For Jasmine, knowing God in this way means a rejection of the "old logic," in favor of this personal experience that leads to change.

> To have that experience so that they will know, because that is the only way they will know, to have that experience . . . that is my favorite way of knowing God. Feeling God, is the knowingness, because you can't deny that, not your old logic, none of that will work, it is just there. So if they had personal experience, an awakening, change takes place from that . . . Yes. That is the only kind of justice I would want.

Like others, Sarah would welcome an apology, but realizes that will likely never come. Sarah recognizes that living her life in a healthy way, knowing that those congregations get "no say in it," is justice to her.

> I mean the ultimate justice would be for them to realize that what they did was wrong and apologize, I mean, that is tough one, because you are like, they should know what they did was wrong and I want to prove it to them, you know, and it is that struggle, what is going to help them to change in the long run? Me

coming after them with a vengeance, they are going to throw up their defense, but if you come to them with peace and compassion they might think about it, that is the battle I am having in my current situation, do I go after this really strongly and really push it or do I just push it as far as I can in a respectful way and make them think about it and then go on my own path, because it is, for me luckily, I go to, my need to prove something to someone is not necessarily about me trying to prove myself, I want to prove so that they don't do it to other people, I have learned about myself that I am much better motivated to do things when I know it impacts other people. And living your life in a healthy and respectful way I think is the ultimate justice because you are healthy and they get no say in it.

The acceptance Sarah found in the church is part of learning to be fully herself in a religious community.

Yeah, because you are showing them that your system isn't the only way, there is people I can go over here and be accepted by. And while that is not the most satisfying feeling, I understand that completely, or I can empathize with that, at the end of the day you don't necessarily control them, you control you . . . So I was like, unfortunately when it comes to justice, unlike a physical action that you need to stop, you have to find peace in that the ultimate justice is for you to be able to be you.

Part of the acceptance Sarah has found at her church is reflected in the relationships she has built with both LGBTQIA+ people as well as straight people. The instilling of values of welcome and acceptance in the families in her congregation makes the welcome even more real to her.

All the different inclusive churches are pushing that justice, and I think we talked about this last time, the Lutheran pastor Nadia Bolz-Weber, when she talked about, when she became really popular and famous and all these straight white people started coming and she was like, they are not a part of our community, and then the transgender kid was like, "my parents won't accept me, but these people look like my parents and they will accept me," that is kind of the ultimate justice. It is a reason I like my [church], there is a bunch of people that if I was walking down the street I would not guess that they would be inclusive and want to be a part of a community that believes these values and yet they are here, they believe it, they are instilling in their families.

In this study, the question of what justice looks like after religious trauma went in two directions. First, participants yearned for an apology, a moment when those congregations that were the sites of their trauma could fully understand what had happened to them and could see how they were implicated in the harm that was done. Second, participants felt that they now embodied justice, by living out and claiming their identities as both LGBTQIA+ people and Christians, their life story was a powerful rejection of the theology in the non-accepting church. It is by accompanying these people in their recovery from religious trauma that the accepting church has the opportunity to offer healing for those who have been deeply wounded. Creating an environment conducive to healing while helping LGBTQIA+ people who have been religiously traumatized reconnect with their spirituality is an act of justice.

One participant, Sarah, summed up this tension by suggesting that the "first reaction is not the final reaction," she hoped, along with others, that the non-accepting church would change. She wished that they would understand the harm that had been done, but she saw in them fear, distrust, and uncertainty about what it would mean to revisit such a central tenant of their theology. For many participants in this study, their theology was like a house of cards, and the non-accepting view of homosexuality was foundational. When that card was removed, everything tumbled down. The first reaction of these churches resulted in religious trauma, but, there is hope that perhaps the first reaction will not be the final.

Until that day, April, Lucas, Oliver, Alex, Beth, Jorge, Jasmine and Sarah are living their lives as openly LGBTQIA+ Christians. They are learning about what it means to be people of faith in a changing world, recovering from their own trauma while they also seek to help others. As Beth said, "again, you know, to get to the other side you have to go through, and it sucks, but it is beautiful at the same time." For participants in this study, getting through is what justice looks like, acknowledging the pain, the part that "sucks," the anguish that accompanies the struggle, but on the other side justice is making a life they can finally call beautiful.

NOTES

1. Lang, N. "This is Trump's America: LGBT community fears surge in hate crimes following homophobia attacks." *Salon*. November 13, 2016. http://www.salon.com/2016/11/13/this-is-trumps-america-lgbt-community-fears-surge-in-hate-crimes-following-reports-of-homophobic-attacks/;Southern Poverty Law Center HateWatch. (2016). Retrieved from https://www.splcenter.org/hatewatch/2016/12/16/update-1094-bias-related-incidents-month-following-election.

2. 152 Cong. Rec 14796 (2006) (Statement of Rep. Michael Pence)

3. Root, "Reconstructing the Impact of Trauma," 241.

4. Pence, M. (July 21, 2016). *Vice presidential nominee remarks.* Paper presented at the Republican National Convention, Quicken Loans Arena, Cleveland, Ohio.

5. Advance America. (2015, March 26). Victory at the state house! retrieved from: https://www.advanceamerica.com/2015/03/victory-at-the-state-house/

6. Pence, M. "Ensuring religious freedom in Indiana; our new law has been grossly misconstrued as a 'license to discriminate.' That isn't true." [*Wall Street Journal*] March 31, 2015. Retrieved from http://turing.library.northwestern.edu/login?url=http://search.proquest.com/docview/1667652033?accountid=12861; Stephanopoulos, G. 'Indiana Governor Mike Pence says religious freedom law 'absolutely not' a mistake." *This Week with George Stephanopoulos*: ABC News. March 29, 2015.

7. Brown, "Sexuality, Lies and Loss," 57.

8. Brown, "Sexuality, Lies and Loss," 57.

Bibliography

152 Cong. Rec 14796 (2006) (Statement of Rep. Michael Pence).

Advance America. (2015, March 26). Victory at the state house! Retrieved from: https://www.advanceamerica.com/2015/03/victory-at-the-state-house/.

Alexander, E. "Can You be Black and Look at This?: Reading the Rodney King Video(s)." *Public Culture* 7 (1994): 77–94.

Allen, C. L. *God's Psychiatry: The Twenty-third Psalm, the Ten Commandments, the Lord's Prayer, the Beatitudes.* Westwood, N.J.: F. H. Revell Co., 1953/2015.

Alvarez, L. and R. Perez-Pena, "Orlando gunman attacks gay nightclub," *New York Times,* June 12, 2016, https://www.nytimes.com/2016/06/13/us/orlando-nightclub-shooting.html?_r=1.

American Psychiatric Association. *Diagnostic and Statistical Manual of Mental Disorders: DSM-5.* (5th ed.). Washington, D.C.: 2013.

Aten, J. D. and D. F. Walker. "Religion, spirituality, and trauma: An introduction." *Journal of Psychology & Theology* 40 (2012): 255–256.

Bell, C. M. *Ritual: Perspectives and Dimensions.* New York: Oxford University Press, 1997.

Bergler, E. *Homosexuality, Disease or Way of Life?* New York: Hill and Wang, 1956.

Bergler, E. "Differential Diagnosis between Spurious Homosexuality and Perversion Homosexuality." *Psychiatric Quarterly* 21 (1947): 399–409.

Blue, Ken. *Healing Spiritual Abuse : How to Break Free from Bad Church Experiences.* Downers Grove, Ill: InterVarsity Press, 1993.

Boulanger, G. *Wounded by Reality: Understanding and Treating Adult Onset Trauma* (Vol. 6). New York: Psychology Press, 2007.

Bridgers, Lynn. "The Resurrected Life: Roman Catholic Resources in Posttraumatic Pastoral Care." *International Journal of Practical Theology* 15.1 (2011): 38–56. https://doi.org/10.1515/ijpt.2011.025.

Brock, R. N. and G. Lettini. *Soul Repair: Recovering from Moral Injury after War.* Boston: Beacon Press, 2012.

Brown, L. "Not Outside the Range: One Feminist Perspective on Psychic Trauma." In *Trauma: Explorations in Memory,* edited by C. Caruth, 100–112. Baltimore: The Johns Hopkins University Press, 1995.

Brown, L. S. "Sexuality, Lies, and Loss: Lesbian, Gay, and Bisexual Perspectives on Trauma." *Journal of Trauma Practice* 2 (2003): 55–68.
Calhoun, L. G., R. G. Tedeschi, A. Cann and E. A. Hanks. "Positive Outcomes Following Bereavement: Paths to Posttraumatic Growth." *Psychologica Belgica* 50 (2010): 125–143.
Calhoun, L. G. and R. G. Tedeschi. *Posttraumatic Growth in Clinical Practice*. New York, NY: Routledge, 2013, 5.
Caruth, C. *Unclaimed Experience: Trauma, Narrative, and History*. Baltimore: Johns Hopkins University Press, 1996.
Caruth, C. *Listening to Trauma: Conversations with Leaders in the Theory and Treatment of Catastrophic Experience*. Baltimore: Johns Hopkins University Press, 2014.
Cass, Vivienne C. "Homosexual Identity Formation," *Journal of Homosexuality*, 4:3 (1979) 219–235.
Crocker, B. "Pastoral aid for the abnormal." *Crozer Quarterly* (1945): 242–245.
Chodorow, N. "Heterosexuality as a Compromise Formation: Reflections on the Psychoanalytic Theory of Sexual Development." *Psychoanalysis and Contemporary Thought*, 15 (1992): 267–304.
Davis, R. L. "My Homosexuality is Getting Worse Everyday": Norman Vincent Peale, Psychiatry, and the Liberal Protestant Response to Same-Sex Desires in Mid-Twentieth-Century America." In *American Christianities: A History of Dominance and Diversity* edited by C. A. Brekus and W. C. Gilpin. Chapel Hill: The University of North Carolina Press, 2011.
De La Torre, Miguel A. *Out of the Shadows into the Light : Christianity and Homosexuality*. St. Louis, Mo: Chalice Press, 2009.
Dias, E. "A Change of Heart." *Time*, 185(2), (2015): 44–48.
Driver, Tom. *Liberating Rites: Understanding the Transformative Power of Ritual*. Charleston, S.C: BookSurge, 2007.
Enroth, R. M. *Churches That Abuse*. Grand Rapids, Mich.: Zondervan, 1992.
Finlay, L. *Phenomenology for Therapists: Researching the Lived World*. Hoboken, N.J.: J. Wiley, 2011.
Frank, G. "The Civil Rights of Parents: Race and Conservative Politics in Anita Bryant's Campaign Against Gay Rights in 1970s Florida." *Journal of the History of Sexuality* 22 (2013): 126–160.
Freud, S. *The Aetiology of Hysteria*. In *The Standard Edition of the Complete Psychological Works of Sigmund Freud* edited and translated by J. Strachey, Vol. 3. 1896/1986.
Freud, S. "Analysis of a Phobia in a Five-year-old Boy." In *The Standard Edition of the Complete Psychological Works of Sigmund Freud* edited and translated by J. Strachey, (Vol. 10), 1909/1986.
Freud, S. *Three Essays on the Theory of Sexuality* edited and translated by J. Strachey. New York: Basic Books, 1910/2000.
Freud, S. *Beyond the Pleasure Principle* edited and translated by J. Strachey, New York: Norton, 1922/1989.
Freud, S. *The Future of an Illusion*. New York: Classic House Books, 1927/2009.

Freud, S. "Historical Notes." *American Journal of Psychiatry* 107 (1951): 786–787.
Freud, S. *Civilization and its Discontents* edited by J. Strachey. 1st American ed. New York: W.W. Norton, 1963.
Freyd, J. J. *Betrayal Trauma: The Logic of Forgetting Childhood Abuse.* Cambridge, Mass.: Harvard University Press, 1996.
Gay, P. *Freud : A Life for Our Time* (1st ed.). New York: Norton, 1988.
Geertz, C. *The Interpretation of Cultures: Selected Essays.* New York: Basic Books, 1973.
Grenz, Stanley J. *Welcoming but Not Affirming: An Evangelical Response to Homosexuality.* 1st ed. Louisville, Ky.: Westminster John Knox Press, 1998.
Hatzenbuehler, M. L., J. E. Pachankis and J. Wolff. "Religious Climate and Health Risk Behaviors in Sexual Minority Youths: A Population-based Study." *American Journal of Public Health* 102 (2012): 657–663.
Havemann, E. "The Age of Psychology in the U.S." *Life* 11: 68–82.
Herman, J. L. *Trauma and Recovery* (Rev.ed.). New York: BasicBooks, 1997.
Hiltner, S. *Preface to Pastoral Theology.* New York: Abingdon Press, 1958.
Hiltner, S. *Sex Ethics and the Kinsey Reports.* New York: Association Press, 1953.
Holifield, E. B. *A History of Pastoral Care in America: From Salvation to Self-Realization.* Nashville: Abingdon Press, 1983.
Johnson, D. and J. VanVonderen. *The Subtle Power of Spiritual Abuse.* Minneapolis, Minn.: Bethany House Publishers, 1991.
Jones, J. W. *Terror and Transformation: The Ambiguity of Religion in Psychoanalytic Perspective.* New York: Brunner-Routledge, 2002.
Jones, S. *Trauma and Grace: Theology in a Ruptured World.* Louisville, Ky.: Westminster John Knox Press, 2009.
Klein, M. *The Psychoanalysis of Children.* New York: Grove Press, 1960.
Kohut, H. and C. B. Strozier. *Self Psychology and the Humanities: Reflections on a New Psychoanalytic Approach.* New York: W.W. Norton, 1985.
Kohut, H. and M. Elson. *The Kohut Seminars on Self Psychology and Psychotherapy with Adolescents and Young Adults* (1st ed.). New York: Norton, 1987.
Kohut, H., A. Goldberg and P. E. Stepansky. *How Does Analysis Cure?* Chicago: University of Chicago Press, 1984.
Lang, N. "This is Trump's America: LGBT community fears surge in hate crimes following homophobia attacks." *Salon.* November 13, 2016. http://www.salon.com/2016/11/13/this-is-trumps-america-lgbt-community-fears-surge-in-hate-crimes-following-reports-of-homophobic-attacks/.
Lareau, Annette. "Using the terms hypothesis and variable for qualitative work: A critical reflection." *Journal of Marriage and Family* 74 (2012): 671–677.
Lee, D. J. *Rescuing Jesus: How People of Color, Women, & Queer Christians Are Reclaiming Evangelicalism.* Boston: Beacon Press, 2015.
Legate, N., R. M. Ryan and N. Weinstein. "Is Coming Out Always a 'Good Thing'? Exploring the Relations of Autonomy Support, Outness, and Wellness for Lesbian, Gay, and Bisexual Individuals." *Social Psychological and Personality Science* 3 (2012): 145–152.

Lewes, K. *Psychoanalysis and Male Homosexuality* (1st softcover ed.). Northvale, N.J.: J. Aronson, 1995.

Moore, G. *A Question of Truth: Christianity and Homosexuality*. London; New York: Continuum, 2003.

Myers, David G., and Letha Scanzoni. *What God Has Joined Together?: A Christian Case for Gay Marriage*. First edition. San Francisco: HarperSanFrancisco, 2007.

Muravchik, S. *American Protestantism in the Age of Psychology*. Cambridge; New York: Cambridge University Press, 2011.

Oakley, Lisa, and Kathryn Kinmond. *Breaking the Silence on Spiritual Abuse*. Basingstoke: Palgrave Macmillan, 2013.

Pence, M. *Vice presidential nominee remarks*. Paper presented at the Republican National Convention, (July 21, 2016) Quicken Loans Arena, Cleveland, Ohio.

Pence, M. "Ensuring religious freedom in Indiana; our new law has been grossly misconstrued as a 'license to discriminate.' That isn't true." *Wall Street Journal* March 31, 2015.

Pew Social Trends. "A survey of LGBT Americans." June 13, 2013. Retrieved February 21, 2017, from http://www.pewsocialtrends.org/2013/06/13/a-survey-of-lgbt-americans/#religion.

Purcell, Boyd C. "Spiritual Abuse." *American Journal of Hospice and Palliative Medicine*, vol. 15, no. 4, July 1998, pp. 227–231, doi:10.1177/104990919801500409.

Rambo, S. *Spirit and Trauma: A Theology of Remaining* (1st ed.). Louisville, Ky.: Westminster John Knox Press, 2010.

Rappaport, R. A. *Ritual and Religion in the Making of Humanity*. Cambridge, U.K.; New York: Cambridge University Press, 1999.

Reynolds, A. L. and W. F. Hanjorgiris. "Coming out: Lesbian, gay and bisexual identity development." In *Handbook of Counseling and Psychotherapy with Lesbian, Gay and Bisexual Clients* edited by R. M. Perez, K. A. DeBord, & K. J. Bieschke, 35–55. Washington, DC: American Psychological Association, 2000.

Rizzuto, A.-M. *The Birth of the Living God: A Psychoanalytic Study*. Chicago: University of Chicago Press, 1979.

Root, M.P.P. "Reconstructing the Impact of Trauma on Personality." In *Personality and Psychopathology: Feminist Reappraisals*, edited by L. S. Brown & M. Ballou, New York, New York: The Guilford Press, 1992.

Ryan, C., D. Huebner, R. M. Diaz and J. Sanchez. "Family Rejection as a Predictor of Negative Health Outcomes in White and Latino Lesbian, Gay and Bisexual Youth Adults." *Pediatrics* 123 (2009): 346–352.

Ryan, C., S. T. Russell, .D Huebner, R. Diaz and J. Sanchez. "Family Acceptance in Adolescence and the Health of LGBT Young Adults." *Journal Of Child & Adolescent Psychiatric Nursing* 23 (2010): 205–213.

Ruiter, J. and M. Shanklin. "Groups band together to mitigate Orlando's anxiety," *Orlando Sentinel*, June 17, 2016, http://www.orlandosentinel.com/news/pulse-orlando-nightclub-shooting/survivors/os-pulse-anxiety-meditation-acupuncture-20160617-story.html.

Sheppard, P. I. *Self, Culture, and Others in Womanist Practical Theology* (1st ed.). New York: Palgrave Macmillan, 2011.

Southern Poverty Law Center HateWatch. (2016). Retrieved from https://www.splcenter.org/hatewatch/2016/12/16/update-1094-bias-related-incidents-month-following-election.
Snodgrass, J. "From Rogers to Clinebell: Exploring the History of Pastoral Psychology." *Pastoral Psychology* 55 (2007): 513–525.
Stephanopoulos, G. "Indiana Governor Mike Pence says religious freedom law 'absolutely not' a mistake." *This Week with George Stephanopoulos*: ABC News. March 29, 2015.
Stoller, R. J. "The Samuel Novey Lecture: Des Sexual Perversion Exist?" *The Johns Hopkins Medical Journal*, 134 (1), 1974: 43–57.
Swain, Storm. *Trauma and Transformation at Ground Zero: A Pastoral Theology*. Minneapolis: Fortress Press, 2011.
"Tips for Talking with Survivors of Sexual Assault." *RAINN*, www.rainn.org/articles/how-respond-survivor.
Turner, V. W. *The Ritual Process; Structure and Anti-Structure*. Chicago: Aldine Pub. Co, 1969/2008.
Van Gennep, A. *The rites of passage*. Chicago: University of Chicago Press, 1960.
Vines, Matthew. *God and the Gay Christian: The Biblical Case in Support of Same-Sex Relationships*. First edition. New York: Convergent Books, 2014.
Walker, D. F. and J. D. Aten. "Future directions for the study and application of religion, spirituality, and trauma research." *Journal of Psychology & Theology* 40 (2012): 349–353.
Walker, Donald F., Christine A. Courtois, and Jamie D. Aten. *Spiritually Oriented Psychotherapy for Trauma*. First edition. Washington, DC: American Psychological Association, 2015.
Ward, David J. "The Lived Experience of Spiritual Abuse." *Mental Health, Religion & Culture*, 14:9 (2011): 899–915, doi: 10.1080/13674676.2010.536206.
White, H. R. *Reforming Sodom: Protestants and the Rise of Gay Rights*. First Edition. Chapel Hill: University of North Carolina Press, 2015.
Winell, M. *Leaving the Fold*. Oakland, CA: New Harbinger Publications, 1993.
Wormald, B. "Chapter 4: The shifting religious identity of demographic groups," 12 May 2015. Accessed 21 Feb. 2017. http://www.pewforum.org/2015/05/12/chapter-4-the-shifting-religious-identity-of-demographic-groups/#religious-composition-by-sexual-orientation.

Index

bearing witness, 117–18, 122–23; storytelling as, 123
Bergler, Edmund, 29–30, 31
Boulanger, Ghislaine, 122–23
Brown, Laura, 13–14, 17–18, 72, 153
Bryant, Anita, 35

Cass, Vivienne, 62
Chodorow, Nancy, 32

Defense of Marriage Act, 2–3
double coming out, 129–39, 148
Driver, Tom, 123–24, 126, 129

establishing safety, 119, 129
evangelicals and evangelicalism, 33, 35, 37

Freud, Sigmund, 10–11, 12, 27–29, 30, 50, 53; Little Hans, 28–29; *Three Essays on the Theory of Sexuality*, 28, 32
Freyd, Jennifer, 17

Geertz, Clifford, 103–4

hell, 56, 92, 95, 110
Herman, Judith, 10, 118–39
Hiltner, Seward, 34

Holifield, E. Brooks, 25–26
homosexuality, 24, 27, 31; as disease 34–37, 61; as inversion, 27–28, as pathology 31, 32; as perversion, 30, 31; as sin, 24, 56–61, 91–92
hysteria, 10; aetiology of, 10

Jones, James, 53, 60, 72, 91, 117
Jones, Serene, 123

Kinsey Report, 24
Klein, Melanie, 29, 30
Kohut, Heinz, 50–53, 55

Lewes, Kenneth, 31

Peale, Norman Vincent, 25, 35
Pence, Mike, 151–53
post-traumatic stress, 12–13
post-traumatic growth, 140–46
psychology and pastoral care, 25–26

Rambo, Shelly, 118
Rappaport, Roy, 128–29
reconnection, 129
Religious Trauma Syndrome, 4
remembrance, 122–29
ritual, 103–4, 117, 122, 123–29; as acceptance, 105

Root, Maria P.P., 14–17, 94, 151

safety, 119–22
selfobjects, 51–53, 117; God as, 59, 91; idealized, 53–55, 62, 72, 89, 93; internalization of, 51
self-psychology, 50
sexual identity development, 34, 61–73, 92–93
shell shock, 11
Sheppard, Phyllis, 16
spiritual abuse, 3–4
Stoller, Robert, 31–32, 34
suicide: risk of, 6, 89; suicidal ideation, 81, 93

theological imagination, 123–29

transmuting internalization, 60
trauma: betrayal trauma, 17–18; direct trauma, 15, 118, 122, 123, 151; expansion of, 13–19; feminist construction of, 15; history of 9–13; indirect trauma, 15, 118; insidious trauma, 14–17, 18, 118, 151–53; LGBTQIA+ trauma, 17–19; womanist construction of, 16
Trump, Donald, 2, 151

Van Gennep, Arnold, 103–4, 119
Vietnam War, 11

White, Heather, 24
Winell, Marlene, 4–5

About the Author

Brooke N. Petersen is a lecturer in pastoral theology and director of master's programs and Coordinator for Candidacy at the Lutheran School of Theology at Chicago. Brooke is a Licensed Clinical Professional Counselor in Illinois and maintains a small private practice in Chicago.

www.ingramcontent.com/pod-product-compliance
Lightning Source LLC
Chambersburg PA
CBHW020122010526
44115CB00008B/941